KT-365-966

DEVOLUTION IN PRACTICE 2006

PUBLIC POLICY DIFFERENCES WITHIN THE UK

EDITED BY JOHN ADAMS AND KATIE SCHMUECKER

ippr

The **Institute for Public Policy Research** (ippr) is the UK's leading progressive think tank and was established in 1988. Its role is to bridge the political divide between the social democratic and liberal traditions, the intellectual divide between academia and the policy making establishment and the cultural divide between government and civil society. It is first and foremost a research institute, aiming to provide innovative and credible policy solutions. Its work, the questions its research poses and the methods it uses are driven by the belief that the journey to a good society is one that places social justice, democratic participation and economic and environmental sustainability at its core. ippr north is our Newcastle-based office.

For further information you can contact ippr's external affairs department on info@ippr.org, you can view our website at www.ippr.org and you can buy our books from Central Books on 0845 458 9910 or email ippr@centralbooks.com.

Our trustees

Chris Powell (Chairman)
Chai Patel (Secretary)
Jeremy Hardie (Treasurer)
Lord Puttnam (Chair of ippr north)

Professor Kumar Bhattacharyya
Lord Brooke
Lord Eatwell
Lord Gavron
Professor Anthony Giddens
Lord Hollick
Jane Humphries
Roger Jowell
Lord Kinnock

Richard Lambert
Frances O'Grady
Sir Michael Perry
David Pitt-Watson
Dave Prentis
Sir Martin Rees
Ed Sweeney
Baroness Williams
Baroness Young of Old Scone

© IPPR 2005

Contents

Part I: Introduction

Acknowledgements   v

About the authors   vi

Preface   1

1   Introduction and overview   3
    John Adams and Katie Schmuecker

Part II: Different priorities but national solidarity?

2   Devolution and divergence: public attitudes   10
    and institutional logics
    Charlie Jeffery

3   Divergence in priorities, perceived policy failure   29
    and pressure for convergence
    Katie Schmuecker and John Adams

Part III: Public services

4   Devolution and divergence in education policy   52
    David Raffe

5   Devolution and divergence in education policy: 70
    the Northern Ireland case
    Bob Osborne

6   Devolution, social democracy and policy diversity   76
    in Britain: the case of early-childhood education and care
    Daniel Wincott

7   The politics of health-policy divergence   98
    Scott Greer

8   Devolution and divergence in social-housing   121
    policy in Britain
    Robert Smith

Part IV: Poverty and economic development

9   Regional economic development   141
    in a devolved United Kingdom
    John Adams and Peter Robinson

10 Devolution and the economy: a Scottish perspective   160
    Brian Ashcroft, Peter McGregor and Kim Swales

11 Child poverty and devolution   172
    Liane Asta Lohde

Acknowledgements

The editors would like to thank all those who have contributed to the ideas contained in this book, through seminars and informal discussions. In particular we would like to thank all the authors for their time and hard work.

We would further thank the following staff and volunteers at ippr and ippr north for their contributions to this publication: Michael Brunskill, Simone Delorenzi, Guy Lodge, Rory Palmer, Howard Reed, Peter Robinson, John Schwartz, Sue Stirling, Loraine Sweeney and Daniel Wilson Craw. Many officials in Whitehall and the devolved institutions provided significant help, but prefer to remain anonymous. Our apologies go to those we have failed to mention. It must be pointed out that, while we have benefited from much advice and assistance from many quarters, responsibility for the final version rests with the editors alone.

ippr north gratefully acknowledges the support for this research project from the ESRC Devolution Programme and the Greater London Authority. Without their willingness to invest in and contribute to independent and original research, this project could not have been undertaken. The findings of our research, however, do not necessarily reflect the views of our funding partners.

About the authors

John Adams is Director of Research at ippr north, the Newcastle office of the institute for public policy research. He was responsible for setting up and then launching ippr north in January 2004. Previously, John was a Special Adviser at the Welsh Office during the 1997 devolution referendum.

Brian Ashcroft is Policy Director at the Fraser Allander Institute for Research on the Scottish Economy, at the University of Strathclyde. He is also a co-director of the Scottish Economic Policy Network and a member of the Scottish Executive's Economic Consultants Group and Economic Statistics Group, and, in 2002, was appointed to the Scottish Industrial Development Advisory Board.

Scott Greer works at the School of Public Health at the University of Michigan, Ann Arbor. He was formerly a lecturer in public policy at the School of Public Policy, University College, London, and a research fellow at the Constitution Unit. His book *Territorial Politics and Health Policy: UK health policy in comparative perspective* was published by Manchester University Press in 2004.

Charlie Jeffery is Director of the Economic and Social Research Council (ESRC) research programme on Devolution and Constitutional Change, and Professor of Politics in the School of Social and Political Studies at the University of Edinburgh. During 2004, he was Specialist Adviser for the Committee on the Office of the Deputy Prime Minister in the House of Commons.

Liane Asta Lohde works for the World Bank in Washington. She was previously a researcher at ippr in London, where she worked on the Social Policy team.

Peter McGregor is a Professor in the School of Economics at Strathclyde University. He was editor of *Regional Studies*, the journal of the Regional Studies Association, from 1991-1996. He has also been a member of the Bank of England's panel of academic consultants.

Robert Osborne is Director of the Social and Policy Research Institute at the University of Ulster.

David Raffe is Professor of Sociology of Education and Director of Research at the School of Education at the University of Edinburgh. He is a member of the Programme Board, which is overseeing the implementation of *A Curriculum for Excellence* (the Scottish Executive's review of the 3-18 curriculum), and was a member of the Tomlinson Working Group on 14-19 Education in England

Peter Robinson has been Senior Economist at the ippr since October 1997. He leads the ippr teams dealing with economic and employment policy and public-service reform. He is also a research associate at the Centre for Economic Performance at the LSE.

Katie Schmuecker is a researcher at ippr north, the Newcastle office of the institute for public policy research.

Robert Smith is a director of the Regeneration Institute at the University of Cardiff. He has previously undertaken research for DoE/DETR, the Welsh Office and the National Assembly for Wales.

Kim Swales is a Professor of Economics and Research Director of the Fraser of Allander Institute at the University of Strathclyde. He is on the management committee of the ESRC Urban and Regional Economics study group and the Regional Science Association's International, British and Irish section. He was, until recently, associate editor of *Regional Studies*.

Daniel Wincott is Reader in European and Comparative Politics at the University of Birmingham. His chapter is based on the project 'Devolution and the Comparative Territorial Analysis of the Welfare State', which he ran as part of the ESRC Devolution and Constitutional Change programme.

Preface

This publication is the result of a joint project undertaken by ippr north and the ESRC Devolution and Constitutional Change Programme, between April 2004 and November 2005. It follows on from a successful venture in 2002, when we published Devolution in Practice: Public policy differences within the UK.

Devolution and Constitutional Change is one of the research programmes funded by the UK's Economic and Social Research Council. It is a major, £4.7 million investment in social-science research, set up by the ESRC in 2000 to explore the impact of the devolution dynamic and to feed the research into policy debates.

More information on the activities of the ESRC Devolution programme is available from:

Professor Charlie Jeffery
Programme Director
ESRC Devolution Programme
University of Edinburgh
Adam Ferguson Building
George Square
Edinburgh
EH8 9LL

Tel: 0131 650 4266
Fax: 0131 650 6546

Web: www.devolution.ac.uk

1 Introduction and overview

John Adams and Katie Schmuecker

The creation of devolved institutions is not just a constitutional reform. Devolution has profound implications for public services within the UK, yet there has been comparatively little attention paid to the consequences of differentiated policy-making. The first volume of *Devolution in Practice* remains one of the few attempts to systematically examine public-policy divergences.

Since the last edition of *Devolution in Practice* (2002), there have been elections in the devolved territories and for the House of Commons, devolution to Northern Ireland has again been suspended and Wales has moved from a Labour-Liberal Democrat coalition to a situation of minority-party rule. Perhaps, more importantly, a further three years of life in a devolved United Kingdom have passed. This has given time for change to bed down and for the devolved administrations to make some headway with their planned programmes of government. As we discuss further in chapter 3, it takes a number of years for policy changes to filter through into policy outputs and outcomes. However, six years into devolution, we are starting to see some interesting shifts in policy and a complex relationship between forces for divergence and convergence within the UK.

This overview chapter will not attempt to summarise the contributions made to this publication, but we do aim to draw out some of the key issues and themes common to each policy area. We outline experience of both divergence and convergence, before discussing the tricky issues of how to balance equity and diversity and how to achieve subsidiarity and solidarity (Morgan 2002).

Forces for divergence

The headline policy divergences of devolution are well-known: free long-term care and no upfront tuition fees in Scotland; abolition of school league tables in Wales; free bus travel for the elderly in Northern Ireland; and the congestion charge in London. However, these are only the tip of the iceberg, and the contributors to this publication explore the real impact of devolution in practice.

Policy choice within a permissive settlement

Perhaps the most influential force for divergence is the fact that there are now new centres of political power making public-policy decisions within the UK. A number of our contributors have made the point that the devolution settlement is highly permissive of divergence, for example Jeffery in chapter 2, Greer in chapter 7 and ourselves in chapter 3. The UK settlement has no mechanisms to provide for common standards or a social minimum, and the 'block grant', though which the devolved administrations are funded, provides for total flexibility in how the funds are used. As Jeffery points out, the lack of robust institutions for co-ordination are also likely, at some point in the future, to fuel divergence and intergovernmental rivalries.

As we discuss in chapter 3, the 'block grant' provides the devolved administrations with flexibility to allocate funds in whichever manner they think fit. Our conclusion, that increases in expenditure in health and education have been larger in England than in Scotland, Wales and Northern Ireland since the devolved administrations were established, is a significant divergence in public policy. It would suggest that the devolved administrations are responding to different policy priorities, which is likely, in time, to lead to differing outcomes.

There are also significant divergences in policy choices between the different administrations. As Greer notes in chapter 7, the health policy of the Welsh Assembly Government has been significantly different to its English and Scottish counterparts, with a much greater emphasis on public health and promoting healthier communities, rather than tackling illness. Greer also argues that there is less faith in market forces (or quasi-market forces) in healthcare in the Scottish Executive or Welsh Assembly Government than in Whitehall.

In chapter 4, Raffe concludes that, in education policy, Scotland and Wales emphasise the links between schools and communities, and the need for common content and standards of provision across all schools. In England and Northern Ireland, policy places greater emphasis on choice, institutional diversity and collaboration. In the field of housing, Smith, in chapter 8, discusses the different approaches between the devolved administrations and Whitehall, with England seeking to find a balance between need and choice, but Scotland and Wales more explicitly prioritising need. Wales has expanded the categories of those perceived to be at risk, to include care-leavers, ex-offenders and those leaving the armed forces; while Scotland is committed to abolishing the notion of priority need, so all homeless persons have the right to a home.

Furthermore, devolution has enabled the devolved administrations to address long-standing concerns that it was difficult to find time for at Westminster. As Wincott discusses in chapter 6, the distinctive Welsh approach to early-childhood education and care policies, and the move towards a rights-based approach, is highly influenced by long-standing concerns about abuse in care homes, which precede devolution.

A final way in which divergence has occurred, is through policy innovation within England, rather than in the devolved territories. For example, Raffe argues in chapter 4 that, while there are divergent attitudes to comprehensive education in the UK, this reflects a refusal by Scotland and Wales to follow English policy direction, rather than positive changes on their part. Far from being 'laboratories of democracy', the devolved administrations have viewed much of the policy experimentation in England with antipathy.

Political parties and policy communities

These divergences beg the question as to how new policies and approaches are developed in the devolved territories. The fact that devolution creates new political spheres and new centres of power is a force for divergence, as there are new opportunities for policy communities and for political parties in the devolved territories. A number of contributors point out that the pattern of party politics in the devolved territories is different. In particular, Jeffery (chapter 2) and Greer (chapter 7) note that, in the devolved territories, the major political opponents to the administrations are on the left of the political spectrum. They argue that there is a pull to the left of centre in Scotland and Wales as a result of Plaid Cymru, the Scottish Nationalists and the Liberal Democrats. However, in England, the major challenge to the Labour Government comes from the Conservative Party on the centre-right.

Furthermore, policy communities have been able to be rather more influential in some areas in Scotland and Wales. While this is, in part, a result of a more inclusive approach to policy-making, it is also a reflection of weaker capacity in the devolved administrations, leading them to rely on external input. For example, Wincott, in chapter 6, discusses the highly influential input of the early-childhood education and care (ECEC) community into policy-making in Wales. He questions whether the more open policy-making process was the result of the underdeveloped nature of the ECEC policy in Wales at the time of devolution, and a lack of entrenched interests. Greer, in chapter 7, also discusses the influence of policy communities, and suggests that the divergent health policies have been, in part, the result of the well-established and highly influential policy communities in existence.

Divergent rhetoric

The ability to forge a more left-wing agenda than was acceptable to (middle) England was, for many, an attractive argument in favour of devolution. But it is a claim predicated on an assumption that the people of Wales and Scotland have a more progressive, more left-wing set of values than those in England. However, as Jeffery discusses in chapter 2, the best available evidence suggests that Wales and Scotland have a broadly similar set of values to those in England.

However, this does not mean that the politicians in the devolved administrations are not different to those in Whitehall, and this fact is best exemplified by Rhodri Morgan's statement that he wanted to create 'clear red water' between the Welsh Assembly Government and Whitehall. Lohde, in chapter 11, argues that the debates around poverty in Scotland and Wales have placed a stronger emphasis on social and economic equalities; whereas the debates in England have focused more on extending equality of opportunity, with less concern for overall inequalities; and in Northern Ireland, debates have taken a rights-based approach. However, she also advises caution as to the extent to which rhetorical differences are reflected in actual policy action. She concludes, in relation to child poverty, that every part of the UK has made tackling poverty and social disadvantage a priority, and the tools they use to do so are broadly similar, with the differences, perhaps, to be found more in emphasis.

Forces for convergence

Despite assumptions to the contrary, divergent policies are not an inevitable consequence of devolution and there are significant countervailing forces for convergence in policy.

Public opinion, values and policy preferences

As we noted above, there is no evidence that the people of the devolved territories have a different set of political values to those in England. While the complexion of politics differs in different parts of the UK, Jeffery's analysis of attitudinal surveys concludes that the values that the general public hold across the UK are broadly consistent. He concludes that, if Scotland is to be characterised as a social democratic country, then England must also be.

Furthermore, not only are people's values broadly similar, their policy expectations are, too. In chapter 3, we argue that public opinion is one of the most important mechanisms for limiting policy divergence and preserving some degree of common standards across the UK. As an example, we use the issue of health waiting times, and the perceived policy failure of the Welsh Assembly Government, compounded by perceptions of policy success in England. This led to demands for policy to be re-examined, for the disparity in services with England to be addressed and for lessons to be learned from England.

The common market

The combination of the interdependencies of the economies within the UK, the largely common tax regime and the (in part) UK-wide labour market is another powerful force for convergence (Keating 2002). Raffe illustrates the importance of this point when he notes that the integrated nature of labour markets within the UK has proved a powerful force for convergence of qualifications. The desire of the Welsh Assembly Government to create a 'Welsh Bac' was constrained by the fact that, in the event that students wished to seek work in England (a highly possible outcome), the qualification needed to be understandable to English employers. Furthermore, the substantial flow of staff and students between institutions across the UK creates pressure for common, or at least compatible, qualifications.

Dominant narratives

While the rhetoric used by the devolved administrations may differ in emphasis in some areas, Adams and Robinson (chapter 9) note that, on occasion, there are certain trends in intellectual and policy thinking that are common across the whole of the UK, and, indeed, other developed nations. For example, they point to key narratives around globalisation and the 'knowledge economy' that, while flawed, have influenced thinking about economic development in all parts of the UK. Their argument is not that policy-makers consciously follow policy initiatives in other territories, but that, within a broad overarching framework, there is a convergent evolution of policy towards a similar end point.

The lack of intergovernmental structures

One of the key issues that troubles constitutional experts and academics is the lack of a robust framework of intergovernmental relations within the UK, as Jeffery concludes in chapter 2. At some stage in the future, the political complexion of the United Kingdom will change, and the Labour Party will not form administrations in Scotland, Wales and Whitehall. The challenge of managing devolution when that happens should not be underestimated, nor should the pressure that a tight fiscal climate will impose.

However, until that time, the current system does provide some pressure for convergence. Jeffery discusses, in some depth, the role of informal links between officials, the continued existence of territorial Secretaries of State in Westminster, overlaps of competence, mechanisms like the Sewel convention, the role of the European Union and policy spillovers from England, all of which act as forces for convergence.

Devolution, divergence and social justice

One of the most important debates within the devolution literature has been the need to reconcile liberty with equity, subsidiarity with solidarity. This has been a particular problem for centre-left thinkers, because of the premium placed on equity as a core value. Some elements of the left in British politics have always worried that creating opportunities for policy divergence would lead to different standards of provision of public services, and undermine a sense of UK solidarity, equity and the welfare state (see, for example, Walker 2002). As Jeffery notes in chapter 2, 'postcode lotteries' are potentially damaging to a sense of common British citizenship. It is for this reason that Bevan, in 1944, famously said 'there is no Welsh problem', expressing the disquiet on the left that territorial concerns could undermine traditional class solidarities on socio-economic grounds.

There is a strong contrary argument that the centralised provision of services does not lead to uniformly high standards. The centralised provision of service results in rigidity and inflexibility, making services poor at responding to changing circumstances and limiting joining up of services at the local level (Paxton and Gamble 2005). Invariably it is the worst-off in society who suffer from these failures.

There is good reason for those concerned with social justice to see devolution as an opportunity. Political devolution can create space for policy experimentation, innovation and learning. New and successful ideas can be adopted, for example the Welsh introduction of a Children's Commissioner has been taken up in Northern Ireland, Scotland and now England (see Wincott, chapter 6), and it is in this sense that the devolved territories have been referred to as 'policy laboratories'. Policy-learning between the administrations can lead to a virtuous circle, pushing up overall standards. Such policy-learning can potentially help combat worries over inequalities, as any inequalities that result from policy divergence can prove to be merely a temporary aberration in the general drive towards higher standards all round.

To some, it is surprising that the UK constitution has no agreed, negotiated set of common standards or floor targets, as is found in Spain, for example. It also surprises some that the UK does not make use of concurrent legislation in the way that a more formally federalised system would. However, given the *ad hoc* and incremental manner in which the uncodified UK constitution evolves, such omissions are very much par for the course. It is, of course, still technically possible to set minimum standards within the UK through negotiations between Whitehall and the devolved administrations, or through the system of concordats (Paxton and Gamble 2005), although neither would be legally binding.

Evidence from other countries suggests that, even where there are no formal minimum standards set by the centre, in practice there tend to be only small variations around common national standards (Banting 2005). More fundamentally, the political challenges in agreeing such negotiations are enormous and likely doomed to failure, not least because the devolved administrations would see this as an attempt to reopen the devolution settlement decided in the referendums of 1997 and 1998. Nevertheless, Adams and Robinson, in chapter 9, argue that central government still has a quasi-federal role, and that it has been slow to adapt to this new role. Even without negotiated minimum standards, they argue that central government needs to rethink its attitude to devolution, to ensure that there are no unacceptable inequalities within the UK and to use the concept of territorial justice to ensure some degree of national solidarity.

As Jeffery notes in chapter 2, people are, on balance, opposed to the idea of territorial policy variation but, simultaneously, they have a desire for greater devolution, driven, in a large part, by a desire to reclaim ownership of politics. Such inconsistencies are the right of the electorate, but it does provide for a difficult balancing act for politicians and policy-makers in all corners of the UK.

The question of how to secure 'equality in diversity' will continue to need to be addressed by the UK Government, by the devolved administrations and by all those who wish to maintain the unity of the UK.

References

Adams J and Robinson R (eds.) *Devolution in Practice: Public policy differences within the UK* ippr

Banting K (2005) 'Social Citizenship and Federalism: is the federal welfare state a contradiction in terms?' in Greer S (ed.) *Territory, Democracy and Justice: Territorial politics in advanced industrial democracies* Palgrave McMillan

Bevan A (1944) *Hansard* 10 October 1944, col 2312

Keating M (2002) 'Devolution and Public Policy in the United Kingdom: divergence or convergence' in Adams J and Robinson P (eds.) *Devolution in Practice: Public policy differences within the UK* ippr, pp. 3-21

Morgan K (2002) 'The English Question: Regional Perspectives on a Fractured nation' in *Regional Studies* 36:7, pp. 797-810

Paxton W and Gamble A (2005) 'Democracy, Social Justice and the State' in Pearce N and Paxton W (eds.) *Social Justice: Building a Fairer Britain* ippr, pp. 219-239

Walker D (2002) *In Praise of Centralism* available at http://www.catalystforum.org.uk/pdf/walker.pdf

2 Devolution and divergence: Public attitudes and institutional logics

Charlie Jeffery

Devolution was a deceptively simple thing to do. The devolution reforms have done little more than democratise the distinctive administrative arrangements that had emerged over time for delivering UK policies in Scotland, Wales and Northern Ireland. The devolution Acts essentially transferred the functions of the Scottish, Welsh and Northern Ireland Offices, as departments of UK government, to new, directly elected institutions in the non-English nations: the Scottish Parliament, the National Assembly for Wales and the Northern Ireland Assembly. They transformed intragovernmental arrangements for differentiated territorial administration into arrangements for democratic self-government conducted in parallel, and in loose intergovernmental co-ordination, with a UK government responsible for a residual mix of UK-wide and England-only functions.

Because devolution rests so centrally on established institutions and practices of territorial administration, it was easy to introduce. The UK has not seen the kinds of intergovernmental tensions that have accompanied decentralisation debates and reforms in other places. In that sense, the grafting of democratic process onto existing arrangements has been an extraordinary short-term advantage. But it is remarkable how little effort was put into thinking through some of the longer-term consequences of introducing devolved democratic processes, of changing territorial *administration* into territorial *politics*.

The introduction of democratic process – the articulation and aggregation of interests, party competition, elections and government formation – may mean that what 'Scotland' (or 'Wales', or 'Northern Ireland') wants becomes different to, or inconsistent with, what the rest of the UK prioritises through parallel democratic processes. No other set of decentralisation reforms has involved less thought into how to deal, post-devolution, with the accommodation of territorial interests within UK-wide interests. Put another way, there has been little attempt, either at UK or devolved levels, to articulate what the UK is for, after devolution, and how a more complex set of governing arrangements, now better able to express narrower territorial interests, is also to express UK-wide purposes and solidarities. A number of commentators have seen that omission as an act of complacency, nurtured by the reassuring continuity of pre- and post-devolution practice; they suspect this complacency brings with it a tendency to underestimate the dynamics and implications of post-devolution territorial politics. They expect those implications to be revealed in intergovernmental conflicts (for which governments at UK and devolved levels are unprepared) as soon as governments run by different parties are in power at UK and devolved levels (House of Lords 2002; Trench 2001, p. 173; Hazell 2003, pp. 300-01; Jeffery forthcoming a).

This contribution is an attempt to work through some of the implications of the UK's new territorial politics. It has a dual focus on public attitudes and institutional logics. It starts by looking at how citizens conceive of multi-levelled politics in the UK, by exploring how the attitudes of the general public define the boundaries of territorial interests and UK-wide solidarity. We find that those attitudes express a tension between shared values and policy preferences that barely vary across the UK, and a desire for even fuller 'ownership' of politics at the devolved level. That tension in public attitudes is not exceptional; in Canada and Germany, for example, there are similar patterns (Jeffery 2005). What is exceptional is the absence in the UK of institutional arrangements that express and – crucially – balance that tension. The institutional logics of devolution appear, instead, primed to favour territorial divergence of policy outcomes over the maintenance of common UK-wide outcomes.

Public attitudes: shared values, shared risks

There is ample data available on public responses to devolution in the UK.[1] It shows that there is little desire for territorial policy variation.

Left and right

The Scots and the Welsh are not more 'left-wing' than the English. Scottish 'leftness' is long assumed to have animated support for devolution in Scotland in the long era of Conservative UK government from 1979-1997 (see McCrone 1998). Views about the stronger left-wing credentials of the Welsh have become prominent since devolution in Wales, too. But, in fact, cross-national differences between UK nations are small, with the Scottish defining themselves as, marginally, the most left-wing; the Welsh, the least left-wing; and the English, in the middle (table 2.1).

Table 2.1: Left and right in the UK (2003)			
Scale	Scotland	England	Wales
Economic Left-Right	2.41	2.53	2.58

Note: The scales are scored from one (the most left-wing) to five (the most right-wing).
Source: Wyn Jones and Scully (2004).

1   See the websites of the two main research programmes funded by the Economic and Social Research Council at www.devolution.ac.uk and the Leverhulme Trust at http://www.ucl.ac.uk/constitution-unit/nations/. The data presented in the following tables is mainly from the British Social Attitudes (for England), Scottish Social Attitudes, Welsh Life and Times and Northern Ireland Life and Times Surveys.

Values and policy preferences

At a more detailed level, much the same picture holds. Table 2.2 shows responses in England and Scotland (and, in two cases, Wales; and, in one, Northern Ireland) to a series of questions designed to reveal broader left-right values (questions one to three) and attitudes on more detailed policy issues (questions four to six) over the years 1999-2003. On some of these questions, there are persistent differences. Throughout the period, rather more Scots have felt unemployment benefits are too low (question one), and that entrance to secondary schools should not be by selection (question six). The Scots want fuller equalisation of risk of income inequalities and fuller equality of oppor-

Table 2.2: Policy attitudes in the UK (1999-2003)

	1999	2000	2001	2002	2003
1) Benefits for the unemployed are too low and cause hardship					
Scotland	36	43	41	41	45
England	32	40	34	28	36
2) Increase taxes and spend more on health, education and social benefits					
Scotland	55	54	63	60	58
England	58	51	60	61	51
Wales	58	-	64	61	58
3) Ordinary working people do not get their fair share of the nation's wealth					
Scotland	58	71	61	64	54
England	60	61	58	61	60
Wales	61	-	61	60	59
Northern Ireland	62	60	55	62	59
4) No students or their families should pay towards the cost of their tuition fees while studying					
Scotland	-	38	31	-	29
England	-	30	33	-	28
5) Government should be mainly responsible for paying for the care needs of elderly people living in residential and nursing homes					
Scotland	86	-	88	-	88
England	80	-	86	-	84
6) All children should go to the same kind of secondary school, no matter how well or badly they do at primary school					
Scotland	63	-	63	-	65
England	49	-	51	-	48

Source: Curtice (2004) on Scotland and England. Wales data provided by Roger Scully. Northern Ireland data from the Northern Ireland Life and Times survey at http://www.ark.ac.uk/nilt/results/polatt.html.

tunity in education. But, on all the other questions, excepting trendless blips, the differences between Scottish and English (and, where they are available, Welsh and Northern Irish) responses have been marginal.

Significantly, opinion on two areas of policy where the Scottish Parliament has introduced significant policy divergence from the UK baseline – abolition of upfront tuition fees for university students and free long-term care for the elderly – there is close to zero difference in Scottish and English opinion. Scotland and England appear 'for the most part to share the same values and similar policy preferences' (Curtice 2004, p. 11).

As John Curtice (2004) has put it: 'If Scotland is to be characterised as a predominantly social democratic country then England qualifies for that description as well' (p. 8). There are implications for two of the points discussed earlier. First, the Scots and English (and, as far as we can tell, the Welsh and Northern Irish), by and large, do not distinguish between particularly 'Scottish' or 'English' policy challenges, but are concerned with much the same kinds of issue in much the same ways. And, second, it seems unlikely that the momentum established for devolution in Scotland after 1979 had a great deal to do with the Scots being more left-wing than the English; they do seem to be a little more left-wing, but not much. This point, about what devolution was for, is taken further below.

Attitudes to policy variation

That understandings of policy challenges are quite uniform across the UK is revealed in questions about the legitimacy of policy variation (table 2.3). In England, Scotland and Wales there are clear majorities in support of standard provision of the main public services, with the strongest support in England. And, in Scotland and Wales, similar majorities (fifty-five to sixty per cent) endorse standard provision both of unemployment benefit (reserved to the UK level and delivered uniformly across the UK) and in devolved policy areas where divergences from England have emerged since devolution (tuition fees in Scotland and prescription charges in Wales). The endorsement of uniformity, even under devolved responsibilities, does not necessarily imply an endorsement of the distinctive devolved policy as right for the UK as a whole; as table 2.2 above shows, Scottish and English attitudes on tuition fees are very similar, with both supportive of the policy that applies in England (by contrast, opinion in England and Scotland overwhelmingly favours the policy on long-term care introduced by the Scottish Parliament and rejected at Westminster).

What table 2.3 does appear to imply is a preference for sharing risk and equalising opportunity on a UK-wide basis. It is, unfortunately, not clear whether that preference has risen or fallen since devolution, since the relevant questions have not been asked in a longitudinal series. It is also not that clear whether this pattern of opinion is unusual comparatively, though equivalent

Table 2.3: Attitudes towards policy variation in Great Britain (2003)

A: Should be the same in every part of Britain (%)
B: Allowed to vary (%)

	A	B
England		
Standards for services, such as health, schools, roads and police	66	33
Scotland		
Standards for services, such as health, schools, roads and police	59	40
Level of unemployment benefit	56	42
University tuition fees	56	40
Wales		
Standards for services such as health, schools, roads and police	55	44
Level of unemployment benefit	57	41
University tuition fees	58	40
Cost of NHS Prescriptions	63	37

Sources: British and Scottish Social Attitudes 2003; Wales Life and Times 2003. Data provided by John Curtice.

data for Germany appears to show even stronger preference for uniform, state-wide policy standards (Grube 2001 and 2004). In the German context, that preference has a constitutional underpinning, both in provisions for federal competence in certain (wide) circumstances to override regional competence and in an elaborate fiscal-equalisation scheme, intended to equip each regional government, despite differences in economic structure and performance, with a more-or-less equal financial capacity to deliver uniform standards. Indeed, fiscal equalisation is an especially potent expression of a concern to share risk across different territorial circumstances. And, both in Germany and in Canada, there is strong public support, in both recipient and donor regions, for the principle of territorial equalisation of risk (Jeffery 2005). It would be revealing to see whether similar support for that principle might exist in the UK. However, though the reduction of regional economic disparities and the notion of 'territorial justice' (Adams *et al.* 2003; Morgan 2002) have entered the political lexicon in the UK, we lack an institutional expression for the inter-regional equalisation of risk, against which public attitudes might be measured. But there is, perhaps, one indicator that suggests public acceptance of something loosely interpretable as equalisation, that is, the traditionally higher per-capita public-spending allocations in Scotland as compared with England, which have a loose grounding in perceptions (back in the 1970s) that Scotland has exceptional expenditure needs. Perhaps counterintuitively, almost half of the English think this is 'pretty much fair'; very few (around ten per cent), that it is an unfair advantage; and rather more (over twenty per cent), that the situation is 'more than fair'.[2]

Public attitudes: devolution, identity and ownership

The data presented above tells a fairly clear story of a UK-wide 'solidarity community', committed to sharing risk and opportunity on a state-wide basis. People in all parts of the UK are, at most, marginally left of centre; with few exceptions, hold much the same values and policy preferences; are, on balance, opposed to the idea of territorial policy variation; and even seem open to inter-regional resource equalisation.

If that is the case, one might ask just what devolution, in the public mind, is for, if not to do different things to reflect different preferences in different places. One obvious route to an answer lies in differences of identity. There is, for example, a strong sense of national community in Scotland, which is defined, in large measure, by drawing a distinction vis-à-vis the English. There is a similar, though less tightly drawn, distinction in the relation of the Welsh to the English. These distinctions are set out in tables 2.4 and 2.5, which provide different perspectives on the common ground that the Scots, Welsh and English share in their claims to an overarching British identity. Table 2.4 'forces' respondents to make a choice between either their Scottish/English/Welsh national identity or Britishness. It shows that the English are much more likely than the Scots to claim a British identity, and the Scots more likely to give precedence to their 'local' identity.

Table 2.4: Trends in 'forced choice' national identity (1999-2003)				
	1997	1999	2001	2003
England				
English	34	44	43	38
British	59	44	44	48
Scotland				
Scottish	72	77	77	72
British	20	17	16	20
Wales				
Welsh	63	68	57	60
British	26	14	31	27

Source: Curtice (2004) on Scotland and England. Wales data provided by Roger Scully.

2   Data supplied by John Curtice.

Table 2.5 allows respondents to combine different identities in 'weighted' mixes on the 'Moreno' scale. In this case, respondents in Scotland and Wales do claim a rather bigger element of Britishness, but almost two-thirds in Scotland, a bare majority in Wales, and just around a third in England give clear precedence to their 'local' identity.

Table 2.5: Moreno national identity (2003)

	Scotland	Wales	England
X, not British	31	23	17
More X than British	34	28	19
Equally X and British	22	30	31
More British than X	4	9	13
British, not X	4	10	10

Note: X refers, in each case, to the nation in the respective columns, so thirty-one per cent of Scots felt Scottish, not British; twenty-three per cent Welsh, not British, and so on.

Sources: Curtice (2004); Wyn Jones and Scully (2004).

This data, in different ways, shows that the three British nations perceive different intensities of a shared, Britain-wide community, with the Scots and the Welsh marking out their narrower communities as their primary loyalty, and the English prioritising Britishness. To invert the perspective, Britishness is more closely associated with Englishness than Scottishness/Welshness (unsurprisingly, given the historical and contemporary economic and population dominance of England in Britain). For the Scots and the Welsh to demarcate their own identities from Britishness is, in large measure, to distinguish themselves from the English.

This distinction of territorial community in Scotland and Wales is reflected in public attitudes to – and levels of satisfaction with – current constitutional arrangements (table 2.6). The status-quo position of the two nations is highlighted in table 2.6. A steady twenty-five to thirty per cent of Scots want to move beyond a very extensive devolution settlement to achieve full independence. Other data shows that a good sixty per cent or more of Scots would like the devolved Parliament to have even more powers.[3] And, while little more than ten per cent of the Welsh prefer independence, at least thirty-five per cent – again a proportion that has held steady over time – want to move beyond their current, much more modest devolution settlement to establish a legislative parliament on the Scottish model.

3   Data supplied by John Curtice.

In a similar vein, there is a very steady majority pattern of opinion that is critical – in both Scotland and Wales – of the high level of influence that the UK government, despite devolution, is still held to have over how those nations are run, and a similarly vigorous majority that wants the devolved institutions to have 'most influence' over how they are run.

Table 2.6: Constitutional preferences in Scotland and Wales (1999–2003)

	1999	2000	2001	2002	2003
Scotland					
Independence	28	30	27	30	26
Parliament	50	47	54	44	48
Assembly	8	8	6	8	7
No elected body	10	12	9	12	13
Wales					
ndependence	9	-	12	-	13
Parliament	35	-	37	-	36
Assembly	35	-	25	-	25
No elected body	18	-	23	-	20

Sources: Data provided by John Curtice from Scottish Social Attitudes Survey (1999–2003), Welsh Assembly Election Study (1999) and Wales Life and Times Survey (2001 and 2003).

There is, in other words, a strong demand for, and approval of, devolution. That demand, as we have seen, is not driven by a desire to pursue different policy objectives in different places, but, much more, expresses the strength of bonds of Scottish/Welsh identity, as distinguished from an Anglo-Britain embodied in UK-government institutions. James Mitchell (forthcoming a) has remarked on the striking absence of concrete policy objectives as drivers of the devolution debates in the different parts of the UK. The Scottish Constitutional Convention, which animated the debate in Scotland, did not, for example, deal in terms of policy objectives. Rather, it built a vision of devolution that was much more about symbolic politics, grounded in a claim of popular sovereignty on a territorial scale narrower than the UK as a whole (the 'claim of right') and suffused with a rhetoric of civic inclusion, participation and consultation. Wales had a paler version of the same debate, and Northern Ireland a different debate, but with similar echoes in ideas of cross-community engagement.

Devolution in all these senses was about reclaiming ownership of politics. In Northern Ireland, it was about building the civic engagement necessary to embed peace. In Scotland and Wales, it was about reconnecting the Scots and

Welsh with a democratic process felt increasingly, but especially in the Thatcher-Major years, to have become closed, even hostile, to Scottish and Welsh concerns at the UK level. Devolution, in that sense, was to provide some level of protection against 'majoritisation' by the more numerous English.

There is a rub. Though devolution was not motivated by a demand for policy difference, fuller ownership of the democratic process through devolved institutions is likely to produce difference. This is not an unusual scenario. In other decentralised and federal states, there are also broadly shared, state-wide values and preferences (which imply uniformity of policy outcomes) standing in tension with devolved or regional institutions with significant decision-making powers, which are buttressed by public desires for greater 'proximity' of decision-making (which imply region-by-region divergences of policy outcomes) (see Jeffery 2005). What those other states generally have, are mechanisms designed to 'hold the ring', to express and balance the tensions in public attitudes between shared state-wide values and preference for locally 'owned' decision-making. Such mechanisms in the UK are either absent, under-institutionalised, or operate as unanticipated spillover effects of decisions taken by the UK government, for England. The next two sections explore the institutional logics that either favour divergence or support uniformity of policy outcomes in the UK, allowing an assessment in the final section as to how effectively those logics map onto the public's simultaneous demands for a) state-wide solidarity based on shared values and a commitment to shared risk, and b) decentralised ownership of the political process.

Institutional logics: the divergence machine

Scott Greer (2005a) has written about devolution as a policy 'divergence machine'. His focus is on health policy, which is, of course, alongside social security, the heartland of state-wide risk-sharing, and is based on imagery of a (UK) National Health Service buttressed (see table 2.3) by public expectations of common standards of provision (which are also confirmed, more anecdotally, in controversies over both 'postcode lotteries' generally and the local service closures that have propelled independent representatives into the House of Commons, the Scottish Parliament and the Northern Ireland Assembly). Greer shows, convincingly, that, irrespective of imagery and public preference, the logic of healthcare policy and delivery in the UK is one of divergence. There is little to suggest that his analysis does not also apply in other fields of public policy where devolution has decentralised decision-making powers. The following discussion is loosely based around Greer's divergence criteria.

The devolution settlement
The devolution settlements around the UK are highly permissive of policy divergence. There is an element of path dependency here, as divergences were

common under the territorially differentiated administration of UK policy before devolution. But the scope for divergence is bigger now:

- In Scotland and Northern Ireland, devolution is based on the **separation of** reserved and devolved **powers**. There are few equivalents of the categories of framework legislation (in which state-level parliaments set common or minimum standards) or concurrent legislation (areas in which both state-level and devolved legislatures can make laws, but where state-level laws take precedence under specified conditions) frequently used in other decentralised systems, which allow the central state to set state-wide policy standards. In the Welsh case, such possibilities do exist, with empowerments of the National Assembly normally made as provisions for differential implementation of a common 'England and Wales' legislative framework. But, even there, the tendency under the existing devolution settlement, and more so in the changes proposed in the 2005 White Paper, is for the National Assembly to exercise its powers with growing discretion and declining Westminster regulation (in other words, declining 'England and Wales' commonality) (Wales Office 2005). One striking example of the weakness of the UK institutions' 'grip' on the devolved territories is the UK Government's policy on regional economic disparities. The Government's concern is that disparities are too wide. Although Wales and Northern Ireland rank low in UK-wide regional economic league tables, they are not included in the Government's targets on reducing gaps in regional growth rates, because the UK Government believe the policy instruments are outside its remit since devolution. It is odd, but also a logical consequence of the devolution settlement, that a central government with a UK-wide mandate is unable to roll out a policy UK wide that would appear to chime with public attitudes on UK-wide risk-sharing.

- **Intergovernmental co-ordination** between central and devolved governments in the UK is, comparatively speaking, weakly institutionalised. There is little strategic policy discussion at senior official or ministerial levels in which the balance of UK-wide and devolved objectives in, say, health policy or transport, is problematised. Asymmetrical devolution also encourages bilateral, rather than multilateral (or UK-wide), discussion of policy ideas and objectives. Even in fields where there is a UK-wide forum (such as DTI-led discussions on the inter-regional spillovers of regional economic development initiatives) and a solid, UK-wide rationale (prevention of 'beggar-thy-neighbour' development policies in the context of a single UK economic market) there are no hard sanctions available to prevent harmful spillovers if one of the participating governments determines to go ahead anyway (see Adams and Robinson, chapter 9).

- The **financial settlement** underpinning devolution is unusually, perhaps uniquely, permissive. Rooted in baseline figures established in the period 1979-1982, and adjusted since by the Barnett formula, funding for the devolved administrations is awarded by the UK Treasury (with only marginal exceptions) as an unconditional block grant. Within the block, the devolved administrations are not tied to a particular spending pattern, can switch across budget headings at will, and are not bound to deliver UK-wide policy objectives. Elsewhere, it is normal for at least some substantial part of the funding for devolved or regional governments to be allocated conditionally by state-level governments, in order to meet state-wide objectives. But the UK government has no mechanism, within fields covered by the block, to 'buy' its way into devolved autonomy to meet such objectives.

The devolved democratic process

- **Elections** to the devolved legislatures are not contested in the same ways as at Westminster. None of the Britain-wide parties that dominate at Westminster stand in Northern Ireland. And the Britain-wide parties are supplemented in Scotland and Wales by nationalist parties, and, in Scotland, by a number of significant smaller parties. The greater diversity of the party system in Scotland is facilitated by a different voting system to that used in Westminster (Wales has a similar system, though less party-system diversification so far). Differences in patterns of party competition, logically enough, tend to produce differences of politics. At Westminster, the main competition is between left and right. In Scotland and Wales, the nationalists pull the terms of party competition to the left of centre. Moreover, voters appear to behave differently in devolved, as compared to Westminster, elections, systematically favouring nationalist over Great Britain-wide parties in the devolved context, and vice-versa in the Westminster context. Different voting systems also produce different types of government. Westminster's single-party majorities are paralleled by what is likely to be permanent coalition government in Scotland and a finely balanced situation in Wales, where we have already seen minority government, coalition government and wafer-thin single-party majority government. Scottish and Welsh governments need, in other words, to be more inclusive, importing into government some of the left-leaning dynamic of party competition. Significantly, some of the main examples of policy variation so far in Scotland – abolition of upfront tuition fees, or the introduction of proportional representation in local government elections from 2007 – have reflected the policy commitments of the junior coalition partner, the Liberal Democrats.

- **Policy communities** are recalibrating since devolution, with some interest groups with a UK-wide organisational structure now working in more territorially differentiated ways, and with more emerging in Scotland-only (or

Wales-only) guises (Keating 2005; Loughlin and Sykes 2004). The emphasis in the devolution debates on civic participation and inclusion has also invigorated, and, in part, territorialised civil-society organisations and activities in the devolved territories. In these ways, territorially bounded policy debates emerge that may, or may not, share the same concerns as those pursued in policy communities centred around the Westminster parliament. Greer (2005b) has noted the greater influence of professional associations in defining healthcare policy in Scotland, and he and others (Jeffery forthcoming b) have pointed to a tendency of local public-sector interests to 'capture' public-policy debates in Wales. Policy debates, processes and, in time, outcomes are becoming, in other words, increasingly particularist in the different parts of the UK.

Institutional logics: forces for convergence

The institutional logic produced by the form of devolution and the establishment of territorially bounded democratic processes is, then, one of divergence. There are, of course, countervailing forces, including:

- Largely **informal intergovernmental linkages**, such as those **among officials** with related functions in devolved and UK administrations. But, these discussions are opaque, their subject matter and impact unclear, and their content unaccountable to either UK-level or devolved democratic processes. They depend on personal working relationships, which need to be reinvented as officials move on. There is some sense that a common home-civil-service tradition of collegiality establishes a framework for UK-wide thinking, but also signs that such collegiality was more easily maintained in the pre-devolution era of territorial administration, and is now limited by the new context of territorial politics. Indications are that intergovernmental dispute between, say, Holyrood and Westminster, perhaps after elections produce different party governments in different places, would override traditional commitments to collegiality (Parry 2003).

- A further link exists in the form of the **territorial Secretaries of State** at the UK level, who (in the official job description) act as mediation points between devolved and UK institutions. The extent to which they are called on to perform such a role is unclear. The Secretary of State for Scotland is now a part-time role, currently combined with the Secretary of State for Transport. When there is a fairly clear separation of Scottish and UK competence, there is not actually much mediation to do; some estimates put the time commitment of the Scotland role at as little as ten per cent. The Secretary of State for Wales does have a substantial mediation role under the current, complex division of labour between Westminster and the

National Assembly, but, even so, is also in a job-share role, also performing the functions of Secretary of State for Northern Ireland. And the Wales and Northern Ireland roles are set to wither further, as Welsh devolution moves slowly towards a separation-of-powers model, and (if and) when stable and enduring devolution is achieved in Northern Ireland.

- Though devolved and reserved powers are generally separated, there are, of course, **overlaps of competence**, for example in housing policy, where housing benefit is part of the UK-level function of social security, but policies on provision of social housing are devolved. There are myriad other such overlaps, especially at the interface of social security with other policies (for example, on social exclusion, early years/childcare, long-term care for the elderly, and active labour market policy). UK social security rules and benefits in these circumstances set boundaries to the options of devolved administrations and, thus, maintain UK-wide floor standards.

- In some circumstances, devolved administrations seek to maintain common UK-wide standards, even in their fields of competence. The **Sewel convention** has, for example, frequently been used in Scotland as a means of ensuring consistency of legislation in some fields between Scottish and Westminster jurisdictions. It was also used (rather more sparingly) when devolution in Northern Ireland was in operation, and is envisaged by the 2005 White Paper for use in Wales, if, and when, there is a move to primary legislative powers.

- The **European Union** has been a force for convergence, either by setting common regulatory frameworks that have to be applied across the UK, or, perhaps more interestingly, by imposing UK-wide discipline on UK and devolved governments (a state can have only one voice in EU-level negotiations, even when the subject at hand falls under devolved competence). A quite systematic practice of intergovernmental co-ordination on EU matters has emerged, based on information sharing and systematic exchange. The only formation of the Joint Ministerial Committee that has met regularly is that on EU matters. Equally, UK and devolved agriculture ministers – whose business is EU-dominated – meet multilaterally on a systematic basis, as do UK and Scottish fisheries ministers. It is remarkable that only where the external rationale of defining a single UK policy for EU negotiations comes into play do we see systematic internal co-ordination between UK governments.

- But, perhaps **the strongest force for convergence across the UK is England**. The UK is an extraordinarily lopsided state, with the preponderant part (England) governed centrally and the peripheral parts (Scotland, Wales, Northern Ireland) self-governing in most fields of domestic policy. England makes up around eighty-four per cent of the UK's population and over eighty-five per cent of GDP. As long as the UK retains a single economic market, a single welfare state (at least in terms of social security, but also, in popular imagery, in health), and a single internal-security area, it is inevitable that decisions taken for the biggest part of those single areas will have impacts on the peripheral parts. For example:

- The existence of a single higher-education market has made it increasingly difficult for devolved administrations to uphold funding mechanisms for universities that diverge from those applied in England. The agenda for the 2005 review of higher-education funding in Wales was, for example, driven by the need for Welsh universities to be able to compete on the same terms as their English counterparts.

- The last UK election produced intensive debates about health policy in Scotland and Wales (which are devolved issues not at stake in UK elections), in particular about the 'failure' of the NHS in Scotland and Wales to meet targets set in Whitehall for the NHS in England. In similar vein, because adjustments to the size of the devolved block grants are made via the Barnett formula, as a result of UK Government decisions on spending programmes in England, it can be difficult not to follow the broad pattern of English expenditure where areas sensitive in public opinion are concerned (to say 'England is spending ten per cent more on health, but we will not' is difficult).

- The Scottish government is committed to an immigration policy to counter population decline, but is dependent on a UK Government reluctant to allow territorial flexibility to a UK immigration policy increasingly understood in policy debates in England as a matter of internal security, not population replacement.

Balancing uniformity and diversity

The preceding discussion has set out:

1. what people appear to want from devolution, which is, at best, limited territorial policy variation, state-wide sharing of risk and opportunity, but decentralised ownership of decision-making;

2. what the institutions of a post-devolution UK are set to deliver, in other words, competing forces for territorial divergence and UK-wide convergence of policy outcomes.

Hardly any effort has been invested by any UK politician into thinking through how the competing institutional logics of divergence and convergence can be harnessed to produce something broadly consistent with public expectations. The single, partial exception is Gordon Brown, who has recognised over decades the problem of reconciling devolution with the traditional social democratic – and state-wide – objectives of the welfare state. He articulated that problem in the aftermath of the failed devolution reforms of 1979:

> No theorist attempted in sufficient depth to reconcile the conflicting aspirations for home rule and a British socialist advance. In particular no one was able to show how capturing power in Britain – and legislating for minimum levels of welfare, for example – could be combined with a policy of devolution for Scotland. (cited in Mitchell forthcoming b).

Since 1997, Brown has made repeated efforts to justify devolution by putting forward arguments about the binding effect of shared values that extend across the boundaries of the UK's nations. But he is at his weakest when addressing the welfare state:

> Today when people talk about the National Health Service whether in Scotland, Wales or England people think of the British National Health Service… And its most powerful driving idea is that every citizen of Britain has an equal right to treatment regardless of wealth, position or race and, indeed, can secure treatment in any part of Britain… When we pool and share our resources and when the stronger help the weak it makes us all stronger… I believe that the common bonds and mutual interests linking our destinies together is as real for other public services: the ideal that every child in Britain should have an equal opportunity in education. And the equally strong belief, widely felt throughout the country, that everyone in Britain who can work has the right and responsibility to do so. When Scots, English or Welsh talk of the right to work, they do not normally distinguish between the rights of the Scottish, Welsh or English miner, computer technician, nurse or teacher. (Brown 1999).

Brown's claims about the strength of common, Britain-wide beliefs are well-founded in public opinion. The problem is that, increasingly, the realities of educational opportunity, labour markets, and healthcare provision do not match the Britain-wide reach of those beliefs, but, instead, vary significantly by national territory. In Scotland, for example, there is less selection in secondary education than in England, teachers are paid more, and healthcare is delivered differently. This is Greer's 'divergence machine' in operation, an institutional logic based on the terms of the devolution settlement and embedded by territorially bounded and distinctive democratic processes.

There is a pessimistic, almost knee-jerk response to this, as expressed by Vernon Bogdanor who laments that 'devolution marks the end of … the belief that a benign government at Westminster can secure the distribution of benefits and burdens on the basis not of geography but need (Bogdanor 1999). But, there is, of course, the countervailing convergence logic that, through mechanisms based in informal exchange among officials, competence overlaps, Europe, and the overweening weight of England, places some limit on the level of divergence. The real question is whether those mechanisms are adequate to the task of expressing the UK-wide solidarities and commitments that citizens appear to want to uphold, while providing for the decentralised ownership of decision-making they favour. They, in most respects, appear inadequate to that task.

There are a number of reasons for that inadequacy. The first is the informality, and, with it, the opacity, of intergovernmental co-ordination. Intergovernmental co-ordination is about the intersection of UK-level and devolved democratic processes. But informal co-ordination is, by definition, opaque, and lacks democratic accountability. It is also based on goodwill, rather than rights. There are circumstances in which goodwill might evaporate, conceivably shutting off devolved access to UK Government thinking. Second, it is doubtful that England's spillovers are a desirable way to contain the autonomy of devolved governments. Those spillovers are not always predictable and rarely intended. They have arisen, instead, in two main ways: a) the failure of UK-level departments to think through, or consult on, the effects of their decisions outside of England (the UK Government famously failed to consult the Scotland government on the content of the 2003 Higher Education White Paper because of the presence of the Liberal Democrats in that government, and despite the considerable implications of the White Paper across a common UK higher-education market); and b) because of a preponderant media focus in Scotland or Wales on the direction and performance regimes of policies decided by Westminster for England (notably on healthcare performance indicators during the 2005 general-election campaign). Third, it is doubtful that many of the forces for convergence would operate easily if there were party-political incongruence between UK and devolved governments.

Having had Labour-led governments across Great Britain since devolution has helped the operation of the forces for convergence listed above. Officials and territorial Secretaries of State have had a relatively easy time in ensuring good lines of communication, because they have been working within a single ideological tradition – even when, as, for example, on long-term care in Scotland, there were differences about how to interpret the overlap of UK-level social security and devolved health-care competences (McLeish 2004). Those lines of communication and dispute resolution would be made much more difficult with, say, a Conservative government in Westminster and a Labour-led coalition in Holyrood. It is, for example, difficult to see a UK government led by one party maintaining the information flows and access to central-government deliberations on EU policy that are possible at the moment, if its counterpart in Scotland were a government led by a different party. It would be more difficult in those circumstances to use Sewel motions so routinely to have Westminster legislate in fields of Scottish competence. Likewise, the practice of finding space in Westminster bills for empowerments of the National Assembly for Wales would be more difficult. Such practices would be harder to manage across the adversarial tradition of British party politics. But, even if a UK government were in non-adversarial mood, it might still be less inclined to open up time in what is always a crowded legislative timetable at Westminster to meet Scottish or Welsh concerns.

And finally, England's spillovers would increasingly become a challenge to the outcomes of devolved democratic processes, as soon as those spillovers reflected decisions made from within a different ideological tradition. This would be all the more the case if those decisions involved a reduction of expenditures in England, for example through a shift to private provision of public services, which then knocked on via Barnett to a Scotland or Wales in which the terms of party competition and interest-group politics might be against replicating the same policy. England's sheer weight within the UK, when amplified by partisan conflict, could quickly generate territorial conflict between devolved and UK administrations.

All this is a longer route to a familiar conclusion: for long-term stability, the operation of a part-devolved political system in a lopsided UK is likely to require more systematic, more formalised and, ultimately, justifiable 'rules of the game' for the co-ordination of UK-level and devolved governments in order to: a) act as shock absorbers for that future point when different parties run different governments; and b) produce the kind of balance of shared values and self-government to which citizens in Scotland, Wales and Northern Ireland aspire. It does not appear likely that some of the practices familiar elsewhere – establishing state-wide framework or floor standards, or bringing some element of conditionality into devolved funding arrangements – could be applied in the UK in order to establish some of those rules. Such measures would require major reforms to the devolution 'constitution', and would require additional guarantees for devolved autonomy, such as input into definition of framework standards or enhanced fiscal autonomy to limit dependence on 'strings attached' funding by the centre. There is little appetite for the, no doubt protracted, constitutional debate such measures would generate.

In other words, any attempt to define more systematic rules of the game needs to build on the framework for intergovernmental co-ordination that we currently have. This was precisely the point made in the very first recommendation of the 2002 report of the House of Lords Constitution Committee on what it called 'inter-institutional' relations in the UK:

> We recommend that further use should be made of the formal mechanisms for intergovernmental relations, even if they seem to many of those presently involved as excessive … Such mechanisms are likely to

become increasingly important when governments of different political persuasions have to deal with each other. (House of Lords 2002, p. 5)

The UK Government's was an equally striking dismissal of that recommendation, amid a confidence that ministers and officials would continue to work together in the way they do now, as a 'second nature irrespective of the political persuasion of the administration involved' (UK Government 2003, p.3). That dismissal sounds like a triumph of hope over any conventional understanding of party politics in the UK, where 'second nature' is that of adversariality, not cross-party co-operation. The oddities of the UK's devolution settlement will require fuller thinking to contain the implications of that instinct for adversariality. The challenge of managing a lopsided state, when electoral processes throw up divergent mandates, is one that should not be underestimated. That it has been underestimated reflects the ease with which pre-devolution practices of intragovernmental accommodation of territorial interests could be transformed into devolved democratic processes. The continuities that have underpinned that transformation have been a tremendous short-term advantage for the implementation of the devolution reforms in a context of pan-British Labour dominance. But the complacency that those continuities have encouraged, threatens to become a crippling disability over the longer timeframe, in which partisan conflict will enter, complicate and disrupt the territorial equation.

References

Adams J, Robinson P and Vigor A (2003) *A New Regional Policy for the UK* ippr

Bogdanor V (1999) 'Constitutional Reform', in Seldon A (ed.) *The Blair Effect. The Blair Government 1997-2001* Little, Brown, pp. 139-158

Brown G (1999) Speech at the Smith Institute, 15 April 1999

Curtice J (2004) *Brought Together or Driven Apart?* unpublished paper

Greer S (2005a) 'The Fragile Divergence Machine: Citizenship, Policy Divergence and Devolution' in Trench A (ed.) *Devolution and Power* Manchester University Press

Greer S (2005b) *Territorial politics and health policy. UK health policy in comparative perspective* Manchester University Press

Grube N (2001) 'Föderalismus in der öffentlichen Meinung der Bundesrepublik Deutschland' *Jahrbuch des Föderalismus 2001* Nomos, pp. 101-114

Grube N (2004) 'Unverzichtbares Korrektiv oder ineffective Reformbremse? Wahrnehmung föderaler Strukturen und Institutionen in Deutschland' *Jahrbuch des Föderalismus 2004* Nomos, pp. 163-175

Hazell R (2003) 'Conclusion. The Devolution Scorecard as the Devolved Assemblies Head for the Polls', in Hazell R (ed.) *The State of the Nations 2003: The Third Year of Devolution in the United Kingdom* Imprint Academic pp. 285-301

House of Lords (2002) Select Committee on the Constitution Session 2002-03, 2nd Report, *Devolution: Inter-Institutional Relations in the United Kingdom*, HL Paper 28, TSO

Jeffery C (2005) 'Devolution and Social Citizenship. Which Society, Whose Citizenship?' in Greer S (ed.) *Territory, Democracy and Justice* Palgrave

Jeffery C (forthcoming a) 'UK Politics beyond Westminster', in Dunleavy P *et al.* (eds.) *Developments in British Politics 8* Palgrave

Jeffery C (forthcoming b) 'Devolution and Local Government' in *Publius. The Journal of Federalism* 36:1

Keating Michael (2005) *The Government of Scotland. Public Policy Making after Devolution* Edinburgh University Press

Loughlin J and Sykes S (2004) 'Devolution and Policy-making in Wales: Restructuring the System and Reinforcing Identity' Policy Papers No. 11, ESRC Devolution and Constitutional Change Programme, available at http://www.devolution.ac.uk/pdfdata/Loughlin_and%20_Sykes_policy_paper.pdf

McCrone D (1998) 'Thatcherism in a Cold Climate' in Paterson L (ed.) *A Diverse Assembly: The Debate on the Scottish Parliament* Edinburgh University Press pp. 205-210

McLeish H (2004) *Scotland First. Truth and Consequences* Mainstream

Mitchell J (forthcoming a) 'Approaching the archangelic: the nature and purposes of devolution' in *Publius. The Journal of Federalism* 36:1.

Mitchell J (forthcoming b) 'Evolution and Devolution: Citizenship, institutions and public policy' in *Publius. The Journal of Federalism* 36:1

Morgan K (2002) 'The English Question: Regional Perspectives on a Fractured Nation' in *Regional Studies* 36:7, pp. 797-810

Parry R (2003) 'The Home Civil Service after Devolution' Policy Papers No. 6 ESRC Devolution and Constitutional Change Programme, available at http://www.devolution.ac.uk/pdfdata/policy_paper_parry.htm.

Trench A (2001) 'Intergovernmental Relations a Year On' in Trench A (ed.) The State of the Nations 2001. *The Second Year of Devolution in the United Kingdom* Imprint Academic, pp. 153-174.

UK Government (2003) The Government's Response to the Second Report of the Select Committee on the Constitution, Session 2002-2003 *Devolution: Inter-Institutional Relations in the United Kingdom* Cm 5780, available at http://www.dca.gov.uk/constitution/devolution/pubs/odpm_dev_609018.pdf.

Wyn Jones R and Scully R (2004) 'Devolution in Wales: What Does the Public Think?' *Devolution Briefings No. 7* ESRC Devolution and Constitutional Change Programme, available at http://www.devolution.ac.uk/pdfdata/Scully_RLJ_Briefing7.pdf.

3 Divergence in priorities, perceived policy failure and pressure for convergence

Katie Schmuecker and John Adams

There were many different reasons why the creation of devolved institutions became politically possible in the latter half of the twentieth century. In the case of Scotland and Wales, it was, in part, bound up in debates about nationhood, and the political representation of identity. In Northern Ireland, conflict resolution was a key driver for devolution. Also, in all three territories, the desire for a new, more open and participatory form of politics was important. However, while the need to find local solutions to local problems and address specific territorial needs is a key rationale for devolution, it is an area that was not fully discussed in the devolution-referendum debates. However, the ability of different parts of the UK to pursue divergent policies and prioritise different issues is an inevitable consequence of political devolution. This has traditionally been a concern for those on the left of British politics who have a commitment to social justice and equity.

As several other authors contributing to this publication have made clear, divergence in policy is not a new phenomenon for the UK. The work of the Scottish, Welsh and Northern Ireland Offices, prior to political devolution, gave these territories the ability to vary policies to suit their particular needs. The move to political devolution has not only made divergence more transparent, but the democratic accountability that accompanies it increases the scope for divergence, as policy-makers now have a level of legitimacy not enjoyed by the Scottish, Welsh and Northern Ireland Offices.

This chapter will consider in more detail where we are beginning to see divergence within the UK. We look at the devolution settlement and the complicated mix of reserved and devolved powers, and the geographical reach of Whitehall departments. We will discuss the priorities of the devolved administrations in comparison to England, by looking at the financial input in different policy areas, and whether different priorities can be perceived. We will look at where there is divergence in the targets and outputs in some key areas, since devolution. Finally, we will consider the questions of policy-learning and perceived policy failure within the UK. First, however, we will consider the scope for divergence in policies in the UK.

The devolution settlement and scope for divergence

In a post-devolution world, policy-making is a complicated matter, with a mix of reserved, devolved and concurrent powers varying between Whitehall, Scotland, Wales, Northern Ireland and London. Modern government does not work on the basis of watertight divisions of functions and competencies. This is a real challenge that needs to be met to ensure that the public sector is effective in its interventions. Policy-makers will need to be clear about the objectives of policy, clear about which policy tools are most appropriate, clear about at which spatial scale these policy tools should be designed and administered, and clear about how they will interact in practice 'on the ground'. It is the people who most rely on government action and strong public services who suffer most from such failures of co-ordination.

Unfortunately, Whitehall is struggling to rise to these challenges, and departments are still unclear about when they operate on an English basis, when they are performing UK-wide functions, and when they are performing a quasi-federal responsibility. Despite this confusion, there is, actually, a little-known but straightforward guide to the geographical extent of Whitehall's spending programmes.

Every two years, as part of the UK Government's Spending Review process, HM Treasury publishes *A Statement of Funding Policy* (HMT 2004a). This document sets out some of the arrangements that apply in deciding the budgets of the devolved institutions, and details the extent to which the public-sector services delivered by United Kingdom government departments correspond to services within the budgets of the devolved administrations. If we can use public expenditure as an indicator of whether or not a programme is devolved, at least as defined by the Departmental Expenditure Limits (DELs), it is relatively simple to determine whether a Whitehall departmental programme extends to England, England and Wales, Great Britain or the United Kingdom.

The term the Treasury uses to describe this is 'comparability'. Officially defined, comparability is 'The extent to which services delivered by Departments of the United Kingdom Government correspond to the services within the assigned budgets of the devolved administrations' (HM Treasury 2004a). If a programme is devolved, the mechanisms that finance the devolved institutions provide monies that would allow the devolved institutions to fund a comparable programme, although the devolved institutions are free to use that money in any way they think fit, and may choose to use the money to fund different programmes creating policy variation. Therefore, if a programme is devolved, the comparability percentage is 100 per cent, as there could be a comparable programme in the devolved territories. If the programme is not devolved, the comparability percentage is zero.

This is clearly not a perfect proxy. First, not all public-policy issues involve public expenditure. In particular, regulation can shape policy without necessarily having large levels of expenditure attached. Second, the Treasury regards a small number of exceptional sub-programmes as unique at the United Kingdom level, such as the Channel Tunnel Rail Link. Third, the DELs do not include some agency-type functions, such as some expenditure under the Common Agriculture Policy. However, the devolved administrations have almost no discretion in this field. Fourth, DELs do not include the revenue-raising sources under the control of the devolved administrations, namely Non-Domestic Rates revenue, Local Authority Self-Financed Expenditure and the proceeds of the 'tartan tax' in Scotland (if it is ever used).

Table 3.1: Comparability percentages for 2004 Spending Review

	Scotland	Wales	NI
Forestry	100.0	100.0	100.0
Education and Skills	99.8	93.5	99.8
ODPM (not local government)	99.6	99.6	99.7
Health	99.5	99.5	99.5
Culture, Media and Sport	95.4	89.1	99.0
Local Government	65.7	100.0	49.3
Environment and Rural Affairs	85.2	80.4	85.2
Transport	71.3	63.8	94.7
Trade and Industry	18.6	18.6	27.6
Home Office	99.6	1.5	3.5
Work and Pensions	6.4	6.4	100.0
Legal departments	96.1	0.0	1.3
Chancellor's departments	0.9	0.9	4.0
Cabinet Office	2.0	2.0	18.7

Source: HM Treasury (2004a)

Table 3.1 lists the Treasury's 'comparability percentages' for each Whitehall Department in the 2004 Spending Review. It should be noted that, while there are numerous different comparability percentages at the departmental level, at the programme level, public expenditure is either devolved or not, and the percentages are either 100 or zero. It is also worth noting that the National Assembly for Wales has limited control over the non-domestic rating system, but, in Scotland and Northern Ireland, this falls within the DEL. This technicality means that the comparability percentages for local government in Scotland and Northern Ireland are misleading, and, in fact, the comparability percentage for Wales of 100 per cent should be taken as indicative for all three territories.

Table 3.2 then goes on to classify Whitehall Departments into rough territorial groupings. We can classify three Whitehall departments as 'mostly English' in the sense that they exercise only very modest reserved powers on behalf of the UK: Health, Education and Skills, and the Office of the Deputy Prime Minister (which has responsibility for local government, planning and housing functions). There are five 'hybrid' departments that have their counterparts in one or more of the devolved territories, but that do exercise some significant reserved powers. There are four 'mostly UK' departments that carry out mostly reserved functions, but also exercise some specifically 'English' functions too. We have classified the DTI as a 'mostly UK' department rather than a 'hybrid' department, because four out of five of its main policy respon-sibilities are exercised at the UK level, although they do not always involve a large amount of money. Finally, we have three departments that deal with international issues.

Table 3.2: Classification of Whitehall departments			
'Mostly English'	'Hybrid'	'Mostly UK'	'International'
Health	DCMS	HM Treasury	Defence
Education and Skills	DEFRA	Work and Pensions	Foreign Office
ODPM	Transport	Trade and Industry	DfID
	Home Office	Cabinet Office	
	Legal departments		

Notes:
• A 'mostly English' department has only very modest reserved powers.
• A 'hybrid' department exercises functions on behalf of England (or England and Wales) that are carried out on a devolved basis in the territories, with departments explicitly covering these functions in Cardiff, Edinburgh and Belfast, but also exercises significant reserved powers.
• A 'mostly UK' department carries out mostly reserved functions, but with some English Functions too.

This settlement would seem to create a highly permissive environment for divergence. The scope for divergence has been further enhanced by the sus-tained increases in the level of expenditure available to the devolved adminis-trations through the block grant. This has meant that tough policy trade-offs about what the priorities are and where public money should be spent have, to some extent, been avoided (Paxton and Gamble 2005).

Furthermore, as tables 3.1 and 3.2 highlight, there is a very high degree of devolution of some of the key public services. Health, education, local gov-ernment and housing are completely, or very nearly completely, devolved. Also, as table 3.1 shows, in Scotland, law and order is fully devolved, follow-ing on from the long-standing separate legal system that the Scots have main-tained. In Northern Ireland, social security is also devolved, although there is an agreement that policy will mirror that of Great Britain. As discussed in chap-ter 1, this devolution of powers is not accompanied by agreed principles of service, minimum standards of provision or floor targets. So, while it may seem unlikely, there would be little, in theory, that could prevent the Scottish Parliament from abolishing the NHS and the principle of treatment free at the point of care, and moving to a different health system should it so wish. This is particularly striking, as Jeffery (2002) notes: variation in economic policy is generally more acceptable to the general public than variation in social poli-cies, yet in the UK the level of devolution is greater in social policy fields than it is in economic policy areas.

However, this considerable scope for divergence does not necessarily mean there will be high levels of divergence. There are complex factors that influence convergence and divergence, and, while the settlement may be permissive of divergence, there are also a number of factors pushing the UK towards convergence, for example the sharing of a common welfare state and a common market across the UK (Keating 2002). These factors also create pressures for convergence in some areas where divergence is legally possible (see Raffe, chapter 4, for a discussion of the pressure for convergence in qualifications due to the common UK labour market).

Furthermore, at present, the Labour Party is in power, or leading a coalition, in all parts of Great Britain, and Northern Ireland is experiencing a period of direct rule. The fact that individuals elected for a political party will share a broad set of values is a significant force for convergence. While the fact that the Labour Party is in power in all four administrations in the UK does not mean there is policy uniformity across the UK, there is an incentive to ensure policies in one part of the country will not be embarrassing or electorally damaging in other parts of the country. Indeed, as Bradbury and Mitchell have argued, party politics has constrained policy-making in Scotland because there is a shortened electoral cycle, with both devolved elections and UK general elections. They argue that this exerts pressure on the Executive to avoid difficult decisions in order to avoid making unpopular decisions in the run-up to either set of elections (Bradbury and Mitchell 2005). This is despite the fact that the record of the UK Government ought to be the focus of UK general elections, not that of the Scottish Executive. Finally, and importantly, public opinion can be a strong force for convergence. As Jeffery discusses in chapter 2, there is a high level of public expectation for common standards of provision across the UK, particularly in key public services, a point we will return to later.

The remainder of this chapter will explore further the complex relationship between divergence and convergence. However, before going on to consider this issue, it is helpful to get a view of where divergence may be occurring. The next section offers an analysis of the priorities of the devolved administrations in terms of expenditure and targets, and how these may be having an impact on outputs.

Devolution and divergence in priorities?

While it is clear that the devolution settlement creates considerable scope for divergence, six years into devolution it is still difficult to discern the extent of divergence in the UK. Certainly, there is a difference in the processes of policy-making, in terms of how inclusive the devolved administrations are. Wincott, in chapter 6, points out that childcare specialists have been highly influential in early-years education in Wales and, likewise, Greer, in chapter 7, identifies the influence the medical profession have had on policy-making in Scotland, leading him to refer to the Scottish NHS system as 'professionalist'. However, it is not yet clear that these different political processes are leading to divergent policy inputs and outputs.

We have seen a small number of flagship policies that are frequently cited as examples of the devolved administrations 'doing things differently', be it free long-term personal care for the elderly and the abolition of upfront tuition fees in Scotland, or free bus travel for pensioners and the disabled or the abolition of prescription fees for the under-twenty-fives in Wales. However, while it was to be expected that the devolved administrations would seek a number of headline grabbing policies to underline their difference from England and to 'prove their worth', this section will look at some of the underlying trends beneath these headline policies.

This is not a straightforward task. The UK is a relatively small, highly interdependent country, and policy developments in one area will inevitably have spillover effects in other parts of the UK. Also, the weight of existing policy commitments limits the ability of the devolved administrations to radically change policy in such a short period of time (Keating 2002). However, this section will look at this question of divergence in three ways: first, whether devo-

Table 3.3: Time taken for change in public services

Phases	What is it?	Timescales
Changing inputs	Resources devoted to a public service or bits within it	1-2 years for significant budget allocations
Changing processes	How public services are 'produced'	2-4 years for organisational, staffing, process and other changes. Capital investment may take longer
Changing outputs	What public services actually produce, for example hip operations, GCSE results	3-5 years as the inputs work through the system
Outcomes	The ultimate effect of public services, for example better health and education	5-10 at the very least. Some changes (for example care of vulnerable children) may take much longer (not until the children are adults)

Source: Talbot et al. (2004)

lution is changing patterns of expenditure in the devolved territories; second, what targets are being set in England, Scotland, Wales and Northern Ireland; and, finally, where possible, whether devolution is having an impact on public-sector outputs. However, the extent to which this can be achieved in a comprehensive or concrete way is limited by the relatively young nature of devolution. Table 3.3 is taken from Talbot *et al.* (2004) and gives an indication of the time taken for significant change to occur in the public services. It is clear from this that we should certainly be able to discern changing inputs and some early outputs, as a result of early policy changes. However, it is too soon to expect to see divergence in outcomes.

Divergence in inputs

Looking at the spending patterns of the four administrations can help to build a picture of policy priorities, and where these might be divergent. As discussed in the previous section, this focus on spending and planned expenditure only acts as a rough proxy for policy priorities, as other factors can change policy without necessarily appearing in budgets. It is also important to stress that we are simply mapping divergent trends in public expenditure. We will not draw conclusions as to whether Whitehall or the devolved administrations are taking the correct course of action.

However, with these caveats in mind, an analysis of changes to patterns of expenditure since devolution can give an idea of the policy areas in which expenditure is increasing more rapidly, and, therefore, a sense of where the priorities lie. To do so requires us to look at patterns of expenditure since 1999, when the devolved administrations came into existence. It is frequently argued that 1999 should not be treated as 'year zero' for the devolved administrations, as political devolution builds upon an era of administrative devolution, and there was substantial policy divergence prior to political devolution. However, that said, 1999 does mark the beginning of political decision-making in Scotland and Wales (and, intermittently, Northern Ireland), where devolved parliaments and assemblies are in charge of the budgets. Analysing levels of public expenditure in different policy areas since 1999 can, therefore, give an idea of which areas are being prioritised (or indeed de-prioritised) by the devolved administrations, at least in comparison to England.

Ideally, this would only be done with the 'assigned' portion of the devolved administrations' budgets, as they have full discretion over this part of the budget (see Heald 2002 for the detailed workings of the devolved administrations' budgets). Unfortunately, this data is only produced and made publicly available by the Scottish Executive. While the Welsh Assembly Government and the Northern Ireland departments publish detailed spending plans for the coming years, they do not publish outturn figures consistently and across all departments. This is both surprising and disappointing, as a key argument in favour of devolution has been an open and more accountable form of politics. There is also a question here for central government, as most federal governments in most federal countries would produce consistent data across all regions and territories within the nation state, as reliable and comparable data is vital for evidence-based policy-making.

Figure 3.1 shows indexed outturn figures and planned expenditure for the core Scottish departments since 1999. These figures suggest that three departments have seen sustained, above-average increases in expenditure: Health, Education and Development (housing, community regeneration and anti-poverty strategies). As figure 3.1 shows, the policy area that saw the greatest increase in public expenditure was education, which increased by eighty-five per cent over the period 1999/00- 2005/06. In contrast, expenditure on the environment and rural affairs grew by thirty-seven per cent in the same period.

However, to be able to really discern where divergence may be taking place in a UK context and where the priorities may be different, it is important to find figures that are comparable across the UK. It is also important to bear in mind that the devolved territories have traditionally enjoyed higher levels of expenditure per head, under the so-called Barnett formula. Furthermore, while

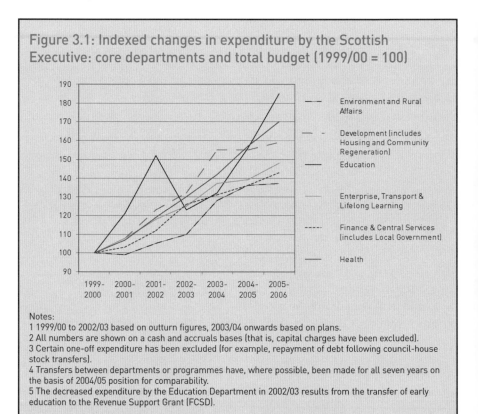

Figure 3.1: Indexed changes in expenditure by the Scottish Executive: core departments and total budget (1999/00 = 100)

Notes:
1 1999/00 to 2002/03 based on outturn figures, 2003/04 onwards based on plans.
2 All numbers are shown on a cash and accruals bases (that is, capital charges have been excluded).
3 Certain one-off expenditure has been excluded (for example, repayment of debt following council-house stock transfers).
4 Transfers between departments or programmes have, where possible, been made for all seven years on the basis of 2004/05 position for comparability.
5 The decreased expenditure by the Education Department in 2002/03 results from the transfer of early education to the Revenue Support Grant (FCSD).

Source: Scottish Executive (2004c) and authors' calculations

much has been written in recent years about the impending 'Barnett squeeze', table 3.4 would indicate that this is not yet evident, certainly in the case of Scotland.

It may well be that a cogent case can be made for higher levels of expenditure in the devolved territories on the basis of need. However, what is clear from this evidence is that the devolved territories continue to enjoy levels of public expenditure per capita that are somewhat higher than in England.

Table 3.4: Index of identifiable public expenditure on services per head in the devolved territories and England (UK=100)

	1999-00 outturn	2000-01 outturn	2001-02 outturn	2002-03 outturn	2003-04 outturn	2004-05 plans
England	96	96	96	96	96	97
Scotland	118	118	119	118	119	118
Wales	114	114	112	113	112	111
NI	132	133	132	133	129	129

Source: HM Treasury (2005b)

In the absence of comparable data from the devolved administrations, the *Public Expenditure Statistical Analyses* (PESA) (HM Treasury 2005b) provides data that can be used to analyse financial inputs. These figures analyse the total identifiable public expenditure – that which can be identified as benefiting a particular geographical area – which now accounts for eighty-four per cent of total public expenditure (HM Treasury 2005b). The remaining sixteen per cent is money spent for the benefit of the UK as a whole, for example on international development or defence. The identifiable public expenditure figures include both local and central government spending, and that of the devolved administrations.

A further benefit of the PESA figures is that they use functional categories that cut across departmental boundaries. This is particularly useful when comparing the constituent parts of the UK, as transfers of responsibility across departments do not affect the series, and neither do the different departmental structures of the devolved administrations. This makes the data consistent and comparable over time (HMT 2005a).

Tables 3.1 and 3.2 in the previous section indicate the areas where Whitehall implements few programmes outside of England, indicating that the expenditure that exists must come from the devolved administrations. Expenditure on health, education, local government and housing is almost entirely at the discretion of the devolved administrations, and that on culture, media and sport, and environment and rural affairs is largely so. Analysing change in public expenditure since 1999 in these areas gives an indication of the relative priority placed on different public services in comparison to England.

This section will look particularly at the key public services of health and education, policy areas that consistently top the list of salient issues that voters most care about (MORI 2005), and which may constitute an important part of shared national identity (see chapter 2). Scotland, Wales and Northern Ireland have consistently enjoyed higher levels of expenditure per capita on these key public services, although, in recent years, every part of the UK has seen substantial increases in public expenditure on both health and education (HM Treasury 2005b). However, if the level of expenditure in 1999 is treated as the starting point for each administration, and the percentage increases of expenditure per head in the constituent parts of the UK are calculated, it seems that the devolved administrations have not increased expenditure on health and education to the same degree as England.

While figure 3.1 suggests health and education have received the largest increases in funding within the Scottish Executive's budget, we see a slightly different story of where the priorities lie if we compare the devolved administrations and England. Figures 3.2 and 3.3 suggest that, while increases in identifiable public expenditure in these areas have been significant in the devolved territories, England has seen notably higher increases. Expenditure on health in England increased by sixty-five per cent in the period 1999/00-2004/05. The equivalent figure in Scotland and Northern Ireland is fifty-seven per cent; and

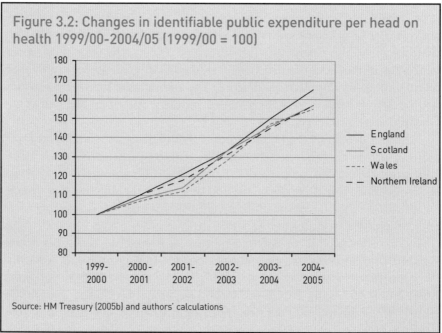

Figure 3.2: Changes in identifiable public expenditure per head on health 1999/00-2004/05 (1999/00 = 100)

Source: HM Treasury (2005b) and authors' calculations

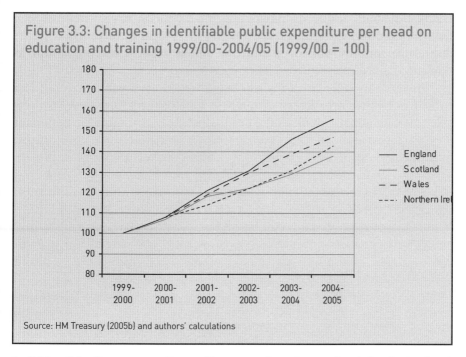

Figure 3.3: Changes in identifiable public expenditure per head on education and training 1999/00-2004/05 (1999/00 = 100)

Source: HM Treasury (2005b) and authors' calculations

in Wales, fifty-five per cent. Expenditure on education and training in England increased by fifty-six per cent over the same period. The equivalent figure in Wales is forty-seven per cent; in Northern Ireland, forty-three per cent; and in Scotland, thirty-eight per cent.

This is particularly surprising, as Scotland and Wales are often regarded as being bigger spenders on education, particularly following high-profile and high-expenditure policies on the payment of university tuition fees and higher teachers' salaries in Scotland. While the Welsh policy on top-up fees has not yet been put into practice, the Scottish policy on upfront payment of tuition fees has been in place since 2000, yet, in terms of increases in expenditure on education and training, Scotland was behind England, Wales and Northern Ireland.

There are a number of possible reasons for this divergence. It may be that the devolved administrations are pursuing improvements to health and education and training in ways that do not require high levels of expenditure. Alternatively, the devolved administrations may consider their inherited levels of expenditure to be adequate and not in need of increase on the same scale as England. On the other hand, it may be that other policy objectives have been prioritised over and above health and education.

If expenditure on health and education has not increased in Scotland and Wales at the same rate as in England, this means that other policy areas must have seen increases greater than in England. Figure 3.4 shows increases in expenditure per head on agriculture, fisheries and forestry, and figure 3.5

shows recreation, culture and religion, again taking 1999/00 as a baseline. This analysis would seem to suggest that the devolved administrations have prioritised these areas in terms of public expenditure to a higher degree than in England. Expenditure on recreation, culture and religion, between 1999/00 and 2004/05, increased by thirty-two per cent in Wales, by thirty-one per cent in Scotland, by twenty-two per cent in Northern Ireland and by eleven per cent

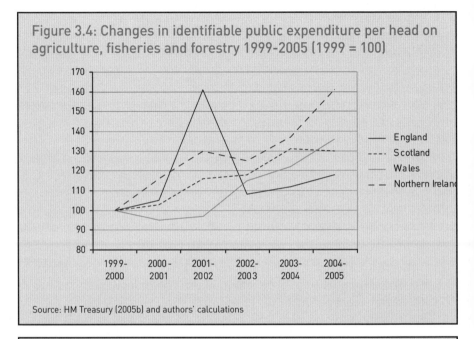

Figure 3.4: Changes in identifiable public expenditure per head on agriculture, fisheries and forestry 1999-2005 (1999 = 100)

Source: HM Treasury (2005b) and authors' calculations

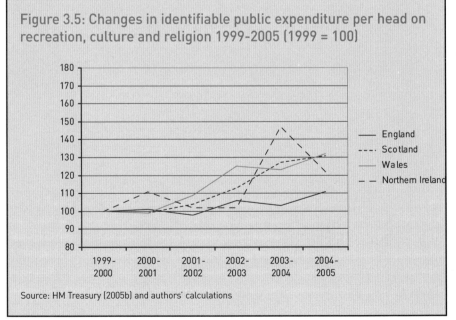

Figure 3.5: Changes in identifiable public expenditure per head on recreation, culture and religion 1999-2005 (1999 = 100)

Source: HM Treasury (2005b) and authors' calculations

in England. In the same period, expenditure on agriculture, fisheries and forestry increased by sixty-one per cent in Northern Ireland, by thirty-six per cent in Wales, by thirty per cent in Scotland and by eighteen per cent in England. While figure 3.1 shows that spending on the environment and rural affairs received the lowest increase in expenditure within the Scottish Executive budget, the growth in expenditure was still considerably higher than in England, although somewhat less than in Wales and Northern Ireland.

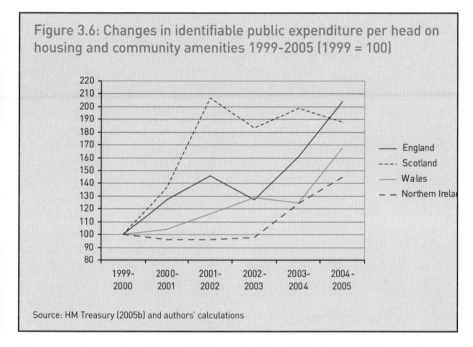

Figure 3.6: Changes in identifiable public expenditure per head on housing and community amenities 1999-2005 (1999 = 100)

Source: HM Treasury (2005b) and authors' calculations

Some care has to be taken with the agriculture, fisheries and forestry figures, for a number of reasons. First, the spike in English expenditure in 2001/02 represents the assistance given to farmers following the foot and mouth epidemic, which was a temporary increase in expenditure due to extenuating circumstances. Second, while agriculture, fisheries and forestry are largely devolved, both agriculture and fisheries are areas highly constrained by EU directives and programmes. While expenditure on the Common Agricultural Policy and the associated Rural Development Plans appear within the devolved administrations' DEL budgets, it is an area they have little discretion over. Indeed, officials in the Scottish Executive suggest that there is discretion over only a quarter to a third of the department's budget. However, in areas where there is discretion, such as agricultural research services, funding for fisheries decommissioning and transitional-aid-schemes expenditure has increased substantially (Scottish Executive 2001, 2002, 2003 and 2004a). This would seem to support the view that rural affairs have a higher political profile in Scotland and Wales (Ward and Lowe 2002)

A rather more mixed picture can be seen in relation to housing and community amenities (figure 3.6), where expenditure per head in Scotland doubled in the first two years, whereas in Northern Ireland expenditure actually fell until 2002/03, when direct rule was reinstalled and expenditure rose sharply. There is a more mixed picture of expenditure in Wales and England, with expenditure in England rising sharply from 2002/03 onwards, coinciding with the publication of the Sustainable Communities Plan (ODPM 2003). In England, expenditure increased by 104 per cent in the period 1999/00 to 2004/05, while in Scotland the equivalent figure was eighty-eighty per cent; in Wales, sixty-eight per cent; and in Northern Ireland, forty-five per cent.

The trends identified here are limited in a number of ways. First, this analysis can only be applied to areas that are either fully or mostly devolved. Second, the approach is rather broadbrush, looking at a functional, rather than a programme level. However, on this latter point, the value of this analysis is that the figures used are comparable, revealing over the short period of devolution so far that England continues to place a higher emphasis on health and education. While increases in expenditure on these areas by the devolved administrations have been significant, they are slightly smaller. Also, it would seem that some other areas, such as culture, and agriculture and fisheries have been prioritised to a greater degree by the devolved administrations. This may simply reflect more difficult or different challenges that the devolved administrations face in these areas. After all, the ability to make political choices such as these is a central point of devolution.

Targets and outputs

The UK Government's headline policy objectives are outlined every two or three years during the spending review process. There are a number of Public Service Agreements (PSAs) setting out targets in all policy areas. These targets can apply to England only, England and Wales, or the UK. Scotland, Wales and Northern Ireland conduct a similar exercise in stating their aims and targets, although the way in which they conduct the exercise varies. Analysing these targets can give further insight into differences in the emphasis of policy in each part of the UK. Looking at the outputs of these policies can also give us an idea of whether devolution is leading to divergence in practice. Care has to be taken with the latter point. As table 3.3 indicates, changing outputs can take between three and five years. As we are only six years into devolution, it is only policies that were introduced soon after the devolved administrations were set up that we can expect to have an effect on outputs.

Target-setting in Whitehall is a tightly focused exercise, which explicitly sets targets for outcomes that are measurable, within a certain timeframe. Over time, the process has evolved so that there are fewer targets, which are ever more outcome-focused (HM Treasury 2004c). They are, however, criticised by some for having distorting effects on policy. In Scotland, a spending review process is conducted shortly after the UK Spending Review, when the Scottish Executive budget is known. The document *Building a Better Scotland* quite clearly outlines the Executive's priorities, budgets and targets in a detailed, yet accessible, way (Scottish Executive 2004b). Similarly the Northern Ireland Office since 2003 has published integrated budgets and targets in a detailed document imaginatively named *Northern Ireland Priorities and Budget 2005-8* (Northern Ireland Office 2004).

The National Assembly for Wales also produces a document *Wales: A Better Country*, which sets out the strategic direction and priorities for the Assembly term (WAG 2003). The 2003 document is more focused on priorities than the previous one, and avoids blanket targets to 'improve' a service with no supporting targets. However, there are a number of targets that are focused on process rather than on outcomes, and are vague with regard to how success will be measured. This would seem to reflect the generally weaker policy community in Wales.

Looking at the targets set by each part of the UK gives an interesting insight into the priorities within policy areas. Of course, with devolution it is to be expected that the devolved administrations would have different approaches, targets and priorities, as they face different problems and different political pressures. To return to the key areas of health and education, the targets set here again give an interesting picture of slightly divergent policies.

Divergent education targets and outputs

Box 3.1 outlines the targets set in the devolved territories and England relating to GCSE (or equivalent) attainment. What is interesting is how tightly focused, measured and time-limited the targets for England, Scotland and Northern Ireland are in comparison to the Welsh aim. Furthermore, the Welsh target appears to be rather ambitious, as the most recent comparable figures available (2001/02) indicate that Wales has the highest proportion of students leaving school with no qualifications, at 7.6 per cent (ONS 2004).

What is also interesting about these targets is the perspective they give on the focus of policy, with England and Northern Ireland firmly focused on raising performance overall, and, in the case of England, raising attainment at a school level as well as an individual level. However, Scotland and Wales both have targets that seek to improve the standards of individual students who are performing badly, effectively trying to ensure that none get left behind. This would seem to be a subtle, but clear, divergence in policy focus. In Scotland, this may reflect the fact that standards were high to begin with, with 57.8 percent of students getting five SCE Standard Grades A*-C (the equivalent of five GCSEs A*-C) in 1998/99, higher than in any other part of the country. With this in mind, it perhaps makes sense for the Scottish Executive to turn its attention to the remaining few that perform badly. However, Wales has the lowest percentage of students getting five GCSEs graded A*-C (47.5 per cent in 1998/99) and, as mentioned above, the highest percentage of students gaining no GCSEs or equivalent (ONS 2004). Therefore, the challenge of widening attainment would be greater in Wales than in Scotland, perhaps reflecting a greater political ambition.

Box 3.1: Targets for GCSE (or equivalent) outcomes across the UK

England:

Objective: All young people to reach age 19 ready for skilled employment or higher education.

- By 2008, 60% of those aged 16 to achieve the equivalent of 5 GCSEs at grades A*-C; and in all schools at least 20% of pupils to achieve this standard by 2004, rising to 25% in 2006 and 30% in 2008

Scotland:

Objective: Ensuring excellence by: maximising achievement and attainment; and providing a basis for Learning for Life.

- Increase the average tariff score of the lowest-attaining 20% of S4 pupils by 5% by March 2008.

Wales:

Commitment: By the end of the decade, no pupil in Wales to leave school without qualifications.

Aim: To enable everybody to be equipped for the modern workplace and as citizens

Implementation: Evidence base of what works established 2003/04. Phased implementation from September 2004.

Northern Ireland:

Objective: To ensure that all young people, through participation at school, reach the highest possible standards of educational achievement, that will give them a secure foundation for lifelong learning and employment; and develop the values and attitudes appropriate to citizenship in an inclusive society.

- To promote improvement in educational attainment so that:
- By 2008, 63% of year 12 pupils to obtain 5 or more GCSEs (or equivalent) at grades A* to C (compared to 59% in 2002/03).
- To reduce differentials in educational attainment so that:
- By 2008, 83% of year 12 pupils in the most disadvantaged secondary schools to obtain 5 or more GCSEs at grades A* to G (or equivalent) (compared to 80% in 2002/03).
- By 2008, 94% of year 12 pupils gaining GCSEs at A* to G (or equivalent) in the most disadvantaged post-primary schools (compared to 89% in 2002/03).

Source: HM Treasury (2004b), Welsh Assembly Government (2003), Scottish Executive (2004b) and Northern Ireland Office (2004)

Despite these signs of divergence in inputs and targets, it is not possible with the current data to discern divergence in outputs that might be attributable to political devolution. Currently, data that is directly comparable is only available up to 2001/02 (ONS 2004), just three years after devolution. It is, therefore, extremely unlikely that any changing trends in outputs at this time can be attributed to policy divergence since political devolution.

Divergence in health targets and outputs

Developments within the NHS have been one of the most controversial policy areas following devolution, particularly after the heavy criticism of the Welsh system for poor standards of service (see Auditor General for Wales 2005; National Assembly for Wales Audit Committee 2005). Furthermore, the management of waiting times in Scotland has been criticised by Audit Scotland (2002); and in the summer of 2005 they stated that they are considering revisiting their earlier review to see if the recommendations have been implemented. Finally, the Northern Irish service has been branded 'unacceptable' by Shaun Woodward, Health Minister in the Northern Ireland Office, as he announced a plan whereby Trusts failing to treat patients within twelve months will see funding to cover the costs of the treatment withdrawn so that treatment can be carried out elsewhere (Woodward 2005).

The key measure of waiting times for hospital treatment has been extremely important for the UK Labour Government, and has caused much controversy in all three devolved administrations. To analyse the health targets set by the devolved administrations would seem to confirm that each admin-

---

Box 3.2: Waiting-time targets across the UK

England:

Objective: **Improve access to services.**
- To ensure that by 2008 no-one waits more than 18 weeks from GP referral to hospital treatment.

Wales:

By 2009 the maximum total waiting time from referral by the GP to treatment to be 6 months, including waiting times for any diagnostic tests required.

Scotland:

A reduction to an 18-week maximum wait for both outpatients and hospital treatment by end-2007.

Northern Ireland

The maximum waiting time for all patients requiring inpatient or day-case treatment (other than in exceptional circumstances) will be reduced to 6 months by 2010.

Source: Department for Health and Social Care (2005), Scottish Executive (2004b), Northern Ireland Office (2004) and HM Treasury (2004c)

---

istration seeks to enhance the speed at which patients receive treatment, although they also reveal the differing standards of service currently available in different parts of the UK on this one measure. Box 3.2 below sets out the targets in relation to waiting times, with England and Scotland aiming for an eighteen-week maximum wait, while Wales and Northern Ireland are still aspiring to reach a six-month maximum.

Interestingly, the Welsh targets in relation to waiting times have been rather inconsistent over the years. The first Welsh Assembly Government pledged to reduce overall waiting times by 2003/04, 'moving closer to levels that compare to the best' (WAG 2001). This rather vague target was clearly not met, as waiting times increased. *Wales: A Better Country*, which set the targets for the second Assembly Government, made no mention of waiting times at all (WAG 2003). The target referred to in box 3.2 seems to have been set in direct response to the criticism of the Audit Commission in Wales. The omission of a target on waiting times in 2003 perhaps reflects the Welsh Assembly Government's different approach to healthcare (see Greer, chapter 7), which argues that policy should seek to tackle the underlying causes of ill health, whereas waiting times could, perhaps, be regarded as a symptom.

There have always been varying standards in the health service, with Wales and Northern Ireland having generally experienced longer waiting times. However, as figure 3.7 demonstrates, while England has reduced the number of patients waiting longer than twelve months to zero, Scotland and Wales, and, until 2003, Northern Ireland, have all experienced increases in waiting times. While it is advisable to be cautious when analysing outputs and attributing them to the policy choices of the devolved administrations after just six years, the experience in England, of a steady downwards trend in waiting times compared to an upwards trend in the devolved territories, would suggest that a concerted focus on waiting times can be reflected in policy outputs relatively quickly. Clearly, the same cannot be said for other policies, such as those aimed at improving public health.

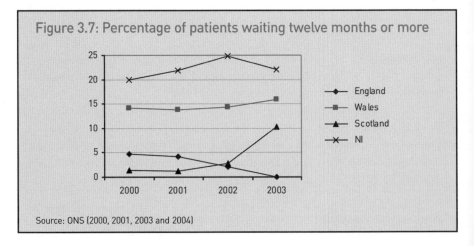

Figure 3.7: Percentage of patients waiting twelve months or more

Source: ONS (2000, 2001, 2003 and 2004)

What is particularly interesting about the policy area of health since devolution is the way in which health became a focus of the 2005 UK general-election campaigns in Scotland and Wales. Indeed, the 2005 general election made for an interesting study in how the centre is struggling to get to grips with devolution, with Tony Blair kicking off the Scottish Labour election campaign with a speech outlining Labour's health record, focusing on improvements in England that do not apply in Scotland (Mitchell *et al.* 2005). In response, Jack McConnell defended Labour's health record in Scotland, despite the fact he was not a candidate for that election. He said:

> We have heard a lot in the last few days about the fact that the National Health Service in Scotland and the National Health Service in England are different. Well, health in Scotland is different to health in England. We made conscious choices to invest in the things that were most important – both in the short term and the long term – for the people of Scotland. (McConnell 2005)

In the speech he stresses the different challenges facing the Scottish health system, yet the public debate around the health service continued to return to waiting times. Similarly, in Wales the health service and waiting times became substantial political issues, with the Secretary of State for Wales, Peter Hain, urging Wales to change its health policy and to emulate English policy on waiting times. The Welsh Assembly Government responded to this pressure by committing to the target outlined in box 3.2 and a pledge to spend £32 million on reducing waiting times (Seaton and Osmond 2005). This has not, however, been accompanied by the type of structural and institutional reforms that have been implemented in England (see Greer, chapter 7). Therefore, in time, this particular area will provide an interesting insight into whether targets and increased expenditure are sufficient to tackle waiting times, or whether English reforms have been central to success.

Partly, this pressure to tackle waiting times reflects the fact that in an area like health demands are similar across the UK, with interest groups operating across boarders and making comparisons between different levels of service (Keating 2002). This again highlights the competing stresses and tensions at play, with the devolved administrations taking a different approach to health policy, and, the devolved administrations would argue, tackling different local circumstances. However, the fact that the English approach has reduced waiting times, and is perceived in Scotland and Wales to have reduced waiting times, is a powerful force for convergence, placing pressure on the devolved administrations to follow English policy. It is this issue of perceived policy failure that we turn to next.

Policy failure and pressure for convergence

As all politicians in all parts of the United Kingdom know, it is not easy to make changes in the public sector. The inertia of the system, historic patterns of public expenditure and the accumulated practices of long-established agencies all conspire to limit the room for manoeuvre (Cornford 2002). However, small changes over a period of time can accumulate and, after a period of some years, can amount to a substantial divergence in public policy.

After six years of devolution, it now seems as if the devolved administrations have begun to prioritise different policy areas to their English counterparts, at least when we examine the growth in public expenditure of different policy areas. While it seems unlikely that there was an explicit decision by the devolved institutions to give greater priority to policy areas such as rural affairs or culture than their English counterparts, the cumulative result of numerous decisions taken in different budget discussions means that the devolved administrations now have notably different priorities to those in England. Health and education still receive the lion's share of devolved budgets, but, after a period when the devolved territories had significantly higher levels of spending in health and education, it is remarkable how that differential has been eroded (HMT 2005b). It is important to note that it is, in some ways, an inevitable consequence of devolution that decisions such as these can be made.

While this chapter is perhaps one of the first attempts to quantify divergent trends in public expenditure decisions, it is relatively well-known that there have been divergent trends in terms of targets and outputs, particularly following the high-profile debates over patient waiting times. This makes, what may have seemed to some, arcane, debates about common standards and national solidarity increasingly relevant.

Divergence is perhaps more palatable if there are strong networks of policy-learning; if 'laboratories of democracy' can produce innovations that are then taken up elsewhere this can push up overall standards. As Raffe and Byrne (2005) rightly point out, policy-learning is more than simply borrowing policies or identifying 'what works', rather, it is about a broader process of understanding and awareness of evidence and practical issues relating to policy development and implementation. Indeed, we have already seen some examples of policy-learning between the devolved administrations and Whitehall that have raised standards or made progress towards social justice across the UK, such as the adoption of a Children's Commissioner in all parts of the UK.

However, there is, perhaps, a reticence among the devolved administrations to learn from Whitehall. When it has been suggested that the devolved administrations could learn from some aspects of the English experience of improving waiting times, politicians from the devolved administrations have been less than enthusiastic. Jack McConnell and Brian Gibson, the Welsh Health Minister, have both argued that English solutions are unlikely to be suitable for the devolved territories (McConnell 2005; Seaton and Osmond 2005). There may be much to this argument, and it is to be expected that politicians from the devolved administrations would seek to take advantage of the room for manoeuvre to create divergent policy that the devolution settlement accords to them. Nevertheless, it will be a sign of the maturity of devolved politics when divergence is not regarded as a necessarily good thing in itself, and there is no political advantage to be gained from either introducing new policy initiatives or decrying various initiatives simply because they appear to be similar to the situation in Whitehall. For a virtuous cycle of raising standards to be realised there has to be openness to policy learning in all parts of the UK, and openness to evidence of what may work.

Perhaps the most significant constraint on divergent public policy post-devolution has been public opinion, and the desire of the populations of the devolved territories for common standards with their English counterparts. The desire for equity and common standards has caused particular concern over the years for those seeking social justice, raising the possibility of 'postcode lotteries', undermining social justice and equality, and potentially damaging a sense of common British citizenship. It is, however, important to note that centralised provision of services over the last fifty years has not led to uniformly high standards. Indeed, a powerful argument can be made that centralised provision of service results in rigidity and inflexibility, making services poor at responding to changing circumstances, and limiting joining up of services at the local level (Paxton and Gamble 2005).

In contrast to other countries with strong sub-national political institutions, the constitutional settlement in the UK provides no framework to protect common national standards. It is, however, important not to overplay this issue, as evidence from other countries suggests that, even where there are no formal minimum standards set by the centre, in practice there tend to be only small variations around common national standards (Banting 2005). While it may be theoretically possible in the future to use the systems of Joint Ministerial Committees and intergovernmental concordats to set some minimum standards within the UK, such an outcome is, politically, highly unlikely. It would be a major revision to the constitutional framework settled following the referendums of 1997 and 1998.

However, the early experience of devolution suggests that such formal mechanisms might not be necessary, and that public opinion provides a *de facto* force for convergence and common standards across the United Kingdom. The most obvious example of this would be the issue of patient waiting times, which became a central issue in the 2005 UK general election. The perception of policy failure in Wales (and, to a lesser extent, in Scotland) put pressure on policy-makers to make changes. The original strategy of the Welsh Assembly Government has been disrupted by demands to address the problem of lengthening waiting times (see Greer, chapter 7; Seaton and Osmond, 2005). In the end, public opinion and public expectations of common standards are, perhaps, the most powerful force for convergence.

References

Audit Scotland (2002) *Review of the Management of Waiting Lists in Scotland* Audit Scotland

Auditor General for Wales (2005) *NHS Waiting Times in Wales* NAO Wales

Bradbury J and Mitchell J (2005) 'Devolution: Between governance and territorial politics' in *Parliamentary Affairs* 58:2, pp. 287-302

Cornford J (2002) 'Foreword' in Adams J and Robinson P (eds.) *Devolution in Practice: public policy differences within the UK* ippr

Department of Health and Social Care (2005) Treatment times in Wales set to fall again' Department of Health and Social Care, available at http://www.wales.gov.uk/servlet/PressReleaseBySubject?area_code=37D4DA73000 83C2000000644000000000&document_code=N00000000000000000000000000 29726&p_arch=null&module=dynamicpages&month_year=3|2005

Heald D and McLeod A (2002) 'Beyond Barnett? Financing devolution' in Adams J and Robinson P (eds) *Devolution in Practice: Public policy differences within the UK* ippr, pp. 147-175

HM Treasury (HMT) (2004a) *Funding the Scottish Parliament, National Assembly for Wales and Northern Ireland Assembly: A statement of finding policy* HMT

HMT (2004b) 2004 *Spending Review: public service agreements 2005-2008* HMT

HMT (2004c) 2004 *Spending Review: New Public Spending Plans 2005-2008* HMT

HMT (2005a) *Guide to HM Treasury Functional Analyses* available at http://www.hm-treasury.gov.uk/media/61D/B1/guide_to_HMT_functional_analyses.pdf

HMT (2005b) *Public Expenditure Statistical Analyses 2005* TSO

Jeffery C (2002) 'Uniformity and Diversity in Policy Provision: Insights from the US, Germany and Canada' in Adams J and Robinson P (eds.) *Devolution in Practice: Public policy differences within the UK* ippr, pp. 176-197

Keating M (2002) ' Devolution and Public Policy in the UK: Divergence or convergence' in Adams J and Robinson P (eds.) *Devolution in Practice: Public policy differences within the UK* ippr, pp. 3-21

McConnell J (2005) Speech to the STUC, Dundee 19 April 2005, available at http://www.scottishlabour.org.uk/fmspeechstuc05/

Mitchell *et al.* (2005) 'Nations and Regions: the dynamics of devolution' in. *Quarterly Monitoring Report, Scotland, April 2005,* available at http://www.ucl.ac.uk/constitution-unit/monrep/scotland/scotland_april_2005.pdf

MORI (2005) *Importance of Key Issues to Voting,* available at http://www.mori.co.uk/polls/trends/importance-of-key-issues.shtml

NAW Audit Committee (2005) *NHS Waiting Times in Wales* NAW

Northern Ireland Office (2004) *Northern Ireland: Priorities and budget 2005-2008,* available at www.pfgbudgetni.gov.uk.

Office of the Deputy Prime Minister (ODPM) (2003) *Sustainable Communities: building for the future* ODPM

Office of National Statistics (ONS) (2000) *Regional Trends* No. 35 London: TSO

ONS (2001) *Regional Trends* No. 36 TSO

ONS (2003) *Regional Trends* No. 37 (revised) TSO

ONS (2004) *Regional Trends* No. 38 TSO

Paxton W and Gamble A (2005) 'Democracy, Social Justice and the State' in Pearce N and Paxton W (eds.) *Social Justice: building a fairer Britain* ippr

Raffe D and Byrne D 'Policy Learning from 'Home International' Comparisons' in *CES Briefing*, No. 24, May 2005 Department of Education, University of Edinburgh

Scottish Executive (2001) *Consolidated Resource Accounts: for the year ended 31 March 2001* Scottish Executive

Scottish Executive (2002) *Building a Better Scotland. Spending Proposals 2003-2006: What the money buys* TSO

Scottish Executive (2002) *Consolidated Resource Accounts: for the year ended 31 March 2002* Scottish Executive

Scottish Executive (2003) *Consolidated Resource Accounts: for the year ended 31 March 2003* Scottish Executive

Scottish Executive (2004a) *Consolidated Resource Accounts: for the year ended 31 March 2004* Scottish Executive

Scottish Executive (2004b) *Building a Better Scotland. Spending Proposals 2005-2008*: Enterprise, Opportunity, Fairness TSO

Scottish Executive (2004c) *The Scottish Executive's Expenditure: Comparative trends: 1996-97 to 2005-06* Scottish Executive

Seaton N and Osmond J (2005) 'Assembly Government' in Osmond J (ed.) *Nations and Regions: the dynamics of devolution. Quarterly Monitoring Programme, Wales, April 2005* http://www.ucl.ac.uk/constitution-unit/monrep/wales/wales_april_2005.pdf

Talbot C *et al.* (2004) *Is Devolution Creating Diversity in Education and Health?* Available at http://www.nottingham.ac.uk/npc/public-policy/content/devolution_v2_3.pdf

Ward N and Lowe P (2002) 'Devolution and the Governance of Rural Affairs in the UK' in Adams J and Robinson P (eds.) *Devolution in Practice: Public policy differences within the UK* ippr, pp. 117-139

Welsh Assembly Government (WAG) (2001) *Plan for Wales 2001* Government of the National Assembly for Wales

WAG (2003) *Wales: A Better Country: the strategic agenda of the Welsh Assembly Government* WAG

Woodward S (2005) Waiting list speech 4 July 2005, available at www.dhsspsni.gov.uk/press_releases/Waitinglist-speech04jul05.pdf

4 Devolution and divergence in education policy

David Raffe

In 1999, the Scottish Parliament, the National Assembly of Wales and the Northern Ireland Assembly were established, with powers including education and training. This chapter asks whether the home countries' education policies have diverged as a result.

In doing so, I aim to distinguish the effects of the political devolution of 1999 from the administrative devolution that began much earlier. Scottish schools have been separately administered, almost from the time that the state acquired its modern role in education; the Scotch (later Scottish) Education Department was established in 1872 and it was incorporated into the Scottish Office when this was created in 1885. Education in Northern Ireland has been separately administered ever since the territory became a distinct political entity with devolved powers under the Stormont Parliament in 1922. Education in Wales developed in closer relation to England; except for a few separate institutions, the process of administrative devolution started in 1970, when the Welsh Office assumed responsibility for education. During the 1980s and 1990s, further responsibilities, including training and higher education, were devolved to the Scottish and Welsh Offices (most had already been devolved to Northern Ireland), and new agencies were established within each territory to deal with such issues as curriculum, assessment, quality assurance and funding. Thus, most of the responsibilities for education and training that were devolved to the new Scottish Parliament and the assemblies in 1999 had already been administratively devolved to territorial departments or agencies of the UK government. The main impact of the 1999 settlement was not to create a new tier of government, but to place an existing tier under democratic control. All three territories already pursued distinctive and (in some respects) divergent policies. Any divergence since 1999 might simply reflect these different trajectories, rather than any direct effects of political devolution.

Devolution is not a uniform process. There are wide differences between Northern Ireland, Scotland and Wales in terms of the devolution settlement, in the change that this represents from previous practice, and in the political and institutional context. This process is further complicated in Northern Ireland by the earlier history of political devolution before 1972, by the delayed start to the Assembly and Executive in 1999, and by their suspension in 2002. There are also regional differences in policy and provision within each country. The effects of political devolution may vary across different areas of education and training policy. And they will unfold, often slowly, over time. Devolution is a process, not an event.

These complexities will be explored by examining two policy areas: choice and diversity of secondary schools, and the design of academic and vocational pathways in upper-secondary education and training. These two areas are an opportunity sample: they are not necessarily representative of all education-policy issues. They may, however, provide case studies that allow us to examine any policy divergence and the processes that promote or constrain it in more contextual detail than a more broadbrush study would allow. Compared with studies of (say) new legislation or policy initiatives, a case-study approach may be useful for identifying non-decision-making, and continuity, as well as discontinuity, in policy.

The next two sections will assess the extent of policy convergence or divergence in the two case-study areas. The following sections draw on this evidence: first to discuss continuities in policy making before and after political devolution; then to argue that, despite these continuities, some aspects of policy divergence can be attributed to political devolution; and then to identify continuing constraints on divergence.

Choice and diversity of secondary schools

In England, the Conservative governments of 1979-1997 introduced a range of reforms to promote markets, choice and diversity in secondary education. They introduced parental choice informed by 'league tables', gave schools more freedom to select pupils, abandoned arrangements for promoting a better social mix in school intakes, reduced or removed local authority powers, combined strong central prescription of outcomes with devolved powers to school governing bodies to achieve these outcomes, encouraged the private sector, and promoted greater diversity among schools. In the eyes of critics, these changes undermined the comprehensive system and helped to reintroduce a system based on hierarchy, selection, inequality and individualism (Gewirtz et al. 1995; Pring and Walford 1997). After 1997, the Labour Government reversed some of these reforms but it continued the drive towards choice and diversity. It introduced new categories of schools, such as Beacon Schools and City Academies, it encouraged faith schools, and it set a target for fifty per cent of schools, initially, and all schools, subsequently, to be able to become specialist schools (DfES 2001 and 2004). It enabled existing specialist schools to acquire a second specialism or become 'leading' schools. It devolved further powers to school managements, and engaged in a discourse of derision about 'bog-standard' comprehensive schools. It articulated a 'vision ... of a new comprehensive system which makes a decisive break with those aspects of the old system that stood in the way of reform and still impact on standards' (DfES 2002, p. 1). This vision was based on specialisation, collaboration, frontline control and strong accountability, compared with the old system based on uniformity, isolation, centralised control and weak accountability.

In Wales and Scotland, the reforms of the 1980s and early 1990s resulted in similar formal provision for parental choice as in England (Adler 1997), but school diversity was pursued less vigorously. Some reforms, such as devolved school management in Scotland, were introduced in a weaker form than in England. Some reforms met local resistance and had less impact in practice: for example, only two schools in Scotland and fifteen schools in Wales 'opted out' of local authority control (Gorard 2000). The opportunity to create new Technology Academies in Scotland or City Technology Colleges in Wales was never taken up. Other reforms, such as specialist schools, were not introduced in Wales and Scotland.

Thus, policies in Wales and Scotland were already diverging from England in 1999. This divergence was associated, at least in Scotland, with a relative increase in attainment, a relative decline in social inequality and (on some measures) a decline in social segregation (Croxford and Paterson 2005; Croxford and Raffe 2005). The devolved administrations did not significantly change the formal opportunities for parental choice, but they abolished league tables, and their school-improvement policies were less centrally driven and relied less upon consumer choice as a lever for change. They expressed strong support for comprehensive education, in contrast to the discourse of derision in England, and they rejected specialist schools. In *The Learning Country*, the Welsh Assembly committed itself to 'non-selective comprehensive school provision in Wales', with close links between schools and the communities they served (NAW 2001a, p. 25). After a meeting with her English counterpart, Jane Davidson, the Welsh Education Minister, issued a press release that praised the success of comprehensive education and distanced her from the English philosophy of school diversity as a strategy of improvement (NAW 2001b).

In 2002, the Scottish Executive launched a 'National Debate' on the school system, in order to develop a policy agenda for the medium term. The debate used questionnaires, discussion groups, seminars, the web and a variety of other measures to engage more than 20,000 people, including pupils, teachers, parents and other stakeholders (Munn *et al.* 2004). The Education Committee of the Scottish Parliament simultaneously conducted an inquiry into the purposes of Scottish education. The debate revealed strong public support for comprehensive education, although participants identified areas for reform, including greater relevance, flexibility and choice in the secondary curriculum. These themes have been reflected in subsequent Scottish Executive policy, including a statement of principles for curriculum reform, *A Curriculum for Excellence*, and a programme of school improvement, *Ambitious Excellent Schools*, (Scottish Executive 2004a and 2004b). The latter document made provision for some schools to develop areas of strength, but in a much weaker form than specialist schools in England, and within the parameters of the principles expressed in the ministerial foreword:

Our comprehensive education system is right for Scotland and it performs in the top class on the world stage.... No one in Scotland should be required to select a school to get the first rate education they deserve and are entitled to. Choice between schools in Scotland is no substitute for the universal excellence we seek and Scotland's communities demand. (Scottish Executive 2004b, p. 2)

Many of the Conservatives' market-oriented changes, including parental choice, league tables and local management of schools, were introduced in Northern Ireland, although they had a different impact in a system based on academic selection and religious segregation (Byrne and Gallagher 2004). Martin McGuinness, the first Education Minister in the devolved Executive, abolished league tables, but school choice may, paradoxically, be extended as a result of devolution. The Belfast (Good Friday) Agreement of 1998 has underpinned a distinctive education-policy agenda, based on the principles of pluralism, equality and social inclusion. In pursuit of this agenda, McGuinness has made it easier to establish new integrated schools; and the draft Bill of Rights for Northern Ireland could potentially enable 'any interest group to establish a separate set of schools to reflect and protect their own cultural interests' (Donnelly and Osborne 2005, p. 151).

In 1997, the direct-rule Labour Government opened up the issue of academic selection by commissioning a research study (Gallagher and Smith 2000). In 2000, the new devolved administration appointed the Burns Committee to review post-primary schooling. Burns proposed to replace academic selection with a system in which parents, informed by pupil profiles, would choose among 'collegiates' or consortia of institutions (PPRB 2001). In 2002, a few days before the Assembly was suspended, McGuinness announced that the eleven-plus tests for transfer to post-primary schools were to end. The new direct-rule Government accepted this decision and appointed the Costello Committee to develop detailed plans (DENI 2003 and 2005). Under the current proposals, the last transfer tests will take place in 2008. Thereafter, schools will be allocated on the basis of 'informed parental choice'; oversubscribed schools will be able to select applicants on the basis of specified family, community or geographical criteria, but not on the basis of aptitude or attainment. In addition, all students will have an entitlement to a range of academic and vocational subjects; in order to deliver this entitlement schools are expected to collaborate with one another, and with colleges, although the proposal for collegiates has been dropped. In 2005, the Government also announced that specialist schools will be piloted in Northern Ireland.

There are, therefore, two distinct models of comprehensive education emerging in the UK. The first, exemplified by Wales and Scotland, emphasises the links between schools and communities and the need for common content and standards of provision across all schools. The second, exemplified by

England and the current plans for Northern Ireland, emphasises choice, institutional diversity and collaboration. There is both convergence and divergence. Northern Ireland is moving towards England and the second model described above, although this convergence is motivated by different political agendas and it reflects the decisions of direct-rule governments as well as devolved governments. Scotland and Wales appear to be diverging from England, although this divergence reflects the refusal of Scotland and Wales to follow policies in England as much as new policy directions by the devolved administrations themselves.

Upper-secondary pathways

In 1999, an Organisation for Economic Co-operation and Development (OECD) review panel described the main weaknesses of the transition from school to work in Britain as 'the academic orientation of mainstream education and, related to it, the previous absence and today the relative weakness of a genuine system of initial vocational education' (OECD 1999, p. 39). Many British policy-makers and commentators would agree. Enhanced vocational provision, it is argued, is needed in order to develop skills needed for the labour market, to motivate disengaged young people, to raise participation, to support smoother transitions to the labour market, and to promote social equality and social inclusion. This analysis is, of course, contested; so are the implications for policy. On one side of the argument are 'trackers', who advocate separate vocational and academic tracks to enable vocational education to develop a distinctive identity and to protect the 'gold standard' of the academic route. On the other side are 'unifiers', who favour either bringing the tracks together within a fully unified system, or a 'linkages' approach that retains separate tracks but creates links between them. Some unifiers advocate Baccalaureate models; others advocate more flexible credit-based or 'climbing-frame' models.

These strands have been present in policy debates in England, Scotland and Wales since the 1980s (Howieson et al. 1997). Unifiers in England have often looked to Scotland for inspiration (for example, ippr 1990; NCE 1993). In 1992, a proposal to replace Scotland's relatively flexible upper-secondary arrangements with a two-track system was almost unanimously rejected in a public consultation. The Scottish Office (1994) then published *Higher Still*, which proposed a 'unified curriculum and assessment system' to incorporate all academic and vocational institution-based learning beyond sixteen, below the level of higher education. This was introduced from 1999 as a climbing-frame model of units and courses at seven levels.

That a Conservative government should propose a unified system for Scotland, while resisting similar proposals for England and Wales, is an indication of the autonomy of the Scottish policy community before political devolution. However, the UK connection constrained *Higher Still* in two respects. It affected the presentation of *Higher Still*, whose vision and rationale as a unified system was consistently underemphasised in order to avoid embarrassing the government south of the Border. And it restricted the unified system to institution-based learning, as work-based learning was part of a UK system of occupational standards and qualifications, and not under the full control of the Scottish Office. These limitations were to have serious consequences. The failure to promote *Higher Still*'s vision of a unified system exacerbated the political fallout from the 2000 exams crisis (Raffe *et al.* 2002) and meant that the devolved Executive, established shortly before the implementation of *Higher Still* began in 1999, never 'owned' the reform or gave it the kind of political leadership that unifying reforms have enjoyed in Wales. The omission of work-based provision exacerbated the academic bias against which some commentators had warned (Weir 1999). The unified system covered academic education more successfully than vocational education and training, and its impact on 'parity of esteem' was more formal than substantive (Raffe *et al.* 2005). An unintended consequence of *Higher Still* was the calling into question of the future of Standard Grade courses for fourteen to sixteen year-olds, as some schools preferred the new *Higher Still* courses, with their stronger progression orientation (Howieson *et al.* 2004). The future of Standard Grade, and its relationship to *Higher Still*, will be determined as part of the policy process initiated by *A Curriculum for Excellence*.

In Wales, there were at least two unifying reform movements in the 1990s: the development of a national credit framework based on the college sector, and proposals for a Welsh Baccalaureate developed by the Institute of Welsh Affairs (IWA). The latter adapted the International Baccalaureate model to provide a Welsh focus and to accommodate vocational as well as academic programmes (Jenkins *et al.* 1997). In their 2000 Partnership Agreement, the coalition Labour and Liberal Democratic parties agreed to pilot the 'Welsh Bac' with the International Baccalaureate as a backup to protect the interests of the students in the pilot. However, by the time the pilots began in 2003, the IWA's model had been rejected in favour of a looser, overarching certificate based on component qualifications such as A levels.

The Learning Country (NAW 2001a) expressed the Assembly's commitment to parity of esteem for academic, technical and vocational pathways; to greater flexibility in the content and pacing of learning; and to reducing the barriers associated with transition at age sixteen. It launched a consultation that was to lead to *Learning Pathways 14-19*, now a flagship policy of the Welsh Assembly Government. The Learning Pathways were developed through a process that involved more than 170 people from different sectors and with stakeholder interests in various working groups; many other people, including young people, took part in focus groups and other consultation exercises (Davidson 2005). The Learning Pathways are driven by the principles of entitlement, inclusion, the community school and new learning pedagogies (Egan 2004). They are based on six elements: individually tailored learning pathways, wider choice and flexibility, a learning core, a learning coach, individual support, and careers advice and guidance (WAG 2004). They, thus, exemplify the 'linkages' approach described above; they do not abolish distinct academic and vocational programmes, but they transform their relationship and, potentially, their content by placing them within a unified framework.

The debates between trackers and unifiers have been less prominent in Northern Ireland, partly because of the different context provided by the selective school system. Since 1999, further education has been administered by a different department from school education (as in Scotland), and policy-making tends to be sectorally based. However, the review of the (school) curriculum was launched in 1999 in the hope that it might lead to a new 14-19 qualifications framework that would promote parity of esteem for vocational and academic learning (Finlay and Egan 2004). The proposed Curriculum Entitlement Framework for post-primary education potentially provides a linkages approach to vocational and academic learning. It would guarantee a range of curricular options, including at least one third of a vocational or applied nature, to all 14-16 and 16-plus pupils, and schools and colleges would need to collaborate to deliver this guarantee.

In England, successive attempts since the 1980s to build up a vocational pathway have fluctuated between track-based and linkages approaches. The Labour Government of 1997 initially pursued a 'standards-based linkages approach' (Hodgson and Spours 2003), which led to the Curriculum 2000 A level reforms. The A level crises of 2001 and 2002 created the political space for a more radical approach, and the Tomlinson Working Group was appointed to make proposals for a unified framework of 14-19 qualifications. The Working Group proposed a system of diplomas at four levels, with a common core, and with flexible opportunities and incentives for progression (Working Group on 14-19 Reform 2004). Later in 2004, Charles Clarke and David Miliband left the DfES. Without their support (especially that of Miliband, an author of *A British Baccalauréat?*) the unifiers lost the battle within a government suffering pre-election nerves. The government proposals, published in February 2005, incorporate some of the Tomlinson proposals but reject the unified framework of which they were part, and consequently lose their underlying rationale (DfES 2005). GCSEs and A levels are retained as the 'cornerstones' of the system. Tomlinson's proposed specialist diplomas, designed as part of a flexible, unified structure, are re-presented as a separate vocational track potentially starting at fourteen years.

After the Tomlinson Report of October 2004, it appeared that the home countries' approaches to upper-secondary pathways were converging in at least two respects: they were all moving towards more unified structures, and they were all moving towards a 14-plus rather than a 16-plus frame of reference.

They differed in other ways: the four countries attempted different compromises between Baccalaureate and climbing-frame models, and the unified frameworks in England and Wales included work-based provision, while those in Scotland and Northern Ireland did not.

By summer 2005, the picture is once again one of divergence. England is committed to a tracking policy in contrast to the unifying policies pursued elsewhere. As in the case of school choice and diversity, the immediate source of divergence – at least in the short term – is a policy change in England rather than in the devolved administrations. And, once again, divergence will only be sustained if the devolved administrations can resist pressures to follow England's lead.

Continuities in policy-making

There has been divergence in both of these policy areas, although it has been neither linear nor consistent across the four territories. In both areas, the divergence is not trivial. The future of comprehensive education and the relation of vocational and academic pathways are subjects of vigorous debate within the home countries. Despite the rhetoric that suggests that policy differences merely adapt common goals to local circumstances (for example, that policies for choice and diversity are less suited to the more homogeneous school systems, more uniform school effects and sparser populations of Wales and Scotland), they are more than this. They also reflect national traditions, identities and aspirations. According to Jones and Roderick (2003, p. 225), *The Learning Country* has the aim of 'providing Wales with an education system based on different social principles, which amounts to a statement about the nature of Welsh society'. Rees (2004), a relatively sceptical commentator on Welsh policy differences, acknowledges that these differences reflect 'profoundly held beliefs about how the education system and the opportunities it provides ought to be organised in Wales'. Policy differences also reflect ideological debates within the Labour Party: closer to European-style social democracy in Scotland and Wales, closer to New Labour social liberalism and developmentalism in England (Paterson 2003).

However, in both case-study areas, the home countries already pursued different policies under the old system of administrative devolution before 1999. *Higher Still* was launched in 1994 and continued a line of policy development in Scotland that began with the modularisation of vocational education in the 1980s. In the 1990s, the Welsh Office already supported unifying reforms, such as credit frameworks, more strongly than the government in England. The home countries' policies for comprehensive education and school diversity diverged under the Conservative governments of 1979-1997, and Phillips (2003) argues that they 'had their roots at least as far back as 1944'. Their roots may lie even earlier. The diversity and liberalism of English education are partly the result of the nineteenth-century accommodation of religious and social diversity (Green 1990). By contrast, the inclusiveness and homogeneity of Scottish schools are partly the product of post-Reformation religious uniformity. Scotland's 'educational philosophy of common schooling as the basis of common citizenship and hence of democracy ... is the secular legacy of four centuries of Presbyterianism, significantly modified in the twentieth century by an infusion of Catholic communitarianism and of social democracy' (Paterson 2002, p. 33). Not only was policy divergence already well-established in 1999, it derived its momentum from deeply rooted social and cultural differences.

A further source of continuity is the education-policy community within each territory. This includes professional bodies, teachers' unions, local authorities and various interest groups, as well as civil servants, the inspectorate and staff of educational agencies. Members of policy communities share 'assumptive worlds' that define policy issues and possible courses of action (McPherson and Raab 1988). They enjoyed substantial autonomy before 1999, although the extent of this autonomy is disputed (Keating 2005). Their power had been increased, especially in Wales, by administrative devolution in the 1980s and 1990s (Jones and Roderick 2003). The autonomy of policy communities and the distinctiveness of their assumptive worlds help to explain the divergence that was already apparent before 1999. They have continued to be powerful since political devolution, especially when the devolved administrations have used them to augment their own meagre policy-making capacity.

The dominant mode of explanation in education-policy studies emphasises how policies are shaped by policy discourses, ideologies and myths, and by the assumptive worlds and collective narratives of policy communities (see, for example, Jones 2003; Ozga 2003). This culturalist perspective is often used to explain continuity, to explain, for example, why national differences persist despite globalisation. It is similarly used to explain continuities in policy in the devolved administrations, especially Scotland and Wales, before and after devolution. However, neither the policy communities nor their assumptive worlds have been as coherent or cohesive as some culturalist accounts suggest. There are conflicts within each policy community, between school and college interests, for example, or between the 'two cultures' of Wales, respectively collective/industrial and rural/cultural (Phillips and Daugherty 2001, p. 90). Educational discourses and ideologies can be remarkably flexible: for example, the 'Scottish tradition' of education has been used at different times to support several alternative models of vocational education. National policy communities have not enjoyed unlimited power either. They did not always get their own way before 1999 (Keating 2005). Indeed, the Conservative governments' perceived threats to Scotland's educational autonomy helped to create the public pressure for a Scottish Parliament (Paterson 2000).

The impact of political devolution

To say that there are continuities in policy-making before and after 1999 is not to deny that political devolution has made a difference. It has done so in at least four ways.

Firstly, the devolved administrations have more successfully resisted the imposition of policy from London. As noted above, national policy communities did not have full autonomy before 1999. Even in Scotland, where the policy community enjoyed most influence, it was able to modify, but not reject, many of the Conservative reforms of the 1980s and 1990s. Wales was even less able to resist policies for choice and management of secondary schools that conflicted with its educational cultures and aspirations (Phillips and Daugherty 2001; Egan and James 2003). After 1999, the devolved administrations could more easily choose not to follow English reforms. Had political devolution not occurred they would have been under stronger pressure to follow the English lead on such issues as school diversity. In Northern Ireland, the introduction of direct rule in 1972 weakened the influence of policy communities: thereafter '[t]he latest [policy] solution was imported from England whether Northern Ireland had a problem for it or not' (O'Callaghan and Lundy 2002, p. 17). Under devolution, politically important decisions in Northern Ireland must have a minimum level of support from both unionist and nationalist Assembly Members. When devolved government is restored, the Assembly may, therefore, be more effective in resisting policies from elsewhere than in agreeing its own policies.

Secondly, several aspects of divergence result from policy initiatives by the devolved administrations themselves. Martin McGuinness, as Education Minister, took the decision to end transfer tests in Northern Ireland. The Welsh Assembly Government decided to pilot the Welsh Baccalaureate, reversing an earlier decision of the Welsh Office, and it initiated the process that led to *Learning Pathways 14-19*. Upper-secondary developments in Scotland have, hitherto, been largely a legacy of the pre-1999 arrangements, but they will gradually acquire the stamp of *A Curriculum for Excellence*, the review initiated by the devolved Executive. Further policy initiatives will follow, as the devolved administrations work their way through their policy agendas. Policy statements such as *The Learning Country* and *A Curriculum for Excellence*, and the Belfast Agreement in Northern Ireland, suggest that these initiatives could lead to divergence. The critical test will come when different political parties control the different administrations (Jeffery 2005). This may result in further policy divergence, just as coalition government has already had an impact. In Scotland and Wales, several policy decisions that have led to divergence, such as tuition fees and the Welsh Baccalaureate, flow from coalition partnership agreements.

Thirdly, political devolution may help to redistribute power away from the old policy communities, to include groups that lacked influence under the former system of administrative devolution. It has been associated with attempts to introduce a new, more open and participative style of politics, such as the National Debate in Scotland, the participative process which led to the Learning Pathways in Wales, and the Burns/Costello consultations in Northern Ireland, which involved an unprecedented level of public participation. The specialist committees of the devolved administrations have also encouraged wider participation. The new politics may also be reflected in changes to structures of governance, such as the abolition of quangos in Wales and the redesignation of the Scottish Inspectorate as an Executive Agency without policy-making powers. The scope for the new politics may be greatest in Northern Ireland, precisely because 'normal politics' and its associated policy communities are least well-established, and because the assumptive worlds of the emerging policy communities may be grounded in the devolution settlement, with its principles of pluralism and democratisation (Donnelly and Osborne 2005).

Close relationships between government and the governed are easier in small polities, such as Scotland, Wales and Northern Ireland, than in a larger country, such as England. However, despite these more favourable circumstances, the future of the new politics is uncertain (Paterson 2000; Keating 2005). The old policy communities have continued to play a leading role in the new structures. The early agenda of the National Assembly of Wales was shaped by the Education and Training Action Group, which was appointed before devolution (Rees 2002). More recent developments, such as the rejection of the IWA's model of the Welsh Baccalaureate, may reflect the continuing influence of established policy communities. In Scotland, the National Debate might not have happened had there been a real chance that its conclusions would have challenged either the assumptive worlds or the current role of the established policy community. And, to the extent that there has been a shift towards a more participative and open style of policy-making, the important question is whether it will survive as the policy cycle moves from policy review and agenda-setting towards the consolidation and implementation of chosen policies.

The fourth reason why political devolution may be encouraging divergence is institutional rather than cultural. Each country has developed a different set of institutions for the governance of education. Even institutions that appear to have parallel functions may vary in their remits, powers and ways of working. For example, the four qualifications bodies – the Qualifications and Curriculum Authority (England); the Scottish Qualifications Authority; the Council for the Curriculum, Examinations and Assessment (Northern Ireland); and Qualifications Curriculum and Assessment Authority for Wales (ACCAC) (soon to be reabsorbed into the Welsh Assembly Government) – have widely varying roles with respect to regulation, accreditation, awarding, the curriculum, and so on. There is similar variation in the bodies responsible for curriculum support, quality assurance and funding. These institutional differences influence the way in which policy agendas are structured. For example, England and Wales have developed policies for a horizontal 14-19 stage, while policy agendas in Scotland and Northern Ireland are structured around school, college and training sectors. These different agendas partly reflect the different institutions of governance: in Scotland and Northern Ireland, school and post-school education come under different government departments, and planning and funding are separately organised for each sector; England and Wales have unitary education departments and planning and funding are organised (partly) on an age basis. Institutional differences also contribute to different modes of policy-making in each country. The Scottish Parliament and the two assemblies have different powers and different ways of reaching agreement. Coalition government has promoted a more measured, predictable style of policy-making. In Northern Ireland, the Belfast Agreement has underpinned a new policy-making ethos, and the new institutions give the Irish dimension a formal place in policy agendas (Osborne 2000; Donnelly and Osborne 2005). There is variation in the role and influence of local government, and of public agencies. Each territory has developed different mechanisms for engaging civil society, and the relative influence of industry and other stakeholders varies across the home countries.

On its own, each of these institutional differences may have only a subtle effect on policy-making. However, their cumulative impact over the longer term may be more significant. Distinctive processes and dynamics of change may be emerging in each home country. At the same time, some of the former mechanisms for co-ordinating policy developments across the home countries have been weakened or removed. Before 1999, the Cabinet Office played a co-ordinating role, and many UK government documents required the signatures of the territorial Secretaries of State, ensuring that their departments were consulted in advance. Since 1999, there has been less consultation, even on issues such as English 14-19 qualifications, which have significant implications for the other home countries (see below). A possible implication is that divergence may occur partly by accident: even in the absence of deep-seated cultural or political differences, 'policies and systems may simply drift apart' (Raffe 2000, p. 24).

Constraints on divergence

However, two factors will continue to constrain divergence. The first is the restricted policy-making capacity of the devolved administrations. Their formal powers are limited, especially within the Welsh Assembly, which has no legislative powers. This could prove a significant constraint if a different political party controlled Westminster and was less willing than at present to support enabling legislation. The devolved administrations have no control over their total funding (except Scotland, which can vary the standard rate of income tax). They can determine the allocation of their budgets between policy areas, but the political scope for this is constrained. Devolved education budgets remain strongly influenced by decisions in Whitehall. The need for education policies to 'join up' with reserved areas is a further constraint. For example, the Duffner Committee felt that the new Careers Scotland should relinquish the careers service's existing responsibility for providing a placement service for school leavers. However, it could only recommend that the Scottish Executive invite the Employment Service, a British agency, to take over this function. Another example is policy for vocational qualifications, which must relate to the occupational standards determined by UK-wide Sector Skills Councils (SSCs). Finally, the devolved administrations have limited capacity and resources for policy-making. Even before devolution, the territorial departments had to 'pick and choose' policy areas for development (Raffe 1998). The new Scottish Parliament and the assemblies have created yet more work for the relatively small number of civil servants (Rees 2000). As a result, many policy areas, such as Modern Apprenticeships, have remained on the backburner since political devolution. The devolved administrations may increasingly respond by 'borrowing' policies, including from each other (Egan and James 2003). Policy-borrowing leads to convergence, but policy-learning – a broader and more open concept – may not (Raffe and Byrne 2005).

The second factor constraining divergence is the interdependence of the home countries' education systems. There are substantial flows of staff and students between them. There is a common qualifications system for England, Wales and Northern Ireland, and there are pressures and incentives for Scottish qualifications to be compatible. Educational processes across the UK are shaped by a relatively uniform social and cultural environment – influences on participation, for example, vary less across the home countries than internationally – and by the integrated labour market of Great Britain (and, to a lesser extent, of the UK). There is limited scope for divergence in policies, such as the New Deal, that rely on common delivery systems. Divergence is also becoming constrained by European developments, such as the emerging credit and qualifications frameworks. These provide an additional incentive for the home countries to co-ordinate their own efforts: the UK's influence over European developments may be weakened if it cannot get its own act together. Finally, the home countries are interdependent politically. There is a strong 'British system' for policy-making (Rees 2002). Many political parties and key stakeholders are organised on a British or UK basis. Labour-market interests, for example, tend to resist any differentiation in education and training across the UK. Many education-policy debates – including debates on comprehensive education and upper-secondary pathways – are conducted across the UK (Taylor 2002).

These constraints have restricted the policy options available to the devolved administrations. The Welsh Baccalaureate was designed as an overarching certificate, which incorporates A levels rather than replaces them, partly in order to protect the position of Welsh students in the UK university and jobs markets. Because Wales has less control over qualifications, the Learning Pathways are based instead around pedagogy and processes; like the Technical and Vocational Education Initiative (TVEI) in the 1980s, they go against the UK grain of qualifications-led reform, and, like TVEI, they may find it hard to 'embed' change. The vocational diplomas to be introduced in England may provide a critical test of devolution. Wales and Northern Ireland (and, to a lesser extent, Scotland) will be under pressure to accept the new diplomas, or to develop close equivalents, and thereby introduce a stronger degree of tracking. This pressure will come from employers and labour-market interests, as well as from those who wish to protect the position of Welsh and Northern Irish learners in the UK qualifications market. The development of vocational diplomas is led by the SSCs, many of which find it difficult to understand educational differences across the home countries, let alone accept the need for them.

These constraints on divergence affect some aspects of education more than others: qualifications more than school organisation, vocational education more than general education, post-compulsory education more than compulsory education. They may also affect Wales more than Northern Ireland (with its less integrated labour market and links with the Republic) or Scotland (with its separate qualifications system, greater critical mass and smaller cross-border flows of students).

Conclusion

This chapter has asked whether the political devolution of 1999 has encouraged a divergence of the education policies of the home countries of the UK. The answer is 'yes, but ...'. There has been divergence, but this has fluctuated over time, across countries and across policy areas. There have also been substantial continuities in policy-making. We can attribute the divergence that has occurred, in part, to political devolution, but we should be wary of *post hoc* determinism. The policy trends described in this chapter have been shaped by a small number of decisions, many of them taken in England, many of which could easily have gone the other way. And policy divisions within each country continue to be as important as policy differences between them.

It is still too early to assess the effects of political devolution. Six years is a short time in the history of an education system, and a short period over which to study comparative policy change. All the devolved administrations have initiated processes of policy review, public debate and agenda-setting, many of which are only now feeding into new policy development. It will take time for the new institutional arrangements to bed in and for new relations between government and civil society to develop. It will take even longer for policy differences to have an impact where it matters most – on the practices, experiences and outcomes of teachers and learners.

Acknowledgements

Work on this chapter was supported by the ESRC project on Education and Youth Transitions (R000239852), led by Dr Linda Croxford. I am grateful to John Hart, Lindsay Paterson and participants at the ESRC/ippr north seminar at the University of Edinburgh for comments on an earlier draft. The responsibility for errors and interpretations is, of course, mine.

References

Adler M (1997) 'Looking backwards to the future: Parental choice and educational policy' in *British Educational Research Journal* 23:3, pp. 297-313

Byrne G and Gallagher T (2004) 'Systemic factors in school improvement' in *Research Papers in Education*, 19:2, pp. 161-183

Croxford L and Paterson L (2005) *Trends in social class segregation between schools in England, Wales and Scotland since 1984* CES, University of Edinburgh

Croxford L and Raffe D (2005) *Secondary school organisation in England, Scotland and Wales since the 1980s* seminar paper, CES, University of Edinburgh, available at www.ces.ed.ac.uk/eyt/publications.htm

Davidson J (2005) Address to Nuffield Review of 14-19 Education and Training, available at www.nuffield14-19review.org.uk.

Department for Education and Skills (DfES (2001) *Schools Building on Success* Cm 5050, TSO

DfES (2002) *Education and Skills: Investment for Reform* DfES

DfES (2004) *Five Year Strategy for Children and Learners* Cm 6272, TSO

DfES (2005) *14-19 Education and Skills* Cm 6476, TSO

Department of Education Northern Ireland (DENI) (2003) *Future Post-Primary Arrangements in Northern Ireland* (Costello Report) DENI

DENI (2005) *New Admissions Arrangements for Post-Primary Schools. Consultation Document* DENI

Donnelly C and Osborne R (2005) 'Devolution, social policy and education: some observations from Northern Ireland' in *Social Policy and Society* 4:2, pp. 147-156

Egan D (2004) '14-19 developments in Wales: Learning Pathways' Working Paper 19 in *Nuffield Review of 14-19 Education and Training* available at www.nuffield14-19review.org.uk

Egan D and James R (2003) 'Education' in Osmond J and Jones JB (eds.) *Birth of Welsh Democracy: The first term of the National Assembly of Wales* IWA

Finlay D and Egan D (2004) 'What policy trajectories are the national governments in England, Wales, Northern Ireland and Scotland following and are they converging or diverging?' Working Paper 20 in *Nuffield Review of 14-19 Education and Training* available at www.nuffield14-19review.org.uk

Gallagher T and Smith A (2000) *The effects of the selective system of secondary education in Northern Ireland* DENI

Gewirtz S, Ball S and Bowe R (1995) *Markets, Choice and Equity in Education* Open University Press

Gorard S (2000) 'For England, see Wales' in Phillips D (ed.) *The Education Systems of the United Kingdom* Symposium Books, pp. 29-43

Green A (1990) *Education and State Formation* Macmillan

Hodgson A and Spours K (2003) *Beyond A levels* Kogan Page

Howieson C, Raffe D, Spours K and Young M (1997) 'Unifying academic and vocational learning: the state of the debate in England, Wales and Scotland' in *Journal of Education and Work* 10, pp. 5-35

Howieson C, Raffe D and Tinklin T (2004) 'The use of New National Qualifications in S3 and S4 in 2002-03' in *Scottish Educational Review* 33:2, pp. 177-190

institute for public policy research (ippr) (1990) *A British 'Baccalauréat?* ippr

Jeffery C (2005) *Devolution: What difference has it made? Interim findings from the ESRC Research programme on Devolution and Constitutional Change*, available at www.devolution.ac.uk

Jenkins C, David J, Osmond J and Pierce J (1997) *The Welsh Bac: educating Wales in the next century* IWA

Jones K (2003) *Education in Britain: 1944 to the present* Polity Press

Jones GE and Roderick GW (2003) *A History of Education in Wales* University of Wales Press

Keating M (2005) *The Government of Scotland* Edinburgh University Press

McPherson A and Raab C (1988) *Governing Education* Edinburgh University Press

Munn P, Stead J, McLeod G, Brown J, Cowie M, McCluskey G, Pirrie A and Scott J (2004) 'Schools for the 21st century: the national debate on education in Scotland' in *Research Papers in Education* 19:4, pp. 433-452

National Assembly for Wales (NAW) (2001a) *The Learning Country: A Paving Document* NAW

NAW (2001b) 'Jane Davidson says education opportunities will continue for all throughout Wales' press release, 15 February 2001, NAW

National Commission on Education (1993) *Learning to Succeed* Heinemann

O'Callaghan M and Lundy L (2002) 'Northern Ireland' in Gearon L (ed) *Education in the United Kingdom* David Fulton, pp. 16-28

Organisation for Economic Co-operation and Development (OECD) (1999) *Thematic Review of the Transition from Initial Education to Working Life: Country Note: United Kingdom* OECD

Osborne R (2000) 'Northern Ireland' in Raffe D and Croxford L (eds.) *The Education and Training Systems of the UK: Convergence or Divergence?* CES, University of Edinburgh, pp. 47-53

Ozga J (2003) 'Pressures for convergence and divergence in education: devolution in the context of globalisation' paper to SERA Conference, CES, University of Edinburgh, available at www.ces.ed.ac.uk/eyt/publications.htm

Paterson L (2000) *Education and the Scottish Parliament* Dunedin Academic Press

Paterson L (2002) 'Scotland' in Gearon L (ed) *Education in the United Kingdom* David Fulton, pp. 29-39

Paterson L (2003) 'The three educational ideologies of the British Labour Party, 1997-2001' in *Oxford Review of Education* 29:2, pp. 165-186

Phillips R (2003) 'Education policy, comprehensive schooling and devolution in the disUnited Kingdom: an historical 'home international' analysis' in *Journal of Education Policy* 18:1, pp. 1-17

Phillips R and Daugherty R (2001) 'Educational devolution and nation building in Wales: a different "Great Debate"?' in Phillips R and Furlong J (eds.) *Education, Reform and the State* Routledge Falmer

Post-Primary Review Body (2001) *Education for the 21st Century* (Burns Report) DENI

Pring R and Walford G (1997) *Affirming the Comprehensive Ideal* Falmer

Raffe D (1998) 'Does learning begin at home? The place of 'home international' comparisons in UK policy-making' in *Journal of Education Policy* 13, pp. 591-602

Raffe D (2000) 'Investigating the education systems of the United Kingdom' in Phillips D (ed.) *The Education Systems of the United Kingdom* Symposium Books, pp. 9-28

Raffe D and Byrne D (2005) 'Policy learning from 'home international' comparisons' *CES Briefing No. 34*. CES, University of Edinburgh, available at www.ces.ed.ac.uk

Raffe D, Howieson C and Tinklin T (2002) 'The Scottish educational crisis of 2000: an analysis of the policy process of unification' in *Journal of Education Policy* 17, pp. 167-185

Raffe D, Howieson C and Tinklin T (2005) 'The introduction of a unified system of post-compulsory education in Scotland' in *Scottish Educational Review* 37:1, pp. 46-57

Rees G (2000) 'Wales' in D Raffe and L Croxford (eds.) *The Education and Training Systems of the UK: Convergence or Divergence?* CES, University of Edinburgh, pp. 25-33

Rees G (2002) 'Devolution and the restructuring of post-16 education and training in the UK' in Adams J and Robinson P (eds.) *Devolution in Practice: Public Policy Differences within the UK* ippr, pp. 114-116

Rees G (2004) 'Democratic devolution and education policy in Wales: the emergence of a national system?' in *Contemporary Wales* 17

Scottish Executive (2004a) *A Curriculum for Excellence* Scottish Executive

Scottish Executive (2004b) *Ambitious, Excellent Schools* Scottish Executive

Scottish Office (1994) *Higher Still: Opportunity for All* HMSO

Taylor K (2002) *Fog in Channel – Continent Obscured: An examination of the European dimension of Scottish and English education and culture policies* PhD thesis, European University Institute

Weir AD (1999) 'Vocational education' in Bryce T and Humes W (eds.) *Scottish Education* Edinburgh University Press, pp. 275-285

Welsh Assembly Government (WAG) (2004) *Learning Pathways 14-19 Guidance Circular 37/2004* Department for Training and Education

Working Group on 14-19 Reform (2004) *14-19 Curriculum and Qualifications Reform: Final Report* DfES

5 Devolution and divergence in education policy: the Northern Ireland case

Bob Osborne

David Raffe's preceding chapter represents an extremely valuable overview, both of some general issues about making policy under devolution and those specific to education. By having education as its subject, the chapter enables some of the 'gaps' in the areas covered in the ESRC's Devolution and Constitutional Change Programme to be filled, as none of the funded projects looked explicitly at education policy. The underdevelopment of the analysis of education policy under devolution contrasts with the analysis of health policy, where Scott Greer's (2004) analysis has set a benchmark for a sophisticated understanding of policy development.

In approaching the comparative analysis of policy under devolution there is an inevitable tension between constructing the general similarities and differences across the three UK devolved regions and assessing the distinctive processes behind policy formulation and implementation in one of the areas. The asymmetrical devolution within the UK that took place in 1998 means that the specificities of each devolved context are as important as the general issues applying to all the devolved regions.

There can be little doubt that the thirty years preceding the 1998 Belfast Agreement and the institution of devolved administration was distinctive in the UK. Northern Ireland was wracked by political violence, resulting in over 3,500 deaths and tens of thousands of injuries, in a society of just over 1.5 million. The various political attempts to resolve this crisis during this period had all been based on devolution, with power-sharing between the political representatives of unionism and nationalism. From 1972, when the original Stormont parliament, created in 1921, was suspended, until the Belfast Agreement, government was by direct rule from Westminster, with only a very short interlude of devolved government from January to May 1974.

The devolved institutions, signed up to by all the political parties except the Democratic Unionist Party (DUP) in 1998, were designed to move Northern Ireland away from violent conflict, led by paramilitary organisations, and towards democratic politics. As such, the Belfast Agreement is loaded with devices to ensure parity of participation and parity of power for the parties representing unionism, the majority, and nationalism, the minority. Moreover, it involves more than devolved government, as is also the case in Scotland and Wales. Carmichael (1999) has termed it 'devolution plus' because of the explicit cross-border institutions created with the Republic of Ireland. These institutions are politically designed to meet the demands of nationalists in Northern Ireland. Nationalists see these bodies as not only providing the symbols for their aspiration for a united Ireland but their existence as an initial basis for its achievement. Unionists recognise the benefits of co-operation on the island of Ireland, but also fear that these institutions may well be used to broaden all-island activities with unity as the aim.

Within the Northern Ireland devolved institutions, there are numerous mechanisms designed to ensure that nationalism and unionism have parity of representation and power. For example, the First Minister and Deputy First Ministers have the same powers and are *de facto* joint First Ministers. Secondly, complex parallel-voting mechanisms within the Assembly ensure that major issues, such as the selection of First and Deputy First Minister, the budget and the programme for government, are consensual decisions involving parties representing unionism and nationalism. For the purposes of this chapter, one of the most significant differences with the other devolved regions relates to the architecture of Northern Ireland devolution, in that the Executive is a coalition, with ministers selected through the d'Hondt principle. After an election, parties nominate ministers for particular departmental portfolios based on party strength in the Assembly. In practice, this has meant that there is no agreed manifesto prior to the election being called and, in effect, no Executive collective responsibility once ministers have taken up their portfolios. True, there was an agreed programme for government, but this excluded so many departmental specifics that there was plenty of room for autonomous individual ministerial decisions. The DUP were quick to exploit this – being in the Executive but refusing to attend executive meetings (see Wilford (forthcoming) for a detailed assessment of the workings of the devolved institutions).

A second important point is that devolution in Northern Ireland has been a start-stop process since 1998, with periods of suspension and the reimposition of direct rule interspersed with the full functioning of all the institutions, until its effective grinding to a halt in October 2002. Elections held in November 2003 produced the DUP as the largest unionist party, replacing the Ulster Unionist Party (UUP), with Sinn Fein replacing the Social and Democratic Labour Party (SDLP) on the nationalist side. As a result of this political history since 1998, policy analysts are faced with the task of trying to unpick what is attributable to direct rule and confirmed under devolution, what is solely and fully attributable to devolution, what was initiated under devolution and is now being carried forward under direct rule, and that which is solely attributable to renewed direct rule.

The development of secondary-education policy, a theme of chapter 4, illustrates the effect of the particularities of devolution in Northern Ireland and the stop-start implementation of the Belfast Agreement.

Academic selection for secondary education was introduced in Northern Ireland in 1947 and came under extensive public debate periodically, for example in the late 1970s under Labour, when it was close to abolition until the return of a Conservative government in 1979. In its most recent incarnation, it started in 1997 after Labour's return to office. The direct-rule minister with responsibility for education made it clear that he needed evidence that there was a demand within Northern Ireland for the abolition of selection before he could take action to begin reform. However, to kickstart the debate he commissioned a major piece of research into the effects of selective education. This research programme represented the largest-ever analysis of the effects of academic selection undertaken in the UK.

By the time the report of the research (Gallagher and Smith 2000) was published, devolution was in place, and it was a devolved-administration minister who set up the Burns Committee to review alternative ways of transferring from primary to secondary education (September 2001). Burns then reported in 2002, again to a devolved-administration minister, recommending an end to academic selection, the adoption of formative assessment, pupil profiling and collegiate co-operative organisation for secondary schools.

During 2002, the devolved Department of Education (DE) launched an extensive public consultation on the Burns proposals. There was initial confusion as to what the Burns Committee was suggesting in relation to 'collaborative colleges', but gradually it became perceived as clearly advocating the end of academic selection. As the political parties digested the recommendations, it became apparent that both unionist parties were concentrating on the proposal to end academic selection and both began to campaign against this prospect, while accepting that the existing 'transfer test' (the eleven-plus) was deeply unpopular and would have to be changed. On the other hand, the two nationalist parties endorsed the central Burns proposal for the abolition of academic selection. (This situation contrasts with earlier debates over selection, when proponents for the retention of selection were able to draw on extensive support from the Protestant and Catholic communities.) At this point, the DE sought to create a consensus for the Burns proposals by 'going to the people'. During spring 2002, all households in Northern Ireland were canvassed via a questionnaire.

However, the strategy backfired. Grammar schools, operating through their co-ordinating body, the Governing Bodies Association (GBA), started mobilising parents and former pupils to vote in favour of academic selection. Newspaper advertisements were taken out showing that a vote against the existing eleven-plus could be coupled with a vote in favour of the retention of academic selection. The results of the household consultation are shown in table 5.1. As can be seen, while a clear majority of the (over 200,000) returns were against the eleven-plus test, a clear majority is recorded for the retention of academic selection. However, as can also be seen in table 5.1, a large-scale opinion poll of the general public, taken at the same time, confirmed these results. This opinion poll data suggested that, while the household consultation may have been skewed by the mobilisation of opinion by the grammar-school lobby, in fact, the results reflect broader public opinion in the apparent desire to retain academic selection.

In the autumn of 2002, with further wrangles between the parties over the decommissioning of paramilitary weapons, the devolved administration was suspended once again. However, the day before suspension, the Education Minister announced that academic selection and the eleven-plus would end from 2008.

The crucial part of these events is that the Education Minister was Martin McGuinness of Sinn Fein. In the share out of ministries at the formation of the Executive, Sinn Fein, which was at that time the fourth largest party in the Assembly, had, under d'Hondt, opted for Education. Hence, in the post-Burns debate, the political parties in the Executive with Sinn Fein, the DUP and UUP, both actively campaigned against a policy being proposed by Martin McGuinness.

	Household Response - 2002			Omnibus Survey - 2002		
Table 5.1: Public responses to abolishing the eleven-plus transfer test and academic selection.						
	Yes %	No %	DK %	Yes %	No %	DK %
Should the current Transfer Test be abolished?	57	32	12	54	27	19
Should Academic selection be abolished?	30	64	7	32	54	14
N		200,551			2,200	

Note: The Household Response was administered to Northern Ireland households during spring 2002 and the Omnibus Survey was administered to the general public in June 2002

With the resumption of direct rule, UK ministers regarded McGuinness's decision as one with democratic legitimacy and announced the confirmation of abolition in 2008, even if it did not accord with either a majority of public opinion, as tested by the household questionnaire and opinion survey, or majority political support (with the two nationalist parties commanding less than fifty per cent of the vote).

In the November-December 2004 period, a deal between the DUP and Sinn Fein for the restoration of the devolved institutions was very nearly achieved. It is widely known among observers of Northern Irish politics that, in the resulting reallocation of portfolios through the d'Hondt principle, following the 2003 elections, the DUP intended securing the Education portfolio and moving towards the reversal of policy: academic selection, if not the eleven-plus, would be retained.

One, perhaps rather controversial, footnote to this discussion is worth raising here. Under the long period of direct rule, it is generally acknowledged that civil servants played an upfront role in policy issues, as direct-rule ministers came and went with highly variable commitment to their portfolios (Carmichael and Osborne 2003). Up to devolution, the DE was noted for its support for the existing system of academic selection, and highlighted the 'better' results from Northern Ireland compared to non-selective England. Moreover, criticisms of the department had been made arising from the predominance of Protestants in senior positions resulting in a perception by those running Catholic schools that they felt remote from the department and that their interests were not always catered for (SACHR 1990). Since devolution, however, the DE has become regarded as an advocate of ending academic selection. Is this simply the case of senior civil servants professionally supporting the minister of the day, or has it also got something to do with the changing profile of senior civil servants, which, instead of being predominantly Protestant, now has a more representative proportion of Catholics, especially at the most senior levels?

It is not yet clear that academic selection is dead. The public is against the test, but in favour of selection. Unionist politicians have noted the return of selection in various guises and the failure to eliminate grammar schools in England. However, it now seems that Catholic schools are determined to abolish academic selection and, in a number of cases, are starting to reorganise secondary schools on this basis (the opportunity to reorganise being driven by falling rolls). If devolution is restored, it is not impossible that the Catholic sector will abolish selection, while the state/Protestant sector retains it (under the direction of a DUP Education Minister). The position of the Catholic middle class will be especially interesting in this situation, since it is not clear that upwardly mobile Catholics, when faced with a choice, will opt for a non-selective school. More generally, if the current proposal to abolish selection by 2008 proceeds, then one further consequence could be the creation of an independent sector for the first time. Most commentators reckon that there is probably only scope for up to two independent schools.

As this story of the proposed abolition of academic selection shows, the particularities of devolution in Northern Ireland create a very distinctive and complex policy-making environment. Traditional ideas of democratic legitimacy, the role of public opinion, and collective responsibility of ministers in an executive or cabinet all have to be reconsidered in the Northern Ireland context.

Finally, it is worth pointing out how the education debate and policy-making agenda varies from the other devolved regions in two other respects. The first relates to the communal conflict and the role education plays in both perpetuating division and resolving the conflict. Hence, issues of rights, in the context of the proposed Bill of Rights, the role of segregated and integrated education, restructuring the curriculum, and related matters, occupy a lot of researchers' time (see Donnelly and Osborne 2005; Donnelly et al. forthcoming).

The second relates to North/South interaction on the island of Ireland. Certain aspects of education were itemised for collaboration in the Belfast Agreement, for example teacher education and education for those with learning disabilities. But there was no institutional representation for these areas –

no cross-border education body. Once again, the political divide determines how much emphasis is likely to be given to developing policy initiatives on this basis. A Sinn Fein or SDLP Minister will want to build this activity up, whereas a DUP/UUP Minister will want to reduce collaboration.

References

Burns Report (2002) *Education for the 21st Century. Report by the Post-primary Review Body* Department of Education

Carmichael P (1999) 'Territorial Management in the 'New Britain': Towards devolution plus in Northern Ireland?' in *Regional and Federal Studies* 9:3, pp. 130-156

Carmichael P and Osborne R (2003) 'The Northern Ireland Civil Service Under Direct Rule and Devolution' in *International Review of Administrative Sciences* 69:2, pp. 205-218

Donnelly C and Osborne R (2005) 'Devolution, Social Policy and Education: Some Observations from Northern Ireland' in *Social Policy and Society* 4:2, pp. 147-156

Donnelly C, McKeown P and Osborne R (eds.) (forthcoming) *Devolution and Pluralism in Education in Northern Ireland* Manchester University Press

Gallagher AM and Smith A (2000) *The Effects of the Selective System of Secondary Education in Northern Ireland*, Volumes 1 and 2, Department of Education

Greer S (2004) *Territorial health politics and health policy* Manchester University Press

Standing Advisory Commission on Human Rights (1990) *Fifteenth Report, Report for 1989-1990* HMSO

Wilford R (forthcoming) 'Inside Stormont: The Assembly and the Executive' in Carmichael P, Knox C and Osborne R (eds.) *Devolution and Constitutional Change in Northern Ireland* Manchester University Press

6 Devolution, social democracy and policy diversity in Britain: The case of early-childhood education and care

Daniel Wincott

By winning three consecutive general elections, Tony Blair fashioned an unprecedented opportunity to reshape British politics and society. The urgent question for his third term is what, if anything, New Labour's enduring progressive legacy will be – how might existing policies be modified to maximise their long-term significance? Clearly, constitutional reform – including devolution – is a key legacy. These changes, introduced soon after the 1997 election, altered the political landscape of Britain irreversibly, democratising long-standing territorial administrative, institutional and public-policy variations across the historic nations of the UK. This analysis brings devolution together with another potentially crucial element of the Labour policy legacy – early-childhood education and care (ECEC). Supporters and critical friends of the Labour government pin considerable hope on ECEC. The ippr position is typical; its showpiece publication *Social Justice* (which might be read as a centre-left prospectus for the creation of a permanent progressive legacy from New Labour) puts ECEC centre stage. In their introduction, Nick Pearce and Will Paxton argue:

> Embedding entitlements to childcare and early years education in a high-quality, publicly regulated and comprehensive service should form the centrepiece of progressive institution-building in the early 21st century, just as the NHS did in the immediate post-war era. (2005, p. xxi)

ECEC is also the first social justice priority in the concluding chapter (Paxton, Pearce and Reed 2005).

Ironically, Labour launched its *National Childcare Strategy* (NCS – making ECEC a 'national' (state-wide) policy priority for the first time), deploying the symbolism of the *nation*, just as, by enacting devolution, it acknowledged the UK's multinational character (Wincott 2005). More broadly, in Britain and beyond, social democrats traditionally support policies that build (on) state-wide solidarity, typically viewing devolution as a policy of divide-and-rule. Yet, this irony does not amount to a necessary contradiction: devolution did, or does, not automatically undercut ECEC expansion. Indeed, viewed historically, the anti-democratic spirit embedded in the centralist, but territorially variable, British state during the putative 'golden age' of the welfare state helps to explain the stalled development of key social services like ECEC before New Labour (Wincott forthcoming a). Quiet decisions, taken behind closed doors in Whitehall during the 1960s, stymied potential ECEC expansion (Randall 2000). Starting in the 1970s – but particularly under Thatcherite auspices in the 1980s – the central stranglehold on local democracy squeezed the life out of promising local ECEC policies (Randall and Fischer 1999), especially in the doomed English metropolitan authorities. In Britain, centralism was hardly the handmaiden of progressive ECEC provision. In fact, the significant, if uncertain, degree of autonomy generated for local government by administrative devolution in Scotland allowed certain authorities to pursue progressive ECEC policies, even during the heyday of the Conservative government. Strathclyde Region, for example, developed a radical, education-based Pre-Fives Initiative between 1986 and 1996 (Cohen *et al.* 2004).

In contrast to the dominant Labour tradition – and at odds with the conventional wisdom of comparative political economy (see, for example, Swank 2002) – some British social democrats argue that devolution may limit welfare retrenchment, and, perhaps, even aid its expansion (Paxton and Gamble 2005; Cohen *et al.* 2004). The Strathclyde example provides historical depth to this intellectual current, but it also offers a warning against ignoring the administrative roots of political devolution; at times, administrative devolution had a similarly protective effect. Some pro-devolutionary social democratic arguments are predicated on perceptions that Scotland and Wales are more progressive than England as nations or polities, more fundamentally committed to welfare 'universalism' rather than 'means-tested selectivity'. These arguments may require modification. While devolved political debate has a distinctive tenor and these party systems have a more left-wing centre of gravity, there is little evidence of a systematic difference in public values (Jeffery 2005). Moreover, Schmuecker and Adams (see chapter 3) raise questions about the putatively radical policy priorities in Scotland and Wales, finding that funding for core welfare services has grown more in England than in Scotland or Wales since devolution.

None the less, if Paxton and Gamble's optimistic vision, that devolution – as a form of democratisation – may interact positively with the welfare state, is utopian, it is not impossibly so. But this positive interaction will not necessarily be achieved simply by following the existing course. Considered together, ECEC and devolution highlight some deficiencies in New Labour political strategy, and these gaps place its ability to construct an historic legacy at risk. The focus here is on a deep dilemma for contemporary social democracy: the reconciliation of equality and diversity. This has proven to be a 'tension in a lot of our reforms', as former Number Ten advisor Peter Hyman observed, perspicaciously (2005, p. 6).

Although some close to New Labour imply that direct redistribution is the mark of 'classic' social democracy (a measure, according to which, this government performs rather well) (Mulgan 2005a; 2005b), this is an Anglo-centric misreading of the wider social democratic tradition. It also misconstrues

UK political history. While the (latest) British 'third way' espoused moving beyond neo-liberalism *and* 'traditional' social democracy (Giddens 1998), its image of the latter was distorted. It misunderstood the Nordic social democratic heartland systematically (Ryner 2002). In Britain and Norden, classic social democratic successes were won through the development of high-quality, universal, public services. Walter Korpi, an intellectual guardian of Swedish social democracy, has argued forcefully that universal services generate a large class of welfare-state beneficiaries and hence, potentially, a big social democratic constituency (Korpi 1980; 1983). While direct income transfers may effect a more immediate redistribution of resources from the better- to the worse-off, a solid pro-welfare constituency for universal services makes them more sustainable politically; in the end, they achieve greater redistribution than direct transfers. Of course, in a mature welfare state, questions of equity and justice become more acute within such apparently comprehensive, universal services (for example, see Rothstein (1998) for a fascinating discussion of the individualisation of maternity services in Sweden).

The concept of 'progressive universalism' shows that some in Labour are thinking along these lines. Progressive universalism could become an important weapon in the government armoury, especially where the ability of (established) universal services to serve the interests of less advantaged social groups may appear compromised. In contrast to the welfare state's formative period, the management of established public services presents distinct challenges. The ability of middle-class citizens to gain premium services from, say, the education system or the NHS is well documented. A strong egalitarian case exists for strategies that target greater resources on the relatively deprived within such services. The 'progressive universalism' approach is particularly associated with politics at Westminster. In Scottish and Welsh public discourse, at least, traditional universalism is celebrated, and counterpoised to (especially means-tested) targeting (see, for example Morgan 2002). Yet, Schmuecker and Adams (chapter 3) observe targeting of less advantaged groups within devolved universal services, including targets to raise the performance of the worst-qualified section of school-leavers in Scotland. In terms of political strategy, progressive universal strategies need to walk a narrow line; by neutralising middle-class relative advantages, such strategies may complicate the logic of social democratic coalition building.

Increasingly, English early childhood education and care seems to be framed by progressive universalism. The case for universal elements in ECEC is strong, while even the most generous systems overseas include some income-related parental payments. However, if it means that better-off families (or locations) pay for services that share only a 'brand' with government-funded services elsewhere, this is unlikely to build a deep cross-class political coalition. Indeed, where politicians are concerned to avoid alienating any group, coalition-building strategies are unlikely to succeed. Thus, for example, while ECEC might appear to be a classic 'motherhood and apple pie' issue, relatively speaking it must privilege families with children. So, while the British 'child free' movement has not achieved the political visibility of its US counterpart, the substantial shift towards supporting children undertaken by New Labour could provoke political opposition, and, hence, might require an explicit popular justificatory narrative. It is unlikely that ECEC can become the cornerstone of a new progressive welfare settlement for the twenty-first century, as Pearce and Paxton hope, unless it is placed at the centre of Labour's strategic vision, and not sacrificed to (admittedly important) shorter-term tactical considerations. While the record of longer-term policy development is encouraging, there is little evidence of a cohesive or co-ordinated narrative about early-childhood policies as a social foundation for pan-UK citizenship. Through the rough-and-tumble of events, is anyone taking the longer-term strategic view about the kind of institutions currently being built, or how well they match up to progressive aspirations?

This chapter makes a modest contribution to addressing these questions: first, considering the role of UK-wide powers relating to public finance and expenditure before second, and at greater length, considering the devolved responsibility for the ECEC provision. The second part is itself subdivided, addressing the historic character of the UK ECEC policy in Wales, Scotland and England respectively (dealing with such issues as policy integration, central-local relations, 'new' politics and relative generosity of funding, as well as characterising the approach to the policy), with a final section concerned with what, if anything, might the role of the central UK authorities be. The conclusion returns to the issue of democracy and devolution.

The politics of public finance and expenditure

Normally loquacious, New Labour has remained strangely quiet about its redistribution to support working families with children, particularly with their ECEC costs. The absence of a public discourse about (and justifying) UK-level inter-individual transfers has not, however, meant that the Government has avoided criticism for their impact. For example, many ECEC advocates are critical of the Government's decision to subsidise childcare through the demand side, arguing that the construction of a robust system requires greater direct support of supply. An even stronger case can be made against demand-side subsidy in Scotland, where we will see that the post-1997 expansion of ECEC was rooted in a comparatively strong tradition of local authority provision, which might have underpinned a more fully 'public-sector' ECEC strategy. Channelling public resources through the demand side made the pursuit of such a strategy more difficult for the Scottish Executive (see the critique in Cohen *et al.* 2004). Others have countered that the demand-side subsidy may, in effect, have 'ring-fenced' the support, removing it from the pressure of

Scottish Executive or local authority budget rounds (Law 2004). The findings of Schmuecker and Adams (chapter 3) – that the devolved governments' expenditure on welfare-state functions has not increased to the same degree as in England – may support this latter argument.

Even recent revisionist scholarship questioning the received wisdom that devolution (and federalism) hamper welfare-state development (see Obinger, Liebfried and Castles 2005) accepts that direct redistribution is most effective when conducted at the highest-possible level of government within a state (to pool risks on the largest scale). There is, then, a strong intellectual case for the 'reservation' of these powers to Westminster. Among the most important of New Labour innovations are those to the tax-benefit system to the advantage of working families with children. Labour's silence on these policies is particularly difficult to understand. But if the tax-credit system excites social policy wonks, it has not (yet) provided the basis for an explicit attempt to shift the climate of opinion, to reshape political preferences or build solid new political coalitions and constituencies.

The perplexing fact is that New Labour seems deliberately to have eschewed such a strategy. Geoff Mulgan – until recently, a close advisor of the Prime Minister – was recently disarmingly explicit on this point, stating that the Labour leadership judged 'over a number of years' that they should not be 'talking too much about redistribution'. The tactical justification for this silence is also revealing. Mulgan argued that emphasising redistribution draws it to the attention of middle-class swing voters and 'you therefore undermine your support' (2005b). Equally, New Labour assumed that those who benefited from the redistribution would credit the Government for the improvement in their situation. Mulgan recognises that this assumption has proven misplaced. As Labour decided not to claim political credit for these policies, those in the electorate that have benefited do not seem to attribute this to government policy. So Labour has not reaped the expected electoral reward. But there is a deeper flaw in this tactical logic. The logic of this redistribution is distinctive and potentially morally engaging. Particularly when cast in terms of supporting children, it is one to which many, although not all, people would subscribe. But Labour ambivalence about making these arguments undercuts their ability to construct this potential constituency and so entrench the new welfare settlement.

Devolution and early childhood education and care: design and delivery

Divergence?

Discussion of devolution and public policy is often framed in terms of divergence – (how far) has it allowed different territories to develop distinctive policies? But divergence may not provide the best conceptual route in to understanding ECEC. In common with many other public services, it is too easy to assume that Britain was 'unitary' prior to political devolution. Significant pre-devolution policy variations are hidden by the powerful myth that the British welfare state was once based on 'need not geography' (Wincott forthcoming a). Mitchell's (2004) general caution against 'year zero' assumptions in devolution analysis certainly applies to ECEC. Administrative devolution allowed important differences in early-childhood and family services to develop – particularly between Scotland and England (such as the Strathclyde Region Under-Fives policy). Indeed, across Scotland, provision for families with young children was generally more fully developed and better defended than English local provision.

The Scottish situation notwithstanding, historically ECEC had been a 'Cinderella' of British social policy. Against this backdrop, the commitment of the 1997 Labour Government at Westminster provided a common, pan-UK impetus to ECEC expansion. Given prior territorial variations, it might even be appropriate to characterise this common growth as *convergence* in a policy area previously subject to scandalous neglect. While the counterfactual question of whether the devolved governments might have expanded ECEC provision *in the absence* of a pre-existing push towards expansion at the UK level is impossible to answer precisely, detailed analysis of post-devolution policy trajectories can help. It suggests that, while novel Scottish and Welsh policies have developed, Westminster, nevertheless, served as one important trigger for them. If this characterisation is accurate, it is striking how little attempt has been made from Westminster to claim credit for it across the UK.

Nevertheless, as for some other major care services (see, particularly, Greer 2005 on health), devolution has generated significant differences in ECEC provision between the historic nations of Britain. Thus far, these are probably better characterised as differences of emphasis as policy is adapted to local circumstances, rather than fundamental variations in the quality or level of service available across the nations. 'Diversity within common expansion' might serve as an appropriate slogan. Indeed, as long as no part of the UK is perceived as sharply falling behind, the existence of differences could prove valuable from a progressive point of view. A system flexible enough to allow for some policy experimentation also creates scope for innovation and policy diffusion (Paxton and Gamble 2005). But this potential is far from being fully realised. This failure results from, and reflects, wider problems with devolution. These include the absence of effective, formal and transparent (even by the murky standards of federal systems) intergovernmental relations, the continuing traditions of 'territorial management' (as conflict avoidance and denial) on the part of the British civil service, and the ambiguity of central-local relations within England.

Wales

Since devolution, policies with a clear '*Made in Wales*' identity are easy to spot. Despite the fact that the National Assembly for Wales (NAW) has the weakest formal powers, its ECEC policies are strikingly distinctive. At least initially, the absence of fiscal powers may have concentrated Welsh minds on 'regulatory' rather than 'expenditure' aspects of public services (Wincott forthcoming b). That is, the Welsh Assembly Government (WAG) has concentrated on the redesign of provision for early childhood; although it is difficult to generate accurate, comparable data, Welsh ECEC expenditure may even have fallen behind those in England (Wincott forthcoming b). In one sense, this emphasis on regulation might sit uneasily with the general stress on universal welfare services in the public discourse of the WAG and Rhodri Morgan (2002) in particular. It reflects a broader truth about the character of devolution; none of the devolved governments has the autonomy to embark on a comprehensive universalisation of the welfare state. Yet, as we shall see also for Scotland, in Wales considerable attention has been focused on 're-engineering' existing early-years policies, including (elements of) existing universal provision.

Two major, innovative, policies frame Welsh ECEC. The first is a radical new curriculum that integrates pre- and primary schooling. Defining a new 'Foundation Phase', this policy provides a seamless curriculum for children from three to seven (see Richards 2005; Wincott forthcoming b). It represents a landmark effort to 're-engineer' the universal – indeed compulsory – early years of school, and could make Wales an international leader (especially given that the UK generally has a young school-starting age). With roots in the Hanney Report (2000), and, thus, drawing on extensive international evidence, this new approach imports a distinctive early-years pedagogy into the early years of compulsory schooling, potentially transforming its ethos. Faced with an educational system in which the philosophy of formal schooling is being driven ever downwards into infant, reception and even pre-school settings, some social democrats are considering *raising* the school-starting age in England. The emerging Welsh practice suggests an alternative, that an integration of pre- and infant schooling might transform the culture and ethos of the first years of 'formal' education, which might be fruitfully integrated into recent English debate (Reed and Robinson 2005; Paxton, Pearce and Reed 2005).

The second innovation takes the form of 'Integrated Children's Centres' (ICCs). Again, these centres have roots in Hanney's important report, in which she called for 'Integrated Early Years Centres … staffed by multi-professional teams' (2000). The Childcare Task Force (CTF, formally the National Childcare Strategy Task Force) picked up this vision of multi-professional children's centres, recommending that childcare should be developed through integrated children's centres on a 'core and cluster' model (National Childcare Strategy Task Force, 2001, see also the *Childcare Action Plan* (WAG 2002)). However, the integrated centres do not provide universal coverage. Like current English provision, they are located in deprived areas, with at least one in every local authority. In contrast to the early English experience, however, the precise location for centres was left to local authorities.

The ICCs developed through intensive co-operation between a number of departments, particularly Health and Social Services, and Education and Lifelong Learning. Pre-dating England's 'Children's Centres' as an initiative, the ICCs share some of their features. They seek to integrate a range of different services – acting as a one-stop shop for families with young children, while also providing facilities older siblings as well. They are intended to be exemplary (Seaton 2005).

How did children and early-years provision become prominent features of the political agenda in Wales? The explanation mixes structural with contingent factors. Thus, for example, bilingualism is a structural feature of Wales that casts early-years provision in a particular light. Moreover, the character of devolved government and its interaction with civil society may have had unexpected consequences. More generally, the relative weakness of organised civil society may have allowed more scope for 'Welsh' level innovation than, say, the Scottish Executive, with its greater formal powers, but denser and more constraining domestic interests. Additionally, the lighter legacy of (distinctive) pre-devolutionary ECEC in Wales may also have enhanced WAG's room for manoeuvre.

Equally, as historical institutionalists suggest, the particular sequence and combination of events at the 'formative moment' of Welsh devolution is important. For example, long-standing concerns with abuse in children's homes in North Wales culminated in the institution of the UK's first Children's Commissioner. This helped to infuse policy impacting upon children with the discourse of children's rights. Equally, partly in the context of issues surrounding the Welsh language, and, initially, prior to devolution, Jon Owen Jones (the then Welsh Office Education Minister) made a Parliamentary Statement announcing a review of the playgroups (Owen Jones 1999). *The Playgroup Review for Wales* was delivered to the devolved Assembly in April 2000. It recommended placing 'play' and a 'child centred' approach to provide 'a national plan for the support and development of services for young children 0-6 years which shows clear linkages between existing strategies' (Pre-16 Education Committee 2000a). This report sent an early signal that the early years of childhood would be understood as a distinct 'stage of life' in Welsh policy debate.

Next, beyond the general pressure to enhance ECEC provision, the UK-wide *National Childcare Strategy* had a decisive, and paradoxical, impact in Wales. Before devolution, (somewhat) different versions of the NCS appeared for the four constituent parts of the UK. The 'version' for Wales was roundly criticised by Welsh MPs at Westminster as being insufficiently attuned to Welsh circumstances, culminating in a critical report of the Welsh Affairs Select Committee (1999). While this ire was directed towards the Welsh Office, by the time the report was published, the NAW had taken over responsibility for ECEC. Very early in its life, then, the task of responding to the Select

Committee report fell to the new devolved authorities. Ironically, Jane Hutt, who became the Assembly Secretary (as the 'Ministers' were then known) for Health and Social Services, was specialist advisor to the Committee on this report (while employed in the voluntary-sector organisation Chwarae Teg ('Fair Play')). In fashioning the NAW's response, the (now defunct) Pre-16 Education Committee and Rosemary Butler (Education Assembly Secretary under Michael) appointed Margaret Hanney as Special Adviser. Her rapidly produced and wide-ranging report set the tone for a deeper 'national' reflection on the purposes of ECEC (see Wincott forthcoming b). When Jane Davidson replaced Butler in the Education portfolio, she took up the ECEC agenda with gusto.

The paradox that greater pressure for devolution may have constrained the scope for policy innovation more in Scotland than in Wales finds an echo 'new politics'. While the drive for Scottish devolution was marked by a 'new politics' mood, political mobilisation for Welsh devolution was more limited and muted. Indeed, enthusiasts for devolution as a form of social democratisation of British politics look to Scotland more than Wales (Paxton and Gamble 2005). The expansion of ECEC has drawn new actors into the policy process – the dismal British record prior to 1997 meant that government lacked an 'in house' capacity in this sector. Nevertheless, post-devolution, the opportunity for new actors to become involved in ECEC policy-making appears to have been greater in Wales. Considerable ECEC expertise was newly marshalled into the policy-making process both through special advisers (such as Margaret Hanney and Shan Richards) and extensive public/professional consultations. Partly a product of the limited internal resources of the WAG, this kind of engagement has long outlived the initial period when the (then) Labour leadership embraced a 'body corporate' image of the NAW, and Alun Michael expounded his notion of 'golden threads', linking it to professionals and the voluntary sector. Again, the relatively large post-devolution change in Wales partly reflects its less distinctive pre-devolution ECEC policy community. It suggests that the more obvious political manifestations of 'new politics' are not necessarily the best predictors of its sustainability or impact in particular policy sectors. Developments in equality of opportunity policy suggest that these observations may have relevance beyond ECEC (Chaney 2004).

The 'novel' character of (at least) some aspects of Welsh policy-making also shows the effect of other, unpredictable, elements of devolution. For example, the relatively long tenure of two women with extensive relevant professional experience in the statutory and voluntary sectors prior to devolution (Jane Davidson and Jane Hutt) in the two key cabinet positions (Education and Lifelong Learning, and Health and Social Services) undoubtedly enhanced the attention given to ECEC by policy-makers in Wales. Neither Scotland nor England has enjoyed a remotely equivalent level of continuity in the relevant cabinet portfolios, never mind one involving politicians so committed to

ECEC. While it hardly amounts to a general claim that Wales has been converted to 'new politics', these factors may provide an enduring legacy for Welsh ECEC policy.

Partly echoing the 'new politics' analysis, as in Scotland, the relationship between the central and local government is generally closer in Wales than in England. Yet the pre-existing pattern of Welsh local authority ECEC provision was more variable than that in Scotland. For example, while the general level of preschool provision for four-year-olds was considerably higher than in England, some local authorities had little or no provision. This variability made it less likely that the policy would be largely handed over to local government, which, as we shall see, happened to some extent in Scotland.

Perhaps the most important feature of the Welsh experience is the wide-ranging 'public' – if not 'popular' – debate on the purposes and delivery of ECEC policies, which is engaging and animating experts in the field. It is the absence in England of precisely this sort of debate that Peter Moss regrets (Moss 1999). The Welsh debate, in contrast to the English and, perhaps, also Scottish, began with a return to first principles and rebuilt policy up from them. This experience shows the positive potential of devolving policy-making, particularly when the population enjoys a clear sense of identity and contains a previously underused reservoir of expertise. In addition, the relatively small scale of Welsh political life has also mean that the cross-departmental work that is a prominent feature of ECEC policy-making has proven relatively easy to engender. Interestingly, in Wales, attempts at formal, interorganisational integration of policy responsibility have largely foundered (see Wincott forthcoming b); yet, WAG's small scale (one interviewee said of the WAG administration 'we all eat in the same canteen'), together with the commitment of the relevant ministers, has meant that informal relationships have prospered. While it works well (politics on such an intimate scale can be highly effective), when left to be largely informal, it might also prove prone to navel gazing and petty infighting.

However, the concentration on the design and philosophy of ECEC policies in Wales may also reflect the lack of fiscal-policy tools, together with the lower level of public expenditure per head compared to Scotland. Moreover, Schmuecker and Adams (chapter 3) indicate that, judged against the metrics of spending changes, welfare provision does not appear to be as clear a priority for Scotland and Wales as for England. Even within 'welfare' budgets, resources may not be matched to putative policy priorities – or the political process may dictate a shift away from the apparent priority given to ECEC. Taken together, these factors may have detrimental consequences for ECEC in Wales. In England, the Treasury has been able to back each new early-years policy initiative with funds. For example, recent decisions to offer Welsh-domiciled university students at Welsh institutions an annual grant of £1,800 may have implications for other education budgets. A recent editorial in *agenda* – the journal of the Institute of Welsh Affairs – worries that 'some other part of the Government's education budget will be raided'. It went on to ask 'can it be justified to reduce spending on early years, primary or secondary education in order to fund deferred top-up fees for largely middle class university students who can afford to pay?' (2005, p. 1)

Although the situation later seemed to improve, by 2003 Wales had fallen behind the rapid growth of funding for childcare in England. Thus, a briefing for the Children and Young People Cabinet Sub-Committee noted that a 'further injection of some £23.5 million per annum by 2005-6 would be needed to provide an equivalent population share. To create a universal impact on the accessibility and affordability of childcare would require even greater additional investment' (WAG 2003, p. 2). Given that levels of need are almost certainly higher in Wales, the effective gap with England may have be wider still. More generally, after a period of reflection on the principles and purposes of ECEC policies, resources questions are likely to bite hard in the next phase of rolling out the policies. This is true of the new Foundation Phase curriculum, which makes potentially expensive recommendations about teacher-pupil ratios for the three-seven age group, as well as for childcare strictly defined.

Scotland

As in Wales, the initial early childhood education and care move in Scotland was universalistic. The Scottish Executive set (and largely met) a target of a free half-day nursery place for all three- and four-year-olds by September 2002. In making this move, Scottish policy-makers were able to build on a substantial legacy of preschool and family-service provision. In many parts of Scotland, local authority preschool education was more-or-less universally available for those families wishing to take it up. To a degree, this provision was a corollary of the decision not to introduce reception classes for the rising fives in Scotland. It also reflected an implicit territorial compact that – at least until the Poll Tax – allowed the Scottish Office to provide some protection from Thatcherism for local government north-of-the-border. This gave Strathclyde Region the scope to develop a radical, education-based Pre-Fives Initiative between 1986 and 1996 (Cohen *et al.* 2004), while the capacity of English local government to develop ECEC was increasingly reined in by Westminster (Randall and Fischer 1999). Although the extension to three-year-olds did follow in England, this commitment did mean that Scottish policy-makers could pride themselves in remaining 'ahead' of developments in England, immediately after devolution. In Scotland, local government had long played a larger role in preschool education and family services.

As responsibility for ECEC provision was devolved, during a flurry of policy activity across the UK, the pre-existing tradition of local authority preschool and family centres significantly influenced Scottish policy development.

Indeed, rather than one clear 'Scottish' strategy, distinctive approaches were adopted in each of the thirty-two local authorities. From their creation, the Early Years Development (and Childcare) Partnerships (EYDCPs) in Scotland were led by local authorities, although partnership arrangements across the private and voluntary sectors have certainly sprung up. Higher levels of largely public-sector provision may also have had another impact. While underpaid throughout the UK, in Scotland, local authority nursery staff engaged in sustained strike action in protest against their pay and conditions. Emphasis on local government should not be allowed to obscure the difference made by new national institutions in Scotland. Crucially, additional time is available to consider children's issues in the Scottish Parliament. Prior to devolution, finding time for Scottish legislation in Westminster was becoming increasingly difficult. For example, the Children's Act (for England and Wales) was passed into law in 1989; time was not found for its Scottish equivalent until 1995.

Of course, local 'ownership' of ECEC provision may well be appropriate. Nevertheless, this tradition both restricted the room for manoeuvre at the national level in Scotland and left it more vulnerable to the vagaries of electoral politics. Even the comparison with Wales makes it hard to disentangle the relative influence of these two factors as they coincided. While some Scottish politicians have placed considerable emphasis on early-childhood provision – notably Sam Galbraith during Donald Dewer's period as First Minister, and, latterly, Cathie Jamieson – it has not received the sustained attention it enjoyed in Wales. At the same time, the instability of the Scottish Cabinet has not allowed any minister long enough in office to give this complex and long-term issue the attention it deserves.

If conventional politicians have not kept it high on the political agenda, ECEC might have been expected to benefit from the 'new politics' that, its advocates believe, devolution engenders (Paxton and Gamble 2005, p. 226). New politics certainly characterised the campaign for devolution in Scotland, particularly through the Scottish Constitutional Convention, to which gender issues, including the representation of women, were central (see Mackay 2004). For ECEC, however, distinctive Scottish legacies in local government and education appear to have dominated the policy space, perhaps limiting the impact of 'new politics'. More generally, since devolution, as new institutions have settled into routines, the political space for 'new politics' may have been squeezed (Paxton and Gamble 2005). Its proportional election system means that Scottish politics does not conform to Westminster style; but, arguably, the open style, characteristic of the devolution campaign, has not been sustained.

Scotland may come to benefit from the smaller scale (and distinctive character) of its new national administration. In contrast with Wales, where the 'joining up' of early-years policy has been informal (at least where it has been successful), the Scottish Executive embarked on an ambitious, large-scale and formal process. Perhaps partly a legacy of the Scottish Office's wide range of substantive policy concerns, although by no means easy, this scale and depth of cross-departmental integration would be unimaginable in the larger-scale, more deeply institutionalised, context of Whitehall. The result, in early-years policy, is a document expounding an *Integrated Strategy for the Early Years* (ISEY) (Scottish Executive 2003). It aims to bring together health, social services, education and childcare. While joining up national-level policy-making is no guarantee of integration of services on the ground, the ISEY ambition was to reconfigure the delivery of services at all levels. It would also draw together services for vulnerable and disadvantaged children into a comprehensive package, including key universally provided elements. Experts believe that a complex policy mix of this sort is the most effective way of identifying and addressing particular problems as early as possible – when the most effective interventions can be made. If successfully implemented, ISEY is precisely the kind of policy that social democratic advocates (Paxton and Gamble 2005) expect devolution to provide. Yet ISEY may prove impossible to digest even in Scotland. Despite its popularity, little has been heard of the strategy since 2003. Nevertheless, even, perhaps especially, if it, ultimately, proves fruitless, ISEY is worthy of close analysis by those interested in the social politics of scale.

If direct policy competence for ECEC was devolved to Scotland, Westminster continued to constrain policy choice north-of-the-border. Treasury-designed demand-side childcare subsidies reinforced the 'mixed economy' policy model developed for English ECEC, which arguably did not reflect, and perhaps even undercut, the more extensive tradition of Scottish local authority provision (Cohen *et al.* 2004). Yet any implication that, but for malign Treasury influence, Scotland would have opted for Nordic-style ECEC provision is highly speculative. Moreover, while counterfactual policy narratives are similarly dangerous, there is little in the record of the Scottish Parliament or Executive to indicate that the first fruits of fiscal autonomy would be invested in the early years.

England

Many politicians have occupied the particular ministries with direct responsibility for English early childhood education and care provision. The departmental location of these responsibilities has migrated around Whitehall. Yet, interest in ECEC at Westminster has been transformed since 1997. It has enjoyed the support of Tony Blair and Gordon Brown – whose tenure in their respective jobs outstrips that of Jane Davidson and Jane Hutt! Without the support and interest of Blair and Brown we would hardly be in a position in which social democrats could envisage ECEC as the early twenty-first century's institutional equivalent of the NHS. Although Government trumpeted a new national strategy in 1998, there was little evidence of strategic thinking (for expert commentary see, for example, Lewis 2003; Moss 1999). In fact, most aspects of ECEC have changed considerably since 1997, and some key aspects remain unsettled.

Although it is sometimes overlooked, the early commitment to support the nursery places of four- and, later, three-year-old children was an important policy change; it offered, in effect, 'universal' support to all families wishing to take it up. The policy contained a peculiar mix of flexible and rigid elements. In the face of the pre-existing mixed economy of local authority, private- and voluntary-sector provision, it sought to support provision flexibly in any approved setting. In effect, providers claim fees on behalf of families. On the other hand, support for five half-day sessions per week could prove inflexible in the face of family needs. In fact, private and voluntary providers, where parents could pay for additional periods of care, often proved more flexible than the local authority sector, which tended to offer a set menu of morning or afternoon sessions. In many areas, particularly less affluent ones, private and voluntary provision was sparse, and hence the nursery school offer did not provide adequate support for working parents.

New Labour rapidly turned to address the issue of childcare directly, through the NCS. However, inconsistency and frenetic activity marked childcare policy. Major new, independently branded, but substantively overlapping, ECEC policy initiatives were announced at a rate of more than one a year during Labour's first half decade in office. Early Years Development Partnerships became Early Years Development and Childcare Partnerships (EYDCPs) little over a year after they were first formed. The NCS was launched in 1998, emphasising Early Excellence Centres. In 1999, Tony Blair launched Sure Start, which has been labelled 'Labour's most ideologically branded initiative' (Quarmby 2003, pp. 50-51). In 2000, the Treasury's Spending Review (SR) showed huge gaps in childcare provision, particularly in deprived areas, and earmarked extra funding for full-day childcare in deprived areas through the Neighbourhood Nursery Initiative (NNI), which directly funds the capital costs of creating new nurseries. Between 2001 and 2004, it has had £203 million of revenue funding through the DfES, and up to £100 million capital funding from the New Opportunities Fund, to create 45,000 new places in some 900 new fifty-place nurseries (DfES 2002). Launched in October 2001, a major Interdepartmental Review of Childcare then proposed the establishment of Children's Centres, intended as an umbrella covering Early Excellence Centres, local Sure Start provision and Neighbourhood Nurseries, but also extending to some new provision (Strategy Unit 2002). Despite identifying confusing 'branding' of ECEC provision as a problem, the Children's Centre label added to, rather than wholly displaced, earlier forms of provision. Both Sure Start and Children's Centres are now entrenched policy 'brands'.

2001 also saw 'Extended Schools' emerge as a national focus for England. The White Paper *Schools: Achieving Success* recommended the introduction of legislation to remove barriers to schools providing more support and services to pupils, families and communities. Following experience in Australia, the USA and Scottish 'New Community Schools', the White Paper proposed the piloting of such 'extended schools' (DfES 2001) and demonstration projects were set up in three areas of England. Subsequently, ECEC was connected to the developing movement to use schools as community resources. Unlike New Community Schools in Scotland, ECEC became a particular focus of English Extended Schools, especially after 2004. Partly under the auspices of the Department for Work and Pensions, Extended Schools Childcare Pilots were launched initially in Bradford, Haringey and Lewisham, focused on returning lone parents to work. Four more English areas (Greenwich, Leicester, Leicestershire and Sandwell) were added from October 2004, together with Scottish pilots in Aberdeenshire and Fife and a Welsh pilot in Torfaen, to which we will return below. At the same time, and again reflecting the frenetic quality of ECEC policy development, the closely related Childcare Taster Pilots were also being run. By 2010, childcare will be offered on school sites for all children under fourteen who require it, through a mixed economy of public-, private- and voluntary-sector provision (DfES 2005).

Just as a child-protection scandal prompted the establishment of the Welsh Children's Commissioner, Victoria Climbié's death also triggered significant developments in England, further elaborating and complicating the policy environment for ECEC. The Government's response, *Every Child Matters*, created an English Children's Commissioner, completing a full set for the UK nations (albeit with rather weaker powers than the Celtic counterparts), but this also held direct implications for ECEC, altering the context within which it operated.

Four interrelated factors explain much of the complexity and hyper-innovation that characterises English ECEC policy. First, as a new, crosscutting area of policy, initiatives emerged from a variety of sources. As a government committed to 'joining up' policy, Labour sought to create a Whitehall 'centre' for ECEC without losing links to other policy fields. Initially, they moved responsibility from Health to the then Department for Education and Employment (DfEE), initially with a distinct Childcare Unit and Early Years Division, and, later, an interdepartmental Sure Start Unit was also housed in the DfEE. By 2002, the DfEE had been broken up, and responsibility for most English ECEC provision was concentrated in one unit. This Sure Start Unit now hung between the new Department for Education and Skills (DfES) and the Department for Work and Pensions (DWP), reflecting its education and employment dimensions. A result of 'muddling through' rather than synoptic planning, it is nevertheless striking that Whitehall both required and achieved a reorganisation of its administrative structures to deliver ECEC expansion. This stands in contrast to relatively smooth *de facto* integration in Wales, and the more ambitious, but as yet unrealised, ISEY process in Scotland, which probably reflects the smaller scale of the institutions. Of course, national-level integration of ECEC, health and child protection will pose further, similar challenges for England as policy-makers grapple with the *Every Child Matters* agenda. Finally, the crucial role of the Treasury in ECEC can hardly be overemphasised, reflecting its general transformation into a domestic policy hothouse. Direct Treasury involvement in English policy has made it possible for funding to be attached to each new ECEC initiative. While this may have encouraged the English policy hyperactivity in this area, it also facilitated a rapid growth in the overall level of funding (in partial contrast to the Scottish and Welsh experience).

Operating on the larger English scale, secondly, the administration of ECEC begs important questions about central-local relations. As well as having clear positive arguments about community involvement in aspects of ECEC, when Labour first came to office it was deeply sceptical about – indeed distrustful of – (some) local government. Labour's ECEC policy might have been designed to avoid handing a new policy responsibility and funding to local government. In contrast to the Scottish practice, English EYDCPs placed local government in a subordinate role. From Sure Start to neighbourhood nurseries, the early ECEC initiatives created new forms of partnership that bypassed local government, or at least limited its role. Part of the rationale was that central government was concentrating its efforts in deprived areas, and developed central techniques for identifying and targeting them.

As government later came to realise (Strategy Unit 2002), EYDCPs were not equipped for the role government envisaged, being of uncertain legal status and unable to hold public funds. Moreover, as New Labour's ECEC commitment grew in scale, it became increasingly difficult to deliver through a patchwork of 'partnerships' without statutory authorities holding the policy field. Starting from the 2002 Interdepartmental Review, and culminating in the Treasury's Ten Year Childcare Plan, local government gradually became central to English ECEC (Strategy Unit 2002; HMT 2004). Arguably, this wheel has turned too far, if ECEC funding is rolled into general local authority budgets in horse-trading, which leaves a ring-fence around expenditure on schools (Toynbee 2005).

The third factor is the changing role of the public sector in English ECEC policy. When first elected, the Government was fiercely critical of its Conservative predecessor's market-oriented approach to ECEC, arguing that it had been left 'almost exclusively to the market. But this simply hasn't worked. And the voluntary sector has been expected to provide, with little government support, most of the services for parents looking after their own children' (DfEE, 1998 p5). New Labour foresaw only a limited 'enabling' role for government in the NCS. If it held high expectations that identifying – and rebranding – a few exemplary Centres and bolstering the market through demand-side subsidy would rapidly trigger a 'national' blossoming of ECEC, it was rapidly disabused. Particularly in more deprived areas, Government has ploughed very substantial sums into building ECEC capacity, from Sure Start and Neighbourhood Nurseries onwards. While it remains committed to a 'mixed economy' of childcare, the public-sector role in ECEC envisaged by Government has been transformed beyond recognition.

Finally, the balance of the underlying rationale for ECEC has also changed. At first, New Labour appeared strongly committed to an economic rationale for childcare. Enabling parents – particularly mothers – to work was crucial. Here, ECEC dovetailed with Labour's welfare-to-work agenda, and especially its drive to get lone parents into employment. This policy rationale remains clear, but it has been powerfully augmented by a child-development rationale, which is further tied to a long-term egalitarian argument. This had always been an element in Labour ECEC policy, providing the philosophy that inspired the designers of Sure Start, as well as underpinning the support for nursery places. In the Treasury's ten-year plan, the first justification for high-quality ECEC is its role in enhancing and equalising children's life chances (HMT 2004, Appendix A).

Although not yet finally settled, a model for English early-years and child-care provision is starting to emerge. The 2005 manifesto commits Labour to develop 'Extended Schools' providing 'wrap-around' care for children up to the age of fourteen, matched by a Children's Centre, covering families with children up to age five, for every community (which might itself be sited in an Extended School) (Labour Party 2005). This combination could provide the institutional framework for a comprehensive provision of early-education and childcare provision. If public resources are particularly concentrated on less-well-off children (or, following existing practice, children in more deprived areas), while the Children's Centres in more prosperous areas amount to more than an empty brand, the 'progressive universal' sobriquet may prove justified for English ECEC.

Conclusion: early childhood education and care, devolution and democracy

Paxton and Gamble rightly argue that democracy is instrumental to achieving social justice (2005); properly understood, TH Marshall's analysis of the relationship between citizenship and the welfare state is grounded on precisely this notion ([1950] 1992; Lister 2005). Yet Marshall's penetrating conceptual analysis rests on and perpetuates the misconception that the UK ever experienced a full national democratisation (Wincott forthcoming a). While in some respects highly centralised, the manner in which political power was shielded from democratic scrutiny and control helps to account for the stalled development of British social democracy since 1945 (Esping-Andersen 1999). Centralism certainly contributed to the stymieing of ECEC expansion in Britain during the 1960s, a decade marked by expansion in many other countries. In 1998, devolution altered the political dimension of citizenship –

arguably filling the democratic deficit generated by a long history of administrative devolution (itself designed to address distinctive Scottish identity and institutions) (Mitchell 2003).

British institutional structure apparently cements devolved social policy autonomy in ways that could maximise the potential for local experiments. Greer notes the absence of formal central constraints on the devolved governments, either in terms of the normative-legal framework or the financial structure, both of which are internationally unusual (2005). International evidence suggests that welfare development is relatively restricted in federal and highly devolved polities (Swank 2002). These factors help to explain why, historically, the British welfare state did not enjoy a 'unitary state bonus' and why the 'devolved penalty' need not be harsh (Wincott forthcoming a).

Even if devolution represents a democratic enhancement, devolved ECEC would still raise questions of UK-wide equity. Paxton and Gamble frame these issues as 'social justice' and 'distributive' tests (2005, pp. 229-233); more graphically Banting and Corbett discuss whether the prospects of a 'sick baby' would or should vary in different regions (2002, p. 19). Here, through its attachment to wider education policy, ECEC is in caught in a particularly sharp historical dilemma. Education is a classic instrument of nation-building, typically representing a homogenising thrust from the centre into the periphery. The peculiarity of British history is aptly caught in the absence of such a nationalising thrust at the UK level, or even within England itself, during the nineteenth century. By contrast, something like a national system did emerge in Scotland at this time. Unimaginable in France, when Paxton and Gamble consider whether education is relevant to national citizenship, they place a question mark against the issue. Education has been, then, an important source of difference with the Anglo-Scottish 'union'. Yet, recent evidence suggests that ECEC can be a crucial influence on a child's life chances. If variations in the quality of a child's medical treatment seem unjust, arguments for mechanisms to ensure acceptable minimum standards and the diffusion of good practice for ECEC are at least as strong.

Yet, formal mechanisms of this sort are strikingly lacking in Britain today. Indeed, Treasury frustration over the weakness of co-ordination, deliberation and direct policy powers for ECEC spilled over in 2002. Gordon Brown turned to the Joint Ministerial Committee (JMC) (Poverty) – a formal forum for discussion of social policy issues across the four nations of the UK – which met for the first time since 2000. The Chancellor 'had become concerned about the Treasury's lack of influence on devolved functions and … he wished to use the JMC as a means to shape devolved policy…' (Trench 2004 p. 180). However, neither of the planned meetings for the 'Poverty' formation of the JMC in (January and June) 2003 took place. The Committee has not met since; now it seems to be viewed as a 'nuclear option' to be used should intergovernmental conflict becomes so intense that it cannot be resolved through informal political or administrative mechanisms.

Of course, all multilevel polities rely on informal mechanisms for political and administrative intergovernmental dispute resolution. What marks the UK out is the comparative weakness of the formal institutions around which such informal relations generally develop. In this respect, Britain shows remarkable continuity in its patterns of interterritorial relations before and after devolution. Continuing the traditions from administrative devolution, civil servants – all within a common Home Service – play a pivotal role. With considerable pragmatic aplomb, the civil service typically seeks to smooth over and disguise intergovernmental conflict. But even the most cursory study of federal and other multilevel polities shows that such conflict is the stuff of their democratic politics. The absence of explicit, public, political discussion of policy issues where reserved and devolved competences meet, but also of those policies from which valuable lessons might be learnt across territory, challenges the democratising potential of devolution.

Instead, even where UK-wide targets exist in policies connected to ECEC – such as the halving, and eventual elimination, of child poverty – the institutional configuration of devolution provides surprisingly little space in which joint political action might take place. The UK 'Centre' has approached these issues crab-wise, for example by funding and encouraging voluntary-sector action. In other cases, such as the Extended Schools Childcare Pilot, it has quietly used the pretext of reserved powers (for example in the DWP) together with funding from its relatively deep pockets to bring influence to bear in the devolved nations. Yet devolved officials insist that, for example, Wales has Community-Focused, not Extended Schools, even while Torfaen is funded from the DWP Extended Schools Childcare Pilot. None of this helps to cast democratic light on these important policies.

Advocates of devolution claim that it generates a new, more participatory and deliberative kind of politics, particularly because of a greater proximity between electors and governors, but also because it can draw previously marginal individuals and groups into politics. Examination of ECEC policy shows that British devolution has certainly introduced some changes of this sort. Yet important continuities with antiquated pre-devolution (un)democratic structures still exist. ECEC and democratic devolution can become foundations for British social democracy, but in both these areas crucial changes have yet to be made.

Acknowledgements

This chapter forms part of a research project on 'Devolution and the Comparative Territorial Analysis of the Welfare State' supported by the ESRC under its Devolution and Constitutional Change programme (award number L219252104).

References

Banting K and Corbett S (2002) 'Health Policy and Federalism: An Introduction' in Banting K and Corbett S (eds.) *Health Policy and Federalism* McGill-Queen's University Press pp. 1-37

Chaney P (2004) 'The Post-Devolution Equality Agenda: The Case of Welsh Assembly's Statutory Duty to Promote Equality of Opportunity' in *Policy and Politics* 32:1, pp. 63-77

Cohen B *et al.* (2004) *A New Deal for Children?* Policy Press

Department for Education and Employment (DfEE) (1998) *Meeting the Childcare Challenge: a Framework and Consultation Document* Cm 3959 HMSO

Department for Education and Skills (DfES) (2001) *Schools: Achieving success* DfES

DfES (2002) *Neighbourhood Nurseries Initiative: Design Competition* DfES

DfES (2005) *Extended Schools: Access to opportunities and services for all. A prospectus* DfES

Department for Training and Education (DTE) (2005) *Extending Nursery Provision for Three Year Olds* DEL

Editorial (2005) *agenda* Institute of Welsh Affairs, p. 1

Esping-Andersen G (1999) *Social foundations of postindustrial economies* Oxford University Press

Giddens A (1998) *The Third Way* Polity

Greer S (2005) *Territorial politics and health policy* Manchester University Press

Hyman P (2005) 'Bring me Alastair' *Guardian* G2 9 February 2005

Hanney M (2000) *Early Years Provision for Three Year Olds: Expert Adviser Report for the Pre 16 Education, Schools and Early Learning Committee of the National Assembly for Wales* NAW

HM Treasury (HMT)/DfES/DWP/DTI (2004) *Choice for Parents, the Best Start for Children: a ten year strategy for childcare* HMT

Korpi W (1980) 'Social Policy and Distributional Conflict in the Capitalist Democracies' *West European Politics* 3:3, pp. 296-316

Korpi W (1983) *The Democratic Class Struggle* Routledge and Kegan Paul

Law J (2004) 'Childcare in Scotland: Perceptions and Realities' presented to the ESRC Workshop on *The impact of devolution on early years education and care policies in the UK* University of Birmingham, 21 September 2004

Labour Party (2005) *Britain Forward not Back: The Labour Party manifesto 2005* Labour Party

Lewis J (2003) 'Developing Early Years Childcare in England, 1997-2002: The Choices for (Working) Mothers' in *Social Policy & Administration* 37:2, pp. 219-238

Mackay F (2004) 'Gender and Political Representation in the UK: the state of the "discipline"' in *British Journal of Politics and International Relations* 6:1, pp. 101-122

Mitchell J (2003) *Governing Scotland* Palgrave

Mitchell J (2004) 'Scotland: Expectations, Policy Types and Devolution' in Trench A (ed.) *Has Devolution made a Difference: The State of the Nations 2004* Imprint Academic pp. 11-41

Morgan R (2002) 'Speech of the First Minister for the University of Wales Swansea' ['Clear Red Water' Speech] National Centre for Public Policy, Third Anniversary Lecture, December 11 2002

Moss P (1999) 'Renewed hopes and lost opportunities: early childhood in the early years of the Labour Government' in *Cambridge Journal of Education* 29:2, pp. 229-238

Mulgan G (2005a) 'What Next For New Labour?' Presentation to the conference *Que reste-t-il de Cool Britannia? Le Royaume-Uni après huit ans de gouvernement Blair,* mercredi 4 mai, available at www.cerium.umontreal.ca/video/coolbrit_mulgan.wmv

Mulgan G (2005b) 'Responses to questions at the conference' *Que reste-t-il de Cool Britannia ? Le Royaume-Uni après huit ans de gouvernement Blair,* mercredi 4 mai, available at www.cerium.umontreal.ca/video/coolbrit_mulgan_questions.wmv

National Childcare Strategy Task Force (2001) *Report* 21 November 2001 HS-16-01 NAW

Obinger Liebfried S and Castles F (2005) *Federalism and the Welfare State* Cambridge University Press.

Owen Jones J (1999) *Hansard* 21 April 1999, available at www.parliament.the-stationery-office.co.uk/pa/cm199899/cmhansrd/vo990421/text/90421w17.htm

Paxton W and Gamble A (2005) 'Democracy, Social Justice and the State' in Pearce N and Paxton W (eds.) *Social Justice: Building a Fairer Britain* ippr, pp. 219-239

Paxton W, Pearce N and Reed H (2005) 'Foundations for a Progressive Century' in Pearce N and Paxton W (eds.) *Social Justice: Building a Fairer Britain* ippr, pp. 355-401

Pearce N and W Paxton (2005) 'Introduction' in Pearce N and Paxton W (eds.) *Social Justice: Building a Fairer Britain* ippr, pp. ix-xxiii

Pre-16 Education, Schools and Early Learning Committee of the National Assembly for Wales (Pre-16 Education Committee) (2000a) Minutes for 12 April 2000 PRE 16-06-00, NAW

Pre-16 Education, Schools and Early Learning Committee of the National Assembly for Wales (Pre-16 Education Committee) (2000b) *Child Care in Wales - Response to the Welsh Affairs Committee Report on Child Care in Wales* PRE 16-04-00, NAW

Quarmby K (2003) 'The Politics of Childcare' in *Prospect Magazine* November 2003, Prospect, pp. 50-55

Randall V (2000) *The Politics of Child Daycare in Britain* Oxford University Press

Randall V and Fischer K (1999) 'Towards Explaining Child Care Policy Variations Among Local Authorities'. Paper presented to the workshop *Child Care Policy* at the Local Level University of Essex, September 17 1999

Reed J and Robinson P (2005) 'From Social Mobility to Equal Life Chances: Maintaining the Momentum' in Pearce N and Paxton W (eds.) *Social Justice: Building a Fairer Britain* ippr, pp. 282-300

Richards S (2005) 'Learning how to learn' *agenda* Summer 2005, Institute of Welsh Affairs pp. 50-52

Rothstein B (1998) *Just Institutions Matter* Cambridge University Press

Ryner M (2002) *Capitalist Restructuring, Globalisation and the Third Way: Lessons from the Swedish Model* Routledge

Scottish Executive (2003) *Integrated Strategy for the Early Years* Scottish Executive

Seaton N (2005) *Development and Implementation of Integrated Centres in Wales* Institute of Welsh Affairs

Strategy Unit (2002) *Delivering for Children and Families - Inter-Departmental Childcare Review* PM Strategy Unit

Swank D (2002) *Global Capital, Political Institutions, and Policy Change in Developed Welfare States* Cambridge University Press

Toynbee P (2005) 'Dig deep to make Sure Start just as brilliant as it can be' *Guardian* 13 July 2005

Trench A (2004) 'The more things change, the more they stay the same: Intergovernmental Relations Four Years on' in Trench A (ed.) *Has devolution made a difference? The State of the Nations 2004* Imprint Academic pp. 165-191

Welsh Affairs Select Committee (1999) *Childcare in Wales* TSO

Welsh Assembly Government (WAG) (2003) *An Update on Childcare Briefing for the Children and Young People Cabinet Sub-Committee, National Assembly for Wales* (CYP(03-04) 10 Annex A) NAW

WAG (2002) *Childcare Action Plan* NAW

Wincott D (2005) 'Reshaping Public Space? Devolution and Policy Change in British Early Childhood Education and Care' in *Regional and Federal Studies* 15:4, pp. 453-470

Wincott D forthcoming a) 'Social Policy and Social Citizenship: Britain's Welfare States' in Publius. *The Journal of Federalism* 36:1

Wincott D (forthcoming b) 'Devolution and the Welfare State: Lessons from Early Childhood Education and Care (ECEC) Policy in Wales' in *Environment and Planning C Government and Policy*

7 The politics of health-policy divergence

Scott L Greer

Aneurin Bevan and his colleagues in the 1945 Labour government were not, by and large, devolutionists. Perhaps that is why they named the NHS as they did: the National Health Service. They clearly meant that it was the National Health Service of the United Kingdom, or at least Great Britain. But the politics of society of the United Kingdom have changed and given us a question: in a multinational democracy such as the UK, what nation does that 'National' mean now?

The extent of health-policy divergence since 1999 adds urgency to the question. Divergence has been striking, with three radically different bets on the best way to save the NHS in England, Scotland, and Wales, and a number of interesting findings from Northern Ireland's subsequent immobility. Divergence can happen so quickly because of the remarkably permissive nature of the devolution settlement; unlike most other systems, devolved health policy in the UK concentrates power in each of the four governments and allows them to run their systems as they see fit, in accordance with their local politics and their local policy debates. And what we have found is that those local politics drive politicians to seek very different solutions to different problems, while the policy debates, which started long before devolution, put different issues on the agendas and leave the ministers buttonholed at different parties by people with radically different solutions. There is reason to question whether the Nation in NHS is still the UK.

The daily differences between the political systems cumulate, as different English, Northern Irish, Scottish and Welsh newspapers flag different issues, different opposition parties in each assembly attack different ministers on different fronts, different policy advocates leap forward to hawk different policy solutions to the time-pressed politicians, and different groups of officials gauge differently the odds that something will work. If four ministers each make a different decision each day, it is not long before their decisions start to cumulate into four trajectories, as far apart as the politics and policy debates in which they participate. And, the NHS systems being easy to change and the devolved governments being free to change them, the result is divergent policy.

This produces in health policy what I elsewhere call the 'fragile divergence machine': a combination of political forces for divergence with an institutional setting that makes it relatively easy to develop different health policies (Greer 2004a and forthcoming a). The machine is effective because it is powered by both political self-interest and the nature of debates in different polities; it is fragile because it requires politics that are tolerant of divergence and a set of interlocking institutions, such as the Barnett formula, that are precarious, poorly understood, and often unpopular.

Why health policy diverges

Three of the four UK health systems, in England, Scotland and Wales, are, politically, quite similar. That is precisely why they are so likely to diverge.

The reason is that their shared characteristics are all conducive to divergent policy-making in health. First, it is because they are national health systems, in other words, integrated systems dominated by a single payer that also either owns or is the dominant contractor for services (Freeman 2000). The NHS and similar systems abroad, in this sense, are unified, large organisations, dependent on general taxation and responsible to the government. As relatively unified organisations, national health services, such as the ones in the UK, are therefore comparatively easy to change, or at least offer a tempting mirage of rapid change to the politician.

Second, it is because the forms of parliamentary government in England, Scotland, and Wales all create governments that are, by international standards, free to do what they like. As long as they have a majority in the legislature, individual ministers and governments can make a broad range of policies. This tendency is most marked in Westminster, but is shared by all three. All three lack the complex interlocking veto points of systems such as Germany or the United States, where interbranch rivalries, courts and different levels of government afford opponents of change endless redoubts from which to fight. Northern Ireland, when devolved, is the reverse; it is so tightly constricted and inclusive that policies there are rare, and generally the output of one minister acting nearly alone.

So the organisational and political costs of policy-making are comparatively low (Greer 2004b). A government in the UK can enact large changes in its health service, either with only a foreordained legislative process, or sometimes only with lesser legal instruments. The odds that three such governments will have similar problems, debates, and policy decisions at the same time are very slim.

Third, the system of intergovernmental relations and finance in the UK permits a broad degree of health-policy divergence. Other systems, such as those in Canada, Spain, or Germany, use different combinations of law, financial controls, and official co-ordination to restrain divergence (Poirier 2001; Banting and Corbett 2002). This includes direct normative supervision over what regional governments can do, as in Spain (where regional health policies must fit with a Spanish basic law). It also includes financial techniques that take advantage of the structural advantages of central states (more free money); this can include co-financing, in which central-state participation helps fund some policy in an area of regional responsibility, but at the price of ceding control. The central state, paying the piper, expresses an interest in the tune. Any combination of normative and financial constraint tends to prove unedifying, frequently leading to heated intergovernmental disputes and elaborate exercises in blame avoidance. More to the point, it tends to reduce the ability of regional governments to adopt divergent policies.

The UK has none of that in Scotland, and in Wales, in health, surprisingly little. There is essentially no normative regulation over what England or Scotland can do; either could abolish the NHS, although if England did, the theoretical consequences of the so-called Barnett formula would convert into a devastating budget cut for the devolved territories. The Welsh situation is more confused, but the scope of secondary legislation in health (if not in other areas) is very broad and affords a great deal of room for policy change without recourse to Westminster. In finance, meanwhile, Barnett might be unpopular and difficult to justify, but it has a great asset: it is a formula-based block grant. It is, therefore, relatively transparent and it blocks significant use of central-government funds to buy its way into devolved policy, while not ring-fencing funds. The result is that there is no effective institutional governor on policy divergence to date.

All this means it is easy to enact different policies and set about trying to implement them. There are also reasons to expect policy divergence, since both the suppliers of policy ideas in the four different parts of the UK and the politicians who 'buy' policies face different constraints and operate on different agendas (this case is made at greater length in Greer 2004a).

Political forces for divergence

Party politics diverges sharply around the UK, and so do politicians' incentives to define themselves and compete for votes. The problem for any party in the UK is that the basic terms of the debate in each country vary. In England, Scotland, and Wales there is a strong and well-known left-right axis, with Labour on the left, the Conservatives on the right, and competition for voters somewhere around the centre. The issues are of commitment to equity, individual and economic liberty, and the role of public and private. Such debates dominate English politics but are joined in Scotland and Wales by a second axis, that of the nationalist-unionist debate. This is the debate over the fate of those stateless nations within the UK, with positions arguing anything from integration (unionism) through autonomy, to separation (nationalism). This makes political life in Scotland and Wales rather complex; Labour, for example, has to demonstrate not just that it satisfies the economic and social preferences of swing voters, but also that it is Scottish or Welsh enough (Seawright 2002). To be seen as an 'English' party in Scotland or Wales is a constant threat for any UK party there, and it is a mortal threat as the recent history of the Conservatives there shows. The result is that Labour and its coalition partners need to show that they are Scottish or Welsh enough – not blindly obeying London, and avoiding policies labelled English, such as foundation hospitals or university tuition fees. Rhodri Morgan, First Minister of Wales, said it best when he suggested in a campaign speech that he wanted to put 'clear red water' between Wales and England (Osmond 2003). The other parties, which are dominant in one country each and scarcely present elsewhere – the SNP (Scotland), Conservatives (England), and Plaid Cymru (Wales) – are likely to be even less constrained in seeking divergence. Finally, just to reinforce a trend to the left in Scotland, the two devolved elections have allowed the Scottish Socialist Party and the Greens to thrive; two parties well to the left of Labour and the SNP nip at their heels, allowing neither party to ignore the concerns of more left-wing voters. Labour in England, shielded by first-past-the-post elections, does not face the same pressure from the left.

The problems facing politicians in Northern Ireland are rather different. English politicians can ignore questions of nationalism and unionism; Scottish and Welsh ones must balance and move tactically between left, right, nationalist and unionist; Northern Irish ones operate almost entirely on a nationalist-unionist continuum. In fact, Northern Ireland essentially has two and a half party systems: a Unionist one, in which the Democratic Unionist Party, Ulster Unionist Party, and some small parties compete to better represent the Unionists; a Nationalist one, in which the Social Democratic and Labour Party and Sinn Fein compete to represent Nationalists; and a few parties in the middle (Alliance and the Women's Coalition), catering to the small non-sectarian electorate. Given the dominance of the internal nationalist and unionist debates, and the difficulties of having devolution at all, it is hardly a surprise that few politicians see much reason to try to focus on health-policy-making in Northern Ireland. In the 'tribal headcounts' that are Northern Irish elections, there are not many votes in public policy.

Divergent policy communities

Policy communities are the political scientists' term for a common phenomenon in politics, namely the people who cluster around political institutions offering advice, selling policies, carping, writing, studying, arguing, and otherwise. These communities nurture some ideas and not others, forming good environments for proponents of some policies and poor ones for others. They are also surprisingly difficult to change.

The English health-policy community, notably, nurtures many more pro-market, pro-management ideas than any other. The English ideological climate has proved suitable for the lush growth of ideas about management, markets, and techniques of new public management. There are abundant and well-funded right-leaning think tanks, such as Civitas, with no real equivalent elsewhere; there are entire Whitehall departments that have internalised new public management and contracting as their standard operating procedures; there is a large academic infrastructure teaching health-services management; even major lobby groups with substantial money and interests in shaping public policy, such as pharmaceuticals, are overwhelmingly located in and around London. In politics, as in institutions, we find with devolution that what we thought was the UK generally turns out to be England.

The Scottish health-policy community, by contrast, reflects the long Scottish history of being a global intellectual centre far out of proportion to its size. Materially, this means a large and well-organised set of medical and professional elites: three Royal Colleges, four university medical centres, and a respect among policy-makers for professionals in social life and the health services often lacking elsewhere. It is not at all hard to find, in Scotland, reputable, important professionals interested in advising on policy. They do not, then, face as many competitors; the think-tank world in Scotland is smaller and often more closely linked to universities, the Scotsman has not proved convincing enough to spark serious neo-liberal debates on its own, and, above all, professional leaders can trade on the existing structure of Scottish policy-making. The Scottish Office, long charged with negotiating the gap between Scottish organisations' preferences and UK policy, did it by relying on the leaders of the professions – the senior academics and doctors in the service. This gave them considerable influence over implementation and priorities; it was a 'reign of professional ideas' (Hazell and Jervis 1998, p. 44) and those networks still remain.

Devolution has, of course, opened up politics and increased the influence of groups previously marginal or invisible in policy debates, such as unions and many advocates of particular diseases or issues. Professional leaders, senior managers and officials are all much more likely to be under pressure from some other group newly empowered by devolved politics, and most complain bitterly about coping with the press. But still, given the vast increase in the importance of policy made in Edinburgh, the professional leaders' switch from dominant influence over marginal issues to preponderant influence over all issues is good for them.

If England has carried on as the UK had carried on before, with its bruising left-right political debate about redistribution, public-private and civil liberties, and Scotland has democratised the reign of professional ideas, Wales has seen a more curious change. Wales lacks both the strong English pro-market, pro-management infrastructure and the Scottish professional elites. For a variety of reasons, Welsh politics gives a far more powerful role in health and most other issues to local government and the trades unions; devolved Welsh politics has had a mix-and-match character in which groups such as those convert their strength in Welsh politics into strength in policy communities, such as health, that had previously taken their lead from Whitehall. The result is that local government and public health, marginal in England, are now at the centre of Welsh health politics. There, they benefit from both a longstanding central role in Welsh political debate unequalled in England or Scotland and an egalitarian political discourse.

Northern Ireland, finally, has a health-policy community suited to its unusual politics. One of the salient characteristics of Northern Irish politics is the lack of bread-and-butter concerns. Elections in Northern Ireland are not won and lost on public services, or on debates between left and right. For much of its recent history, it has been governed by direct rule and ministers from parties that do not campaign in Northern Ireland, and who have little electoral incentive to make major changes in the areas covered by their enormous portfolios (such as health, social services, and education, in one combination). The result is that both Northern Irish politicians, under sporadic devolution, and direct-rule politicians prefer a health system that stays out of the newspapers, does not pick fights, and does not create serious crises or dilemmas for the minister. Managers who can deliver that ministerial tranquillity are then free, much freer than their colleagues 'across the water', to deliver other priorities. The result is extraordinary variation in the style and functioning of Northern Irish health organisations, combined with stability in the managerial cadre. If we want to see what a health service looks like when left alone, without reorganisation or top-down policy, we should look to Northern Ireland.

Divergence to date

The cardinal error of analysing devolved policies is to take England as a baseline. There is no reason to do so; different politics, debates, values and histories all conspire to mean that there is no reason to expect the four systems will line up neatly on some scale of achievement. Perhaps England, with its recent large spending increases (see Schmuecker and Adams in chapter 3), does some things better – it certainly has reduced waiting lists for elective surgery – but there is always the possibility that achievement, will be counterbalanced by some other cost, a cost other systems are not willing to bear. Welsh policymakers insist that elective waiting times for procedures that, by definition, are not urgent are a very poor benchmark for the quality of a health system, and that reducing inequalities and investing in public health will work better in the long run. Indeed, the divergence in specific policies and organisations reflects not just different assessments as to what will solve a particular problem; it reflects different understandings of ends and means.

England: Markets and management

The Labour Government in England, following significant increases in public expenditure on the NHS, has started to construct what it hopes will be a far more robust, effective and desirable internal market than that of the Conservatives. This does not reflect the explicit campaign pledge by Labour in 1997 that it would abolish the internal market; rather, it reflects the party strategy of Labour and the solutions and ideas found in mainstream English health debates. Labour, on one side, is forced to fight on its right flank in England. Untroubled by the SNP, Plaid Cymru, the SSP or the Greens, it instead must contend with a Conservative official opposition that proposes more market forces and choice in the NHS. It is the presence of the Conservatives, as much as any convictions Labour has about growing consumerism, that explains why choice and customer satisfaction are such important goals and so constantly debated. And it is the conviction that English public services need to be reformed if they are to be politically sustainable that explains the sheer volume, and radicalism, of English health policies.

First, Labour is restoring the internal market within the English NHS. This is partly in pursuit of greater healthcare from the fixed sum of money going in, given that Labour, to date, has ruled out co-payments in core services (which evidence suggests tend to be wasteful anyway) and that it lacks the Conservative enthusiasm for building up the private sector as a rival to the NHS. The question for Labour is how to move central government from the business of complex organisational and management design to the business of complex market design.

The English system is built around Primary Care Trusts (PCTs), which are responsible for ensuring adequate healthcare for their populations. PCTs do this by contracting with local GPs; by contracting for acute services with hospitals and other trusts (the relationship at the heart of PCT activity and political debates); sometimes by commissioning services from private providers; and occasionally by providing services on their own. The other providers – ordinary trusts and foundation hospitals – sign contracts with PCTs to provide services to the PCTs' populations. Foundation hospitals are especially unrestrained trusts, chosen from among the best-performing trusts with the best financial stability; their creation, at least in part, is supposed to free them from central micromanagement and enhance innovation. The problem is that, like the rest of the English NHS, they are expected to perform within an internal market while their structure and their accountabilities hem them in (Klein 2003).

In the market model, then, regulatory agencies make sure that competition does not produce problems. The Healthcare Commission regulates quality, a special regulator for the finances of the foundation hospitals demands that they balance their budgets, and the National Institute of Clinical Excellence evaluates technologies (although the latter performs this role for all of the UK). They are pre-eminent among the various 'arms-length' bodies (quangos) that regulate and audit the NHS, and whose name, 'arms-length', is belied by central control over their remits and work programmes (Labour established dozens, and then suddenly merged them without abolishing their functions, see DoH (2004)). As an accounting device to ease contracting, the Government is introducing Payment by Results (PbR). PbR fixes a tariff for each procedure. The goal is to see costs clearly and thereby identify inefficiencies, while permitting contracting on a sensible basis that does not leave PCTs open to exploitation by acute trusts. The complexity of administering such a system and the opportunities for fraud (code-shifting, as it is called by the Americans, who designed the system's ancestor) could be substantial.

Second, English policy is making that market less internal by changing the frontiers between public and private. The drivers are a pair of unobjectionable views: the idea that the English NHS needs additional capital, and the idea that it is not as efficient as it should be. The conclusions drawn by the Government are more contentious. First, that the capital base of the NHS should be expanded through broadbased use of the Private Finance Initiative (and later variations, collectively known as public-private partnerships). Second, the distinctively English focus on greater use of the private sector in provision and management is based on the idea that the private sector can improve NHS provision, whether by bringing in better managers, by introducing some competition, by increasing capacity or by using existing private capacity. Simon Stevens, a former prime-ministerial advisor, now working for a private firm (United Health) that entered the NHS market during his tenure, explained in 2004 that the 'plurality' in provision will 'expand capacity, enhance contestability and offer choice' (Stevens 2004). Improving management involves franchising management of trusts that fail the complex star-ratings system. Novel problems, such as chronic care and different kinds of cancer care, are also being contracted to American firms – such as United Health (Carvel 2004).

A journalist writes, of choice: 'while the political rhetoric has been about patient power and consumerism, for those charged with the implementation of choice it is about planning, capacity- and funding' (Carlisle 2004). There is not enough competition to have much choice because there is not enough capacity, and it would be an irresponsible use of taxes to create real choice on a par with the choice we enjoy in supermarkets or newsagents. Instead, it is about two things. One is service redesign. Most NHS facilities operate on the brink of financial disaster. This is because neither government budgeting procedures nor public-sector accounting encourage the development of surplus funds or reserves. Nor are deficits tolerated. So neither the profits nor the losses of a big listed company are allowed in the NHS. PFIs are particularly finely calculated, with the viability of many deals hinging on the addition or removal of a couple of beds. This means that the threat to divert small numbers of patients from a hospital amounts to a fundamental threat to its finances and the careers of its managers. Viewed this way, the availability of a private-sector alternative makes it possible for commissioners to force the hand of their local NHS hospitals into service redesigns that will produce greater efficiency. Given that it takes only a small change in patient flows to destabilise NHS facilities, two or three per cent private-sector contracting, if used intelligently, might be enough to force service redesign. But the Government judges that ten to fifteen per cent is required to create a big enough market to sustain private-sector competition; it remains to be seen whether ten to fifteen per cent private sector creates too much financial trouble for the existing NHS facilities and their fragile finances.

The other purpose of choice and contestability is the entrenchment of NHS dominance in an English population always more likely than that in other parts of the UK to turn to the private sector. Using the private sector to increase capacity was a policy presaged by a Concordat (DoH 2000), as well as by significant moves such as appointing Chai Patel, head of a private health firm, to the NHS Modernisation Board. The most dramatic policy has been the use of independent treatment centres to set up 'assembly line' operations for simple procedures, such as hip replacements and cataracts, that clog waiting lists.

But the incumbent private sector, Concordat or no, has not done well out of these policies. Simply put: the traditional private sector justified its high costs (shared with doctors otherwise employed by the NHS) through short waiting times and nicer 'hotel' services. As waiting times come down, independent treatment centres come on line, and NHS hospitals improve, it looks to patients like increasingly poor value for money. The chair of the British Medical Association Private Practice Committee said in 2004 that the higher standards and lower waiting lists in the NHS are a 'threat' to private practice incomes. Dennis Skinner, the left-wing Labour MP and a routine critic of the Government, applauded government strategy and Committee Chair Derek Machin's discomfort on exactly these grounds (Watt and Carvel 2004).

Third, English policy is attempting to 'change the terms of trade' with professionals. This is the heart of the service redesign and greater efficiency, as well as tackling the issue of consultants' private work. One of the key problems facing all the NHS systems, although delayed slightly in Scotland, is simple lack of staff. The problem is that the UK has fewer specialists and fewer doctors per head than most equivalent health systems, in large part due to tight medical-education budgets – given time lags in medical education, this is a problem that dates back to previous Conservative administrations. The result is that reducing waiting times, improving satisfaction, and better use of primary care were all hostage to a shortage of professionals. Recruiting professionals from poor countries, already bad for the poor countries, has the practical disadvantage that every other rich country is doing the same thing and some pay much better. So what is required to increase capacity is a strategy for coping with a shortage of doctors, nurses and some allied professions. In English health policy, the solutions to date are policies directed at saving the highly trained (technically, and in professional responsibility) doctors for the most complex tasks, increasing the role of nurses, pharmacist and allied professions in tasks doctors used to perform, and creating new primary-care routes such as a 24-hour telephone service and walk-in centres. This, of course, speeds the end of the continuity of care that had existed when most medical contact was through a single GP (and that was already eroding as GPs, particularly women, entered into larger practices and attempted to balance their work and life).

More to the point, the problem is that the policies amount to managerial decisions to reallocate tasks formerly assigned to professions, which then allocated them onward on a concrete, case-by-case basis. Where, previously, doctors controlled the distribution of tasks in medicine, now managers and ministers are to do so. Professional autonomy is to be replaced by managerial functions – analysis of the organisation's needs and capacities, and organisation to match. Consider pharmacy: pharmacists know a great deal about medicines and seem to be an untapped resource that can assume responsibility for the time-consuming task of repeat prescriptions from GPs; the Health and *Social Care Act* (2001) permits them to do repeat prescriptions. The problem is that letting pharmacists prescribe could create a financial incentive to treat that had been carefully engineered out of the system in the interest of making sure no patient would be treated in accordance with profit rather than need. Meanwhile, redefining the role of doctors creates a new problem of co-ordination: an excellent (and currently nonexistent) medical record, very widely shared, will be required to notify doctors if a pharmacist changes a patient's prescription, and, if it does not work, patients could suffer. Currently, it is not clear if doctors will accept the changes, whether they will work, or whether they will even happen.

In conclusion, English health policy is about markets and management (its public-health policy is kept separate and its lifestyle-focus, dominant). It is part of a very English habit, dating back to the 1983 introduction of a 'depoliticised' management board, or the 1991 internal market, in which ministers try to design the NHS into being a machine that will go by itself, mechanically taking hard decisions about services and process, without political intervention. To date, such efforts have been undermined by a complexity and range of unintended consequences that tend to drag the centre in yet further. Policy focuses on disaggregating the NHS into distinct units, with incentives and goals programmed from above, but managerially autonomous. The ability of the formal structures to absorb information and develop strategy are likely to be limited by the tightly demarcated budgets, poor integration of information, confused responsibilities of organisations above the trust level, and declining expertise in either financing or programme design beyond the trust. Whitehall remains powerful in the system: it defines the structures; it defines the incentives to which their management is to respond; it defines the regulators and their agendas; it defines the remit of regulators; it fixes problems created by the sheer complexity of the system; and the senior managers know perfectly well that the Department ultimately can tell them what to do.

There is one other, overwhelming caveat in the agenda for the English NHS. It is revolutionary; but some scepticism is warranted since neither the extreme complexity of the financial engineering nor politicians' poor track record in controlling doctors suggest implementation will look at all like these schemes. Whitehall is powerful over managers, for whom it designs the incentives, but the fate of its efforts to gain real powers over professionals is unknown, and its ambitious incentive design schemes are notable, primarily, for complexity and unintended consequences. The capacity expansion, well or poorly done, is the most secure legacy of Labour in England.

Scotland: professionalism

Compared to the sheer scale of change in England, combined with the beneficial effects of new health spending there, it is not surprising that today there are worries about the Scottish health system, even though Scotland has picked out just as clear and coherent a path as any other system. There was always a subterranean link between the policy preferences of many Scots elites and their preferences for constitutional change – it did not take very sophisticated constitutional analysis to work out that there would never have been a Margaret Thatcher, or Poll Tax, or NHS internal market in Scotland if Scots had been in control of their affairs (see Mitchell 2005).

After devolution, this meant that there was a coherent Scottish policy direction (the definitive work is Woods and Carter 2003). Its broad tone was professionalist: trust in the professionals who run the system, and lack of trust in, or even antipathy towards, the markets and managers who have been called in, in increasing numbers, to reform the English NHS. This meant the staged elimination of the internal market in Scotland, a process that took time in large part due to the sheer complexity of the issues and of the legislation required. It finished in 2004, though, with the abolition of the trusts and the unification of the system in the fifteen Heath Boards (Department for Health and Community Care 2003). Now, under the slogan 'partnership' Scotland has restored its planning capacity and sharply reduced the role of managers while eliminating the purchaser-provider divide and the market-manipulating policies that English policy-makers use to try and create competition. The obvious beneficiaries of these changes are professionals on the ground, and, to an extent, their leaders. Rolling back firm-like management – which is what the trusts were there to provide – creates broad new spaces open to reoccupation by professionals and managers more interested in partnership with them. In a hospital no longer dominated by a powerful chief executive, but, rather, run by a distant board, there are many opportunities for politically astute doctors and nurses to regain a substantial degree of control and professional autonomy. Logically, also, transaction costs are decreased – England maintains an elaborate (and soon to become much more elaborate) set of bureaucracies to buy and sell care in a 'market', between monopolists and monopsonists, in which there is little or no permitted variation in quality, price or volume. Scotland at least saves that much money.

On questions of public and private, Scotland has chosen a middle ground between England's enthusiasm and Wales's reticence. Scottish politicians are as interested in new facilities as any others, and the Scottish policy community contains both professional leaders interested in improved facilities and a long-standing familiarity with the issues born of sharing a small capital city with the large, sophisticated Edinburgh legal and financial community that played a leading role in inventing the structured finance deals that came to include PFI. Meanwhile, even the unions, the habitual opponents of PFI, often strike more moderate positions, confident as they are of their ability to negotiate. As a result, Scottish new capital investment is often through PFIs, but there is little enthusiasm for greater, or different, use of the private sector (there is little private sector to use in Scotland that is not already contracted by the Scottish NHS).

Scotland's tightly knit policy community, long history of abysmal public health, and obvious problems of poverty and inequality all mean that there was an inherited academic, policy and institutional interest in public health not so present in London. In differentiating the public-health policies, it is important to distinguish between public health and 'new public health'. The latter is based on the analyses produced by academics (or common sense) that show strong relationships between poverty, unemployment, inequality, poor housing, poor education and poor health. The influence of such background social factors is such that it might be thought to overwhelm the impact of traditional medicine (McKeown 1979) or at least make a major difference worthy of policy-makers' attention (Fox 2003).

Scotland and Wales are both more open to the new public-health agenda, with its demand for attacks on inequality, while England's leaders have been much more likely to focus on lifestyle issues and, separately, on targeted measures to remedy 'social exclusion'. In Scotland, this has meant, above all, efforts to ban smoking in public places (Cairney 2005). It has also meant an effort to reallocate funds, and ministerial pressure on local partnerships for public health. There are not many other headline-grabbing new policies, but actually trying to see that managers, local governments and others implement such locally based policies is important. Finally, the Scottish party system is at work on this issue, not just keeping inequality and poverty in focus but also making particular issues salient. For years it has been known that one of the problems in the Scottish diet is inadequate fruit consumption; even the Conservatives, between 1995 and 1997, tried to support the Scottish soft-fruit (basically, berry) industry by running pilot fruit-distribution programmes in schools to increase berry eating, while giving students a taste for fruit. The Scottish Socialist Party, with its populist touch, has since made 'free fruit in schools' a campaign of its own, and the result has been a series of efforts by the Scottish Executive to promote fruit in schools.

A good case can be made for this overall professionalist agenda to provide an efficient, humane and politically sustainable health system. It is supposedly less likely to reform itself, but there is a powerful argument that it is the responsibility of elected politicians to sign off on major policy changes. Something as big as A&E closures or Glasgow hospital restructuring will always be political, no matter how many consultations, managers, regulators, contracts or plans are involved. The problem is, of course, that it takes tremendous political effort to close those hospitals, and it is always tempting to use gimmickry and reorganisation to try to reform the system, when the actual need is for serious use of the planning powers that Scotland (unlike England) formally enjoys.

The Kerr report, a strategy document commissioned by the Scottish Executive from a commission headed by Professor David Kerr, proposed a way forward that clearly grows from Scottish politics and problem perceptions – in other words, that leaves structures alone and focuses on easing the transition to a new pattern of services (Scottish Executive 2005). It starts with an analysis of how health services work (making the well-established point that very little healthcare happens in the hospitals, but most of the money is spent there). It then spends most of its time asking how services can be understood so as to permit reconfigurations that will keep hospitals, or some kind of services, local whenever possible. The answer, according to the report, is to centralise only the most complex high-end services and otherwise try to move care out into the community – even beyond district general hospitals to clinics and the primary-care sector. This clearly stems from both the solid political bases of Scotland's health-service organisation and the fearsome political consequences of the hospital closures that would be required without new thinking about service delivery. Combined with some other changes – a tariff that, on an abstract level, resembles Payment by Results and that improves transparency – the Scottish health-services agenda is increasingly going to be about territorial politics within Scotland.

Before and after the Kerr report, though, there began to be increasingly loud calls for reorganisation. They are based in good part on the relatively small change in Scottish health-service outcomes since devolution; it is odd to compare a major outcome study of health services done just before devolution (Dixon, Inglis and Klein 1999) with one from 2004 (Audit Scotland 2004). Both raise questions about the efficiency and effectiveness of the system. Hence calls for reform. Scotland, of course, already has a policy of working with professions (the professionals, that is, not just their representative organisations) and using its regional planning structures, and it is now bedding down. The question is why another policy is sought. Part of this drive for a new policy is driven by the perception that the English NHS is improving while the Scottish NHS is not. The question in Scotland is whether the demands for reform will crowd out other decisions that need to be made, and whether the Scottish health system will be able to continue to settle down to its innovative model of using professionals to ration and design the system rather than working against them, as is the fashion elsewhere.

Wales: Localism

Wales, meanwhile, has adopted a policy of localism and a focus on the wider determinants of health that goes far beyond most other health systems in the world. The Welsh health system has a series of problems: high sunk costs and a focus on hospitals, extreme inequality of health outcomes, and large populations with serious health and other problems. It also has a distinctive politics of its own, one that makes it much more open to the twin messages of localism and a focus on the wider determinants of health.

Intellectually, the Welsh health agenda, as stated, is one of the most complete endorsements of new public health anywhere. Consider the language of the Welsh health plan, which can be compared with those of England and Scotland (Department of Health and Community Care 2000; DoH 2000; NAW 2001, all reviewed in the appendix of Greer 2001). England and Scotland focus on what their health services will do, and why, with lots of targets and action points. The outcomes will mostly be health-service outcomes, and the tool, the NHS. The Welsh document, by contrast, identifies the objective as health (not medical treatment) and goes on to discuss the NHS as one of many agencies in the public sector that contribute to good population health. Whether other agencies will contribute remains unknown, but the spirit is one of joint working, particularly with local government, to address wider determinants of health and reduce health inequalities.

Practically, though, the interaction of this agenda with a series of last-minute political compromises and inherited weaknesses in Welsh public policy have turned it into something quite different and unplanned. Partly to achieve these goals of greater population health, partly to have a more transparent system that could track funds, and partly to give local government more control over the health services, the National Assembly opted for an unusual new structure. On paper, the Welsh NHS now operates through the commissioning work of twenty-two Local Health Boards (LHBs), similar to PCTs but coterminous with local authorities and tightly bound to them by a number of obligations and councillors sitting on the boards. With technical advice from the centre and the three regional offices, they will commission services from trusts in line with local priorities and demands. The result should be improved local joint working – for example, making sure that the recipient of a hip replacement gets a visit from social services to trip-proof the house – and greater local democratic input. They should also erode acute trusts' power.

In reality, the reorganisation turned into something of a black hole in Welsh health policy, undermining its own goals as well as the functioning of the system overall. The bureaucracy inherited from the Welsh Office was very good at permissive managerial techniques – keeping the minister out of trouble and keeping the system ticking over – but it was inadequate to the challenges of understanding the whole system and redesigning it so that the new version would work well. There was a simple question of overload; much larger organisations in Whitehall with much more practice inventing new organisations make mistakes, but they had a better chance. Furthermore, John Redwood MP, as Secretary of State for Wales, had, with remarkable skill, uprooted the indigenous Welsh focus on patients and outcomes that had developed in the managerial cadre during the 1980s, and which had made Wales a leader in joined-up working (Welsh Office and Welsh Health Planning Forum 1989). What Redwood eliminated – a coherent Welsh management cadre with an agenda and good links to clinicians – has still not returned.

The result was a string of undesired outcomes. The reorganisation proved especially traumatic, distracting managerial and official attention for years while not working very well in many of its details, such as hiring. The effort it took distracted attention from performance management so that Welsh healthcare organisations are bottom of the UK league for the waiting-list indicators that are so politically sensitive, and the Minister and leading managers are under intense public pressure. In 2004 around ten per cent of the Welsh population was on some sort of a waiting list. The Assembly is right that waiting lists should not be the main object of health policy, but they might be indicators of just how much trouble there is in the Welsh health system (there are also important critical reports: Audit Commission 2004; Review of Health and Social Care in Wales 2003). Other studies certainly uncover frightening signs: in a poll of Welsh health leaders (managers, Community Health Councils and leading doctors) only thirty-one per cent said they would want a loved one to be treated in the Welsh NHS (Longley and Beddow 2005, p. 9).

These bad reports raise questions about the political sustainability of the current policies, in turn raising the threat that implementation problems in the reorganisation will scupper this interesting and radical attempt to establish a National Health Service in place of the National Sickness Service found elsewhere. These questions took the form of months of media pressure around the general election of 2005. Labour's UK campaign made great play of the achievements of the English NHS. This strategy made rather less sense for Labour in Wales. Welsh MPs pressed home the message that the National Assembly's health policy was an electoral albatross for Labour. The result was a conviction, particularly strong outside Wales, that change was inevitable. The minister duly changed; Jane Hutt, who spearheaded the effort to expand health policy beyond the NHS, was replaced with GP Brian Gibbons. Rumours flew of more use of the private sector or even a Welsh form of foundation hospitals.

But, as the old *Punch* cartoon said, if you want to get there, you shouldn't start from here. The content of Welsh health-services policy shows real continuity. This should not surprise us; it emerges from entrenched Welsh politics and Welsh policy debate, just like the policy trajectories of the other systems. The most important document at the time of writing is the May 2005 strategy *Designed for Life*, (WAG 2005). *Designed for Life* proposes to address the various deficiencies of Welsh health services through three-year plans, starting with a focus on service design and allocation. It proposes basic policy themes – essentially, good service design, improved quality, and (less explicitly) better integration of health- and social care – and highlights the actions that must be taken to achieve them. The document is as interesting for what it is not as for what it is. It is not an English policy import. There is very little about markets or anything else. It is not reorganising. While the present structure of Welsh health services (and local government) has few admirers, reorganisation, after the experience of the previous few years, has even fewer. The result is that *Designed for Life* is about goals and process rather than organisation, and is rightly read for hints of future hospital closures or investment in badly needed primary care. There are strong reasons to expect both –that Wales, like Scotland, will focus on service allocation rather than organisation in the near future.

Public-health policy, the strong suit of Wales and its historic claim to fame, shows signs of drift. Under the long-serving devolved-administration minister Jane Hutt, there was a clear effort to expand the remit of health policy beyond the NHS (Greer 2004a); the problem now is that the visibility and relative deterioration of health services gave a bad image to not only Welsh health services management, but also to Welsh health policy. Those opposed to the focus on public health were happy to suggest that ministers had their priorities wrong. The result is the dissipation of the new public-health agenda and loss of élan – most visible in the shift from an emphasis on socioeconomic causes of ill health to a focus on lifestyle factors seen in the current Health Challenge Wales, which encourages people to give up smoking. Both are good policy ideas, but a challenge to individuals to give up smoking is much less radical. There is also reason to believe that the unified public-health service has been drawn into the task of advising the small, weak LHBs on commissioning, instead of developing useful public-health interventions. This is exactly what happened in the first (Conservative) internal market (Tuohy 1999). The pressure on planning capacity then, and in Wales now, led managers to draft public-health doctors into advisory roles in service commissioning. The reason was that public-health specialists are trained to collect and understand population-health data and relate it to demand for services. If there are not enough skilled service planners, and Wales now needs enough to serve twenty-two LHBs, then public health is a good second-best source of skills. The price, of course, is that the pressures of commissioning work divert them from doing public-health work.

Outside Wales, there is much scorn for Welsh health policy. Inside Wales, there is much anguish. But the Welsh health-policy community and the Welsh party system remain distinctive, not least in a localist trajectory and a focus on goals rather than on market processes. The result is that not just Welsh policies, but also the resources and ideas that will change them, are distinctively Welsh.

Northern Ireland: Permissive managerialism
Policy change is not just qualitative – the direction in which change goes. It is also quantitative – the extent to which there is change. England is the quantitative champion, announcing major structural changes at a rate that far

exceeds the other systems (although its record in implementation is, of course, far spottier). Scotland and Wales both started off quietly, then made major changes around 2000-2002, and are now under pressure for their supposed lack of change since then, just when their systems are settling down.

Northern Ireland is a different story altogether. Northern Ireland has a political system that operates with very little reference to health policy, or indeed any of the bread-and-butter issues that animate politicians and constituents elsewhere. Furthermore, its devolved assembly has operated only intermittently since 1998, hostage to the wider development (or lack of development) of the peace process (Wilford and Wilson 2000 and 2003; Wilson and Wilford 2001 and 2004). The result is that Northern Irish health policy has been made since 1998 by two wholly different types of regime: the devolved politics of the Northern Ireland Assembly and the politics of direct rule from Westminster. Neither produces much health policy, if, by that, we mean priorities, reorganisations or reallocation of resources.

The most obvious result is that the internal market continued much longer in Northern Ireland than elsewhere. The policy problem lay in identifying a replacement system that would work; the process problem lay in having a much smaller and less policy-minded policy community than elsewhere; the political problem lay in the absence of any political incentive to make large-scale changes. Sinn Fein, like several other Northern Irish parties, does not appear to see much electoral benefit in public-service reform, and knows that, given its overall image, it will probably not win many votes as a steward of public administration. The initial result was stalemate; the Department put forward an idea, loosely modelled on England's system before the development of the PCTs, to replace the most obvious part of the internal market – GP fundholding. After a year's delay, this happened; fundholding was finally abolished and replaced by commissioning by subcommittees of Health Boards that acted rather like PCTs. The rest of the market, including the eighteen organisations the Conservatives had set up (one health service quango per 100,000 people) remained for the rest of the Assembly's short devolved life. Few other headline policies got made; the result is that devolution, for most managers, meant an unhappy combination of micromanagement and permissive managerialism. Members of the Legislative Assembly (MLAs) and the Department went to great lengths to make the system accountable to them, with some demoralising trawls for excess travel expenses by the Assembly and some extraordinary efforts by the Department to centrally decide issues such as the allocation of new electric wheelchairs. Even if the attention of democratic politicians is a necessary attribute of democracy, no matter how much trouble it causes for devolved managers, it is hard to dispute that devolution did not improve policy or day-to-day administration.

What then, of policies? Most of them show a great deal of continuity, because the common denominator between direct-rule ministers (who generally spend a maximum of two days a week in Northern Ireland) and Northern Irish politicians (caught up in more dramatic questions of nationhood and constitution) is that neither has much reason to make policies. The result is that the same kind of permissive managerialist system suited them both equally well. That means a premium on stability, coupled with a permissive attitude towards certain kinds of activity; most prominently it is a good environment for dynamic teaching hospitals, and it is a permissive environment for advocates of new public health, who can point to the obvious connection between social exclusion, bigotry and paramilitarism, in many areas.

The real focus, unsurprisingly, was a series of impassioned campaigns over, naturally, hospital closures. Not only has Northern Ireland been better funded than the UK average for a while, but due to the difficult political context, direct-rule ministers have avoided closing hospitals that are unlikely to have remained open had they been situated elsewhere, in a bid to avoid conflict. This meant that there was a consensus that a devolved Northern Ireland would not just have to sort out its management structure, but also that it would have to rationalise its acute services. The process started out badly when the incoming Sinn Fein health minister made a poorly explained decision to locate a new maternity ward in a hospital in her Falls Road constituency, rather than in mainly Protestant South Belfast; this prompted outcries and went to judicial review (a rather academic review, since the building at the losing hospital was speedily demolished). After that unsatisfying warmup, the Northern Ireland Assembly proceeded to a thornier issue: the slow disintegration of acute care in the southwest (Tyrone/Fermanagh), where there were two hospitals and only enough volume or defensible budget allocation for one. The question was where to put the single hospital, and the two county towns put on excellent campaigns to get the facility. The minister ran out the clock, commissioning consultations and reports, while both counties then elected Sinn Fein MPs and thereby guaranteed that the party would avoid a decision. That ensured that it would eventually be a direct-rule minister who would make the decision: a PFI in Fermanagh.

The future of divergent health policy

It is striking, but explicable, how much health-policy divergence we have seen since 1998. The institutional precondition – the autonomy – was present. The political drivers – different kinds of party competition – were present, as were the different inherited policy communities more than happy to suggest ideas that happened to be different. The question, though, is whether this divergence machine can run indefinitely. There are two clear threats to it, and a question.

The first is the fragility of the UK system of intergovernmental relations. Thanks to the Labour party's dominance and overall coherence since 1998,

there has been a standing incentive for the three ongoing governments to min-
imise their disputes, and ample support for officials in their efforts to identify
and snuff out disputes before they become major. The Barnett formula has the
capacity to offend everybody in the UK by either seeming to underfund them
or cutting their funding. It is easy to imagine it coming under pressure, and a
replacement system being less transparent or more constraining. In addition,
there is no such thing as a competence of just one government; something
always requires help from other governments. Whether such help will be forthcoming with a change in government somewhere is unclear. Official networks,
already degraded in health policy by recent reorganisations, are likely to dete-
riorate further over time. They will be unlikely to be able to prevent conflict if
that is what politicians, out to embarrass each other, are seeking. There is a very
good chance that the system will jam, and make conflicts much more difficult
to resolve, as soon as there are parties of different persuasions in power in different parts of the UK (Trench 2004; Laffin, Shaw and Taylor forthcoming).

The second is Europe (Greer 2005 and forthcoming b). Whether we like it
or not, the EU is developing a health competency and the question is what to
do about it. This is primarily due to the activities of the European Court of
Justice, which has been systematically creating something like a single market
for health services, through decisions allowing patients and professionals to
travel to the system that will treat them most quickly. It has, furthermore, inter-
preted the Working Time Directive so as to redesign medical work across the
continent and accelerate the demise of small hospitals and key departments
around the UK. Finally, and in large part in response to this 'spillover' of EU
law into health, there is demand for an EU health law, inclusion of health in
EU single-market law, or use of the 'Open method of co-ordination' to stan-
dardise health service variation, as well as the various information and net-
working schemes proposed by the Directorate General responsible for health
and consumer protection. Even opponents of the EU role to date – and there
are good reasons to consider it damaging to the NHS systems – are finding that
the solution to uninvited EU activity is EU lobbying to shape that activity in a
more agreeable manner. And in the EU policy-making process, there is no
meaningful role for Northern Ireland, Scotland or Wales. Without special
effort to pay attention and influence policy, and without institutionalised
goodwill between the Department of Health and devolved-territory policy-
makers, the EU member states might make policy harmful to Northern
Ireland, Scotland and Wales without even knowing it. The problem is simple:
nobody is obliged to invite devolved governments to EU councils, and they
cannot vote anyway. It is crucial then, if we are to defend the autonomy and
policy capacity of all the UK systems, that the Department and devolved governments establish the networks, information sharing, and priorities required
to influence EU legislation (Greer 2005; Jeffery forthcoming). Not all devolved
governments or parts of the Department of Health take this issue seriously, and
might find the ensuing policy is not to their taste.

Finally, there is the question that brings us back around to the start of this paper, and the reasons for devolution: what does the public think of it all? Much of the international evidence is that when there is a clash between policy divergence and the welfare state 'the welfare state wins hands down' (Banting 2005; Jeffery 2005). There is a great deal of support for devolution and regional government in comparable countries and the UK, but much less for real variation in citizenship rights (for more on this see Jeffery in chapter 2). That suggests that at the end of this process, politicians will refuse to change citizenship rights too much. Other countries that created regional levels have seen this dynamic: policy divergence, but a real public demand for a levelling up of services and a reduction in the difference between different regions' outcomes over time (Dupuy and Le Galès 2005). On that level, devolution makes divergence more transparent and its creators much more accountable – and we can find out, over time, how much divergence and what citizenship rights the public and political elites really want. The NHS systems remain tax-funded, egalitarian, redistributive and politically vulnerable. How much of that reflects a real consensus across the UK, and how much of it is a result of inertia or satisfaction with the current state of health policies, we do not know.

The interim report, though, is that after the burst of divergence in 2000-2003 we now see it bedding down. England, Northern Ireland, Scotland and Wales all have their distinctive politics and consequent policy styles, and when they move forward they move in their own directions and with their own resources. The Kerr report in Scotland, *Designed for Life* in Wales, Northern Irish somnolence, and the contestability agenda in England are all distinctive to the systems, depend on distinctive mindsets and institutions for their implementation, and are all deeply embedded in the assumptions, preoccupations and debates of their creators and political systems.

For decades 'the' NHS was a symbol of UK national unity; everybody knew what the 'nation' was. Now, ordinary politics and the cumulation of small political decisions mean the 'nation' in the name is Scotland, England or Wales. Understanding this, relating it to deeply held common values, and negotiating its consequences and limits will be one of the crucial challenges for a multinational United Kingdom in coming years.

References

Audit Commission (2004) *Transforming Health and Social Care in Wales*. Audit Commission

Audit Scotland (2004) *An Overview of the Performance of the NHS in Scotland*. Audit Scotland

Banting Keith G (2005) 'Social citizenship and federalism: Is the federal welfare state a contradiction in terms?' in Greer SL (ed.) *Territory, Democracy, and Justice* Palgrave Macmillan, pp. 44-66

Banting Keith G and Corbett Stan (2002) 'Health Policy and Federalism: An Introduction' in Banting KG and Corbett S (eds.) *Health Policy and Federalism: A Comparative Perspective on Multi-Level Governance* McGill-Queens University Press, pp. 1-37

Bell David and Christie Alex (2002) 'Finance – The Barnett Formula: Nobody's Child?' in Trench A (ed.) *The State of the Nations 2001: The Second Year of Devolution* Imprint Academic, pp. 135-152

Cairney Paul (2005) 'Using devolution to set the agenda: The smoking ban in Scotland' Paper given at 55th Political Studies Association Annual Conference University of Leeds, 4-7 April 2005

Carlisle Daloni (2004) 'Choice makes its entrance' in *Health Service Journal* 114: 5923, pp. 10-13

Carvel J (2004) 'US firm linked to No 10 wins NHS cancer contract' in *The Guardian*, 8 September 2004

Department of Heath (DoH) (2000) *For the Benefit of Patients: A concordat with the Private and Voluntary Health Care Provider Sector* DoH

DoH (2000) *The NHS Plan: A Plan for Investment, a Plan for Reform* HMSO

DoH (2004) *An Implementation Framework for Reconfiguring the DH Arm's Length Bodies: Redistributing resources to the NHS frontline* DoH

Department for Health and Community Care (2000) *Our National Health: A Plan for Action, a Plan for Change* HMSO

Department for Health and Community Care (2003) *Partnership for Care: Scotland's Health White Paper* HMSO

Dixon J, Inglis S and Klein R (1999) 'Is the English NHS Underfunded?' in *British Medical Journal* 318, pp. 522-526

Dupuy C and Le Galès P (2005) 'Regional government and civil society' in Greer SL (ed.) *Territory, Democracy, and Justice* Palgrave Macmillan, pp. 116-138

Feachem RG, Neelam A, Sekhri K and White KL (2002) 'Getting more for their dollar: a comparison of the NHS with California's Kaiser Permanente' in *British Medical Journal* 324, pp. 135-143.

Fox DM (2003) 'Population and the Law: The Changing Scope of Health Policy' in *Journal of Law, Medicine and Ethics* 31, pp. 607-14

Freeman Richard (2000) *The Politics of Health in Europe* Manchester University Press

Greer SL (2001) *Divergence and Devolution* The Nuffield Trust

Greer SL (2004a). *Territorial Politics and Health Policy* Manchester University Press

Greer SL (2004b) 'Why Do Good Politics Make Bad Health Policy?' in Sausman C and Dawson S (eds.) *Future Health Organisations and Systems* Palgrave, pp. 105-128

Greer SL (2005) 'Becoming European: Devolution, Europe and Health Policy-Making' in Trench A (ed.) *The Dynamics of Devolution: The State of the Nations 2005* Imprint Academic, pp. 201-224

Greer SL (forthcoming a) 'The Fragile Divergence Machine: Citizenship, policy divergence, and intergovernmental relations' in Trench A (ed.) *Devolution and Power in the United Kingdom*

Greer SL (forthcoming b) 'Uninvited Europeanization: Neofunctionalism and the EU in health policy' in *Journal of European Public Policy* 13:1

Hazell R and Jervis P (1998) *Devolution and Health* The Nuffield Trust

Heald D and McLeod A (2002) 'Beyond Barnett? Financing Devolution' in Adams J and Robinson P (eds.) *Devolution in Practice: Public Policy Differences Within the UK* ippr, pp. 147-175

Jeffery C (2005) 'Devolution and Social Citizenship: Which Society, Whose Citizenship?' in Greer SL (ed.) *Territory, Democracy, and Justice* Palgrave Macmillan, pp. 67-91

Jeffery C (forthcoming) 'Continental Affairs: Bringing the EU Back In' In Trench A (ed.) *Devolution and Power in the United Kingdom* Manchester University Press

Klein R (2003) 'Governance for NHS foundation trusts: Mr Milburn's flawed model is a cacophany of accountabilities' in *British Medical Journal* 326, pp. 174-5

Laffin M, Shaw E and Taylor G (forthcoming) 'The Parties and Intergovernmental Relations' in Trench A (ed.) *Devolution and Power in the United Kingdom* Manchester University Press

Longley M and Beddow T (2005) *NHS Wales Barometer 2004* Welsh Institute of Health and Social Care, University of Glamorgan

McKeown Thomas (1979) *The Role of Medicine: Dream, Mirage, or Nemesis?* Princeton University Press

Mitchell James (2005) 'Scotland: Devolution is not just for Christmas' in Trench A (ed.) *The Dynamics of Devolution: The State of the Nations 2005* Imprint Academic, pp. 23-42

National Assembly for Wales (NAW) 2001. *Improving Health in Wales: A Plan for the NHS with its Partners* National Assembly for Wales

Osmond J (2003) 'From Corporate Body to Virtual Parliament: The Metamorphosis of the National Assembly for Wales' in Hazell R (ed.) *The State of the Nations 2003: The Third Year of Devolution in the United Kingdom* Imprint Academic, pp. 13-48

Poirier J (2001) 'Pouvoir normatif et protection sociale dans les fédérations multinationales' in *Canadian Journal of Law and Society* / Revue Canadienne Droit et Societé 16:2, pp. 137-171

Review of Health and Social Care in Wales (2003) *The Review of Health and Social Care in Wales: The Report of the Project Team* Advised by Derek Wanless National Assembly of Wales

Scottish Executive (2005) *Building a Health Service Fit for the Future: A National Framework for Service Change in Scotland* Scottish Executive

Seawright D (2002) 'The Scottish Conservative and Unionist Party: "the lesser spotted Tory"?' in Hassan G (ed.) *Tomorrow's Scotland* Lawrence and Wishart, pp. 66-82

Stevens S (2004) 'Reform Strategies for the English NHS' in *Health Affairs* 23:3, pp. 37-44

Trench A (2004) 'The More Things Change, the More the Stay the Same: Intergovernmental Relations Four Years On' in Trench A (ed.) *Has Devolution Made a Difference? The State of the Nations 2004* Imprint Academic, pp. 165-191

Tuohy CH (1999) *Accidental Logics: The Dynamics of Change in the Health Care Arena in the United States, Britain, and Canada* Oxford University Press

Watt N and Carvel J (2004) 'NHS puts squeeze on private medicine' in *The Guardian* 3 July 2004

Welsh Assembly Government (WAG) (2005) *Designed for Life: Creating World-Class Health and Social Care for Wales in the 21st Century* National Assembly for Wales

Welsh Office and Welsh Health Planning Forum (1989) *Strategic Intent and Direction for the NHS in Wales* Welsh Office

Wilford R and Wilson R (2000) '"A Bare Knuckle Ride": Northern Ireland' in Hazell R (ed.) *The State and the Nations: The First Year of Devolution in the United Kingdom* Imprint Academic, pp. 79-116

Wilson R and Wilford R (2001) 'Northern Ireland: Endgame' in Trench A (ed.) *The State of the Nations 2001* Imprint Academic, pp. 77-106

Wilson R and Wilford R (2004) 'Northern Ireland: Renascent?' in Trench A (ed.) *Has devolution made a difference? The State of the Nations 2004* Imprint Academic pp. 79-120

Wilford R and Wilson R (2003) 'Northern Ireland: Valedictory?' In Hazell R (ed.) *The State of the Nations 2003: The Third Year of Devolution in the United Kingdom* Imprint Academic, pp. 79-118

Woods K and Carter D (2003) (eds.) *Scotland's Health and Health Services* TSO / The Nuffield Trust

8 Devolution and divergence in social-housing policy in Britain

Robert Smith

It has been argued that devolution represents one of the most significant changes in the political appearance of the UK over the last 150 years (Bogdanor 2001). New centres of political power and policy-making have emerged within each of the four nations that comprise the United Kingdom. While the constitutional reforms introduced by New Labour during its first term of office (1997-2001) have given different sets of powers to each of the four nations, devolution has provided for the possibility of divergence in public policies across the UK. The creation of devolved administrations in Belfast (at least for a time), Cardiff and Edinburgh (as well as the Greater London Authority) has provided a potential for distinctiveness in processes of policy development, variations in policy and differences in outcome.

Devolution has initiated a new era of governance and policy-making. This chapter seeks to examine how the housing-policy agenda in Britain has developed since the late 1990s. It reflects on how the governance and accountability of housing has changed since devolution, and sets the policy-making process in a broader context of the restructuring of the state in the UK and moves towards multilevel governance. It focuses on how aspects of national housing policy in England, Scotland and Wales are changing, and either converging or diverging. There is a growing literature that examines housing in different parts of the UK (Smith *et al.* 2000; Paris 2001; Sim 2004). This has recognised that different parts of the UK have distinctive sets of housing circumstances and that, to a degree, each have developed their own approaches to addressing housing issues. Devolution has contributed to this. However, as Murie (2004) has noted, distinctiveness may reflect local circumstances and influences rather than national ones, that differences within countries (for example between urban and rural) may be more significant than those between countries, and that within the UK the differences between the housing policies and systems may be relatively small compared with differences in housing across Europe (Murie 2004).

While the focus of this chapter is on devolution and housing-policy-making in Scotland and Wales, and how this may be contributing to the development of policies in these two countries that are quite distinct from what is happening in England, it is important to see this in a wider perspective. Other parts of the UK have been affected by the creation of national or regional bodies. Although this chapter does not choose to examine the development of housing policy in Northern Ireland, it could be argued that the history of a distinct national housing policy is stronger here than in either Scotland or (most certainly) in Wales (Fraser 1996; Paris 2001; Paris *et al.* 2003). Since its election in 1997 the Labour Government has not only been concerned with national devolution to Scotland, Wales and Northern Ireland, these constitutional reforms have also been accompanied by a degree of devolution to the English regions, with the strengthening of the Government Offices for the Regions and the creation of Regional Development Agencies (RDAs), Regional Housing Boards, Regional Spatial Strategies and co-ordinating Regional Assemblies (Cole 2003; Robinson 2003), strengthening regional housing policy and strategy, alongside other areas of regional strategic concern, such as land-use planning and economic development.

Thus, we are seeing the emergence of regional differences in housing policy within England, as well as differences between the devolved nations, although it could be argued that one of the downsides of this developing regionalism is a further emasculation of the housing role of local government. While there are strong arguments to support the view that a history of housing policy in Britain over the last quarter of the twentieth century suggests moves towards greater central control, and less local discretion, (Karn 1985; Murie 1985), and, in a number of ways, Labour has continued to put in place centrally driven changes in public policy, the ongoing tide of centralisation has been accompanied by a more recent political shift towards concepts of social inclusion, participation, partnership working and enhanced levels of self-government. However, some of the shifts in policy thinking at Westminster (for example, a move towards consumerist policies, associated with public-choice theory) have found little echo in either Edinburgh or Cardiff. The processes of governing have shifted, both within and beyond the framework of government (Rhodes 1994 and 1997). This has encompassed not only reforming the relationships between central and local government, but also devolving power and responsibilities to (sub)national and regional tiers of government. Devolution beyond Westminster and Whitehall to a range of subsidiary bodies with varying legislative powers, degrees of control over budgets and autonomy has resulted in a 'decentering down' (Pierre and Peters 2000). These shifts, from government to governance and from the national to the subnational and regional, have also contributed to what Jessop has called 'a shift in the centre of gravity around which policy cycles move' (Jessop 1998, p. 32).

The focus of this chapter is to examine changing housing policy in Britain since 1997; in particular, to examine how political devolution to Scotland and Wales has impacted upon the processes of housing-policy-making in these two countries; and, by using particular aspects of social housing policy, to explore policy divergence and convergence within the housing sphere in England, Scotland and Wales. Elsewhere, others have examined different aspects of housing policy divergence at both a national (Satsangi and Dunmore 2003; Walker et al. 2003) and regional level (Slocombe 2003; Robinson 2003). It has already been noted that attention has not been paid in this paper to Northern Ireland, while, given the author's affiliation, the Wales perspective is more fully developed than that for Scotland. However, the latter is covered in a paper by Kintrea (forthcoming), which aims to make an assessment of housing reform in Scotland since 1999.

The chapter sets the scene by looking briefly at the changing nature of housing policy within the UK. It then sets the context for housing-policy development in Scotland and Wales post-devolution, by highlighting how the housing context in these two countries is different from that of England. The paper then goes on to examine the nature of the housing-policy-making process in Scotland and Wales since devolution, before using particular aspects of housing policy in relation to the social sector to examine the evidence of policy difference and similarity. However, it does not attempt a comprehensive assessment of housing policy under devolution in the two countries, but instead elects to focus on specific and important aspects of social housing policy; the future of the public-housing stock, questions of access to the social rented sector and homelessness. It concludes with a tentative assessment of the achievements and limitations thus far, in respect of housing policy in Scotland and Wales, post-devolution.

The changing dimensions of UK housing policy

A whole range of organisations have an involvement with housing and, by implication, policies on housing. However, as Malpass and Murie (1999) have noted, housing policy is usually thought of in terms of the policies of the state, and the interventions of government. Historically, it can be argued that in Britain there was no distinct housing policy prior to 1919, although its origins are rooted in the nineteenth century, with a growing concern over increasing industrialisation and urbanisation and the associated problems of overcrowding, unsanitary dwellings, and ill-health and disease (Gauldie 1974; Burnett 1986).

The overarching objective of housing policy in Britain can be summarised in the words of a government White Paper from 1971: 'a decent home for every family at a price within their means, a fairer choice between owning a home and renting one, and fairness between one citizen and another in giving and receiving help towards housing' (MHLG 1971). Similarly, Labour's 1977 Housing Green Paper suggested the aim of 'a decent home for all families at a price within their means (DoE 1977). In order to meet these objectives, housing policy can be modified to influence the quantity, quality, price, ownership or control of housing (Malpass and Murie 1999). A recent evaluation of English housing policy, covering the period 1975-2000, while re-emphasising these objectives, suggests that governments have also attached more significance to extending consumer choice and improving the efficiency and effectiveness of housing management during this period (ODPM 2005a).

This very valuable review notes that the present housing system reflects a number of key influences, of which housing policy itself is but one. The other important factors that have helped to shape housing over this period have been population growth and demographic change, economic factors (rising real incomes, employment changes, economic restructuring *etc.*), social change (rising expectations, greater household diversity *etc.*) and non-housing policy changes that have impacted upon housing (ODPM 2005a). The research also identified key housing-policy themes (and clusters) that developed over this period. These include policies to deregulate the private sector of housing (and the system of mortgage finance), and encourage the privatisation of social housing, a restructuring of housing subsidies (shifting the emphasis from sup-ply-side to demand-side subsidies) and policies designed to regulate and restructure the social rented sector (ODPM 2005a).

It has been argued that conventional housing policy in Britain has declined in importance (Bramley 1997; Hills 1998) and is now, in Bramley's words, 'to be found living in a different place and under a different name' (Bramley 1997, p. 405). In developing this theme, Malpass (1999) has suggested that housing policy, at least in the sense in which it was understood during much of the last century, has come to an end. Malpass cites the fact that gross over-all housing shortages and extensive poor housing conditions, which sustained housing policy in the past, are now only present in Britain to a much reduced degree. As a result of a diminution in housing problems, those who exercise political and economic power no longer see benefits in continuing policy action (Malpass 1999). However, he does conclude, as Bramley, that housing policy is alive and well, but in a different form, and that the housing dimen-sions of public policy designed to combat social exclusion, promote economic and community regeneration and tackle ill-health, crime and educational underachievement need to be adequately addressed.

Critics of Malpass (Kleinman 1999; Williams 1999a) have taken issue with elements of his argument, but are in agreement that there is a need to integrate housing policy with issues of inequality and social exclusion, pointing not to a past pre-eminence of housing policy, but to its crucial role at the hub of wider public policies. Maclennan, too, has argued that housing should be at the heart of any agenda to address neighbourhood renewal (Maclennan 2000), and, across the UK, housing has increasingly been seen as playing a key role in wider agendas around regeneration and economic prosperity (Smith and Morgan 2005). It might also be argued that, in the last few years, housing's potential contribution to tackling some of these wider socio-economic prob-lems, together with concerns over housing shortages (and problems of afford-ability) in some areas, and failing housing markets (and poor housing condi-tions) in other localities, has meant housing has risen on political agendas.

Of course, housing, unlike, for example, education or social services, is not a core public service – in the sense that the state has never been the dominant service provider (at least not in England and Wales). The private sector has been dominant, and, over the last three decades, central government has explicitly sought to shift the emphasis of the role of local councils to that of enablers, working in partnership with other agencies (housing associations, private developers, voluntary-sector agencies, quangos *etc.*) to deliver services. The state (both central and local) has placed an increasing emphasis on developing its strategic role, providing resources (grants, loans, land, information *etc.*) and using regulatory powers to influence the actions of others (Goodlad 1993).

At the same time, as Bramley and Hills have argued (Bramley 1997; Hills 1998), it would be wrong to see housing policy as something that is entirely self-contained, but, instead, as something that cuts across much wider agendas (poverty, income support, social care, sustainability, regeneration, environmental improvement *etc.*). As such, the need for joined-up thinking (and working) poses particular challenges.

In Whitehall, the Offfice of the Deputy Prime Minister's (ODPM) five-year plan for housing, *Homes for All* (2005b), has identified a number of key policy themes. These have included additional housing provision to meet need (particularly in new growth areas in the South East of England), additional support for sustainable homeownership, policies to revive ailing housing markets, enhanced quality and choice in the rented sector, increased support for the vulnerable, environmental policies towards housing (such as increasing energy efficiency, raising design standards) and shifts towards neighbourhood and community empowerment.

While it can be argued that Labour's Westminster agenda for housing since 1997 has been to continue to develop the policies of previous Conservative administrations (albeit with some evidence of increased social housing investment, even if this is only returning investment levels to those of the mid 1990s), there is some evidence to suggest a reversal in the decline of housing's importance in public policy. However, a recent analysis of the Blair Government's record on housing, which examined a number of key themes (investment, the housing market, homelessness, housing-related welfare and neighbourhood regeneration), while identifying strengths and weaknesses in each area, only gave the Government a 'fair' – one-star – rating for its performance (Roof 2004). At the same time, given the role that housing policy is being increasingly expected to play in achieving broader objectives (regeneration, social justice, social inclusion, resident empowerment, community sustainability), it may no longer be appropriate to evaluate housing policy purely in terms of a set of housing objectives (output, quality, affordability), although, in seeking to take a wider view, it may be more challenging to separate out housing's contribution to these wider agendas.

But in a context of post-devolution Britain, what does this mean for housing policy in Scotland and Wales? Following a period in which there has been a strong tendency towards a centralisation of housing policy, does devolution represent a set of counter moves? To what extent have developments in housing policy diverged or converged since the creation of a Scottish Parliament and a Welsh Assembly, and what might the future hold? These questions are at the heart of the remainder of this chapter.

Housing in Scotland and Wales

The devolved administrations control most aspects of housing policy, although not housing benefit, including responsibility for allocating public resources for housing and setting spending priorities within the so-called Barnett formula, and developing specific sets of housing policies. This has not only involved civil servants working with ministers (and deputy ministers), but cross-party subject committees exercising, at least in theory, a role in both policy development and scrutiny. The Scottish Executive and Welsh Assembly have also had to develop a regulatory framework for both local authorities and housing associations (registered social landlords) and provide guidance and best-practice advice. The Barnett formula funding arrangements (while more generous to Scotland than to Wales) have restricted the freedoms of both the Scottish Parliament and the Welsh Assembly, although, in some areas, the financial framework for housing is more flexible in Scotland than in England and Wales (for example there is greater potential for prudential borrowing). There is a strong argument for Wales in particular to seek a renegotiation of the Barnett formula, as its present form, together with Wales' limited legislative powers, and its reliance upon the Westminster government to enact primary legislation (and a need to ensure that this does not impact adversely upon Wales), have all combined to influence what has been achievable in policy terms since 1999. Of course, while much has changed, devolution is not a fixed outcome. Already, there have been debates in Wales as to the electoral arrangements and powers of the Assembly (Richard Commission 2004) and, at the time of writing, a government White Paper (Wales Office 2005) is out to consultation on proposed changes to the Government of Wales Act 1998, including giving enhanced legislative powers to Wales.

However, before looking at policy developments post-devolution, it is worth beginning by examining the extent to which housing in Scotland and Wales is different, both between the two countries and from England – and, therefore, the extent to which each country has its own set of problems. The obvious starting point is to note that both Scotland and Wales are relatively small countries in terms of population; just under three million in Wales and a little over five million in Scotland, compared with around fifty million in England. A number of the English regions are significantly larger than either country in terms of population and housing stock.

There are also differences in tenure within Britain, with homeownership highest in Wales (seventy-two per cent) and lowest in Scotland (sixty-four per cent), against just under seventy per cent for Britain as a whole. However, the rate of growth in owner-occupation over the last two decades has been much faster in Scotland, where it more than doubled between 1981 and 2001, compared with either England or Wales, where the expansion in homeownership over the same period was only just over a third – a still significant growth, although much less marked. Historically, Scotland has consistently had a higher proportion of its housing stock in council ownership, compared with either England or Wales. The decline in Scotland's public-housing stock over the last twenty-five years has accounted for a significant proportion of the growth in homeownership. It should also be noted that, historically, the dominant form of housing in urban Scotland before the First World War – the tenement flat – differed from the rest of Britain, where workers' housing was often the terraced house (Rodger 1992).

Others have pointed to differences between Scotland and Wales and other parts of Britain in terms of their socio-economic profiles, both historically and in present times. In relation to Scotland, O'Carroll has pointed to relatively poor housing conditions, low wages, high unemployment and expensive rents prior to the First World War, compared with England (O'Carroll 1996). While historical differences are much less well-understood in relation to the development of housing in Wales (although, see Daunton 1977; Fisk 2000), recent analysis has shown that disposable household incomes are, on average, lower than in England, that levels of unemployment (and, in particular, economic inactivity) are higher, that the housing stock is generally in a poorer condition and that the projected growth in household population is lower (Smith *et al.* 2000). In many ways, the housing situations in both Scotland and Wales might be considered more similar to some of the northern English regions rather than to England as a whole. However, it is worth reiterating the point that, as for England, the differences in housing circumstances within each country at the local level may be more significant than the differences between them at a national level, with parts of both Scotland and Wales paralleling to a significant degree the overheating seen in the housing market in South-East England.

While acknowledging that there have been differences in the historical evolution of housing in each country, and differences in the socio-economic contexts in which each housing system has developed and operates, there are, perhaps, other factors that may also explain their uniqueness. There have been political differences at a local level, with much of urban Scotland and urban Wales being dominated during the twentieth century by Labour local administrations. In the case of Scotland (although not Wales), there is also a much longer history of a territorial administration and a separate legal system, which has helped to shape housing policy in Scotland in ways quite different from those in both England and Wales. The Scottish Office dates from 1885, and is the longest established of the territorial ministries within the UK. In comparison, Wales's history of administrative devolution is much more recent, with the creation of the Welsh Office only dating back to 1965, and much weaker. While the Welsh Office (and successive Secretaries of State for

Wales) exercised a degree of control over housing policy in Wales, and, prior to devolution in 1999, there was limited evidence of policy divergence and innovation, civil servants in the Welsh Office were not primarily concerned with policy development. Their main role was essentially administrative, ensuring effective delivery of services and, where appropriate, adjusting Whitehall policies to better suit local circumstances (Smith *et al.* 2000). Scotland has had both a longer and much stronger role in policy formulation.

Housing-policy-making post-devolution

Devolution is still in its early stages. The structures were put in place between 1997 and 1999, and the devolved administrations have only been in place for six years (with just two elections). At the same time, we have seen governments of similar political persuasion in London, Edinburgh and Cardiff, although both the Scottish and, for a time at least, Welsh administrations have involved Labour sharing power with another party (the Liberal Democrats). Thus, while devolution offers the prospect for policy divergence, and for the development of policies to better suit the needs of Scotland and Wales, it may be too soon to expect to see major changes in policy direction.

The previous section began to outline the different contexts in which housing policies are being developed and implemented in Scotland and Wales. It is true that the scale of housing is much smaller in both countries compared with England, and the detailed housing legacies may be different, but, none the less, many of the problems faced, which policies need to address, might be considered common across the UK in broad terms. Concerns about the adequacy and sufficiency of housing supply, affordability and growing housing inequalities, both within and between tenures, are shared by governments across England, Scotland and Wales. The interaction between sets of housing policies and wider social, economic and demographic changes help create the housing circumstances that exist at any one point in time and challenges that still have to be faced. The recent evaluation of English housing policy suggested a number of specific housing legacies. These included:

- Supply-side failures to provide sufficient housing to meet needs and demand;

- Problems of affordability in both the rented and owner-occupied sectors;

- Growing tenure and location polarisation;

- Problems of housing quality and disrepair;

- The inter-relationship between housing policies and broader economic and social restructuring have become more complex and have produced different outcomes for specific neighbourhoods, both between and within regions. (ODPM 2005a)

If these are the main housing legacies inherited from the last century, how have governments responded? During New Labour's early period in office, housing policy initiatives at Westminster were relatively modest (Kemp 1999). Nevertheless, there were broader policy developments (for example, the replacement of compulsory competitive tendering with Best Value) that had implications for housing. However, April 2000 marked a re-emergence of housing as a policy issue on the agenda of the Westminster Government, with the publication of Labour's Housing Green Paper *Quality and Choice: A Decent Home for All* (DETR/DSS 2000). While emphasising the themes of housing quality (across all tenures) and housing choice (with more of a focus on the social rented sector), it made it clear that it was considering housing-policy issues in respect of England, and that only in relation to housing benefit did it apply to Great Britain as a whole. Explicit reference was made to the fact that housing policy in Scotland and Wales was a matter for the devolved administrations. However, in setting proposals for legislative change it failed to acknowledge that primary legislation would affect Wales – although not Scotland, which has its own legislative powers. Of course, it should be fully acknowledged that policy change cannot be equated with legislative change. Governments have a host of levers (or 'sticks and carrots') that can be used to shape policy.

It has already been noted that, prior to devolution, there was evidence that both the Welsh Office and Scottish Office had exercised a degree of control over housing policy in the respective countries, but the proposals to establish a Scottish Parliament and a Welsh Assembly placed an emphasis on developing policy independently of Whitehall and Westminster. In both countries, this process commenced before the new devolved bodies were actually in place. In Scotland, a separate Housing Green Paper was published in advance of the first Scottish elections (Scottish Office 1999) and was subsequently adopted by the new Scottish Parliament. This was followed by a set of housing proposals from the Scottish Executive (2000a and 2000b), to be incorporated in subsequent Scottish primary legislation, for example the *Housing (Scotland) Act*, 2001 and the *Homelessness, etc. (Scotland) Act* 2003. Similar developments took place in Wales, with the July 1999 publication of a *Framework for a National Housing Strategy for Wales* (NAW 1999) and a first-ever national housing strategy, *Better Homes for People in Wales* (NAW 2001).

Almost inevitably, within the first six years of the devolved governments' history, where housing has been located within each administration, and its political responsibility have changed on a number of occasions. In Wales, a separate housing department was created initially, with the merger of the former Welsh Office Housing Division and Tai Cymru/Housing for Wales (the Welsh equivalent of the English Housing Corporation). Subsequently, much of the housing department was located in a Social Services and Communities Group, with a small number of functions going to a Local Government

Group. A third reorganisation has seen the Housing Directorate combined with a Communities Directorate within a Department of Social Justice and Regeneration. Ministerially, since 1999, housing has been first the responsibility of Peter Law (with local government), and subsequently with Edwina Hart (first alongside a finance portfolio and now as part of Social Justice and Regeneration). In Scotland, where there has been a somewhat higher turnover of ministers in relation to housing, it currently rests with the Minister for Communities, alongside responsibility for social inclusion, area regeneration and planning.

All of this may suggest that both the Scottish Executive and the Welsh Assembly have been unclear where housing best fits within the policy-making framework – something often true in England, since it ceased to be an independent ministry (Housing and Local Government) in the early 1970s. However, it also suggests that both administrations have sought to integrate housing, with a view to it contributing not only to housing-specific objectives but also to broader goals, often articulated in higher-level strategies (for example, greater equality, social justice, tackling exclusion, promoting economic competitiveness and prosperity, regeneration *etc.*). This is a point made strongly by Kintrea when he contends that housing reforms in Scotland have the potential to make significant inroads into meeting these higher-level goals (Kintrea forthcoming). It is also a point made by this author and a colleague in relation to housing's potential contribution to regeneration in Wales (Smith and Morgan 2005).

The development of housing policy under the devolved administrations has also been based on encouraging wider consultation on, and participation in, the policy-making process, by the wider housing-policy community. For example, in Wales, a National Consultative Forum for Housing was established in 1998 by the then Parliamentary Under Secretary of Wales, involving a wide range of representative bodies and interest groups. The Forum, which has continued post-devolution (and is chaired by the relevant Assembly Minister), was involved in the development of the Framework document (NAW 1999) and the subsequent strategy (NAW 2001). Forum members were also involved in (and chaired) four task groups that were established in 1999 to consider housing-policy issues and options. Their findings (NAW 2000) were published in April 2000 and have informed the subsequent development of the national housing strategy. In both Scotland and Wales, representatives of the wider housing-policy community, serving a variety of different interests (local authorities, housing associations, private sector, academia, tenants, homeless people, those with support needs *etc.*), have also been involved in a range of housing task forces and groups, often jointly with civil servants, out of which have emerged recommendations for further policy development (for example, Scottish Executive 2002 and 2003; NAW 2001b and 2001c). Last year, an independent task and finish group reviewed the *National Housing Strategy for Wales,* making recommendations for policy action in the second term (WAG 2004).

Early evidence suggests that in the much smaller housing policy communities of Scotland and Wales there has been a willingness on the part of housing representative bodies and other interest groups to engage in the process of policy development. Newly elected politicians and often hard-pressed civil servants have, to an extent, been willing to encourage more inclusive housing-policy-making and, despite complaints of the strain that this has placed on organisations and grumbles that effort has not always led to positive results, this has been perceived as a positive outcome of devolution. However, while such an inclusive approach to policy-making is symptomatic of New Labour's style of government, in a housing context, there are signs that the initial enthusiasm for collaborative working and even an overall consensus may be fraying at the edges. Since the Welsh national housing strategy was adopted (and despite a one-off ministerial Housing Task Force), the National Consultative Forum on housing has been much less active, while in Scotland the Commission of Scottish Local Authorities (CoSLA) withdrew from the Homelessness Monitoring Group – the successor to the Homelessness Task Force.

In broad terms, and, perhaps, not unexpectedly, at a national level the priorities for housing-policy change in Scotland and Wales have not been significantly different from those in England. For example, the *National Housing Strategy for Wales* (NAW 2001a) identifies meeting needs/demand, tackling social disadvantage, promoting sustainable homeownership, improving the quality of housing, and meeting the needs of specific, and often vulnerable groups as priorities for housing policy. However, in order to consider how policy differences and similarities have developed post-devolution, in the next two sections the chapter explores two specific aspects of housing. Firstly, it examines different approaches to encouraging the improvement of council housing in the three countries, and then it considers issues of access to social housing and the treatment of homeless persons. It could be argued that such a focus is a little narrow, and that there is a case for considering other issues, such as policies towards Right to Buy, questions of regulation and inspection, and even the role of land-use planning and the provision of affordable housing, but, given the limited length of this chapter, the issues of stock improvement and access have been selected as a means of exploring policy contrasts.

Improving the quality of council housing

The governments in England, Scotland and Wales are all expecting local authorities to improve the quality of their stock. In England the ODPM has established the *Decent Homes Standard* (DHS), with a timescale of 2010, by which point social landlords are expected to have reached this standard. In

Wales, the Assembly has set the *Welsh Housing Quality Standard* (WHQS), with a target date of 2012, and in Scotland, the *Scottish Housing Quality Standard* is to be achieved by 2015. While there are differences between the individual standards (WHQS puts additional emphasis on the stock being well-managed and located in attractive and safe environments), there are similarities in approach. In the interim, local authorities in England have been expected (by June 2005) to complete options appraisals for the future of their council housing, which are expected to be signed off by the Government Office and integrated within wider regeneration strategies. In Wales, councils have been required to complete Housing Revenue Account Business Plans and to consider how they intend to meet the WHQS. Scottish authorities and registered social landlords have been expected to produce Standard Delivery Plans to be assessed by Communities Scotland.

Stock options, and the use of stock transfer, have also varied across the three countries. The transfer option has been much less widely used in either Scotland or Wales than across England, although Glasgow, Borders, and Dumfries and Galloway councils have transferred council homes to alternative landlords in Scotland, as has Bridgend Council in South Wales, while others are considering the transfer option in the light of the quality standards. However, the range of alternatives (beyond transfer and retention) for the future of the council stock is less in both Scotland and Wales than in England. While the best-performing English authorities have been able to consider Arms Length Management Organisations (ALMOs), as a form of stock retention, with funding available from the ODPM, this has either not been an option or has not been given additional government financial support in Scotland or Wales. A similar position has meant that the Private Finance Initiative has not been a real option for local authorities beyond England as a means of generating additional investment in the council-owned stock. Where stock transfer is being pursued, different models of ownership and governance have been pursued by each administration. In this respect, the community-ownership model is more well-established in Scotland than the emerging Community Gateway model (England) and the Community Housing Mutual, which is the preferred option in Wales.

The evidence suggests that in both Scotland and Wales the establishment of a national housing quality standard has been used, at least in relation to the public-housing sector, to encourage local authorities to think seriously about the options for the future ownership and management of council housing. Indeed, Kintrea (forthcoming) has argued that the need to overcome barriers to local authority housing transfer was at the heart of the Housing Scotland 2001 Act. Where the shortfall in anticipated public investment is most marked, this may encourage the wider use of the transfer option, particularly given the lack of alternatives (compared with England) – or at least a willingness to top-slice housing budgets to fund these alternatives. In Wales, the evidence is of a clearer steer from the Assembly during its second term, although it may well be that the introduction of prudential borrowing for Welsh and Scottish authorities may muddy the waters for some councils. None the less, it would seem, at the present time, that the devolved administrations in Edinburgh and Cardiff are rather more bullish in support of transfer than the Government at Westminster. This is not just in terms of withholding support for other options such as ALMOs, but also in terms of offering the prospect of substantial public funding (as well as Treasury-backed debt write-off) to encourage often reluctant local authorities down the transfer route.

Accessing social housing and dealing with homelessness

One of the key areas of housing policy where post-devolution differences of approach have emerged is in relation to access to social housing (for a fuller discussion see Stirling and Smith 2003). In England and Wales, access to social housing has primarily been via a local authority or housing-association housing register, or by acceptance as being statutorily homeless, often leading to rehousing by the local authority or nomination to a housing association (registered social landlord). The *Housing Act* 1996 introduced the concepts of qualifying persons and a statutory housing register, from which all allocations should be made. However, the *Homelessness Act* 2002 abolished this duty (and the concept of qualifying and non-qualifying persons), while giving local authorities the power to deem applicants ineligible (for example, due to unacceptable behaviour). This new legislative framework has attempted to balance meeting priority needs and promoting choice in the lettings process, with the ODPM, in particular, encouraging a shift to choice-based lettings. In England, there has been considerable government support for the development of choice-based lettings pilots by local authorities and housing associations, with targets set for the implementation of such schemes (ODPM 2002). While Wales has been subject to the same primary legislation, and the *National Housing Strategy* has argued that choice for social housing applicants should be optimised (NAW 2001a), the level of Assembly support for choice-based lettings has been much less marked. In comparison, the *Housing (Scotland) Act* 2001 broadened the entitlement for anyone aged sixteen or over to be registered on a housing list (although not necessarily housed) and gave added impetus (and resources) to the development of common housing registers (CHRs), as a means of widening applicant choice. However, the Scottish Executive seems to have been more cautious in relation to choice-based lettings, with concerns being expressed that those in the greatest need (including homeless people) should not be disadvantaged by enhancing choice for others (Scottish Executive 2002).

The legislative framework for homelessness in England and Wales was also set out in the *Housing Act in* 1996, and subsequently amended by the *Housing Act* 2002. The 2002 legislation requires local authorities to review homelessness within their locality, prepare homelessness strategies, provide advice and assistance to those for whom there is no duty to secure accommodation, and extend the priority-needs groups. However, Wales had used secondary legislation in March 2001 (prior to the *Homelessness Act*) to extend the groups to be considered as in priority need to include sixteen- and seventeen-year-olds, care-leavers, ex-offenders, those fleeing (or threatened with) domestic violence and persons leaving the armed forces. The early developments in Wales reflect the priority given by the Welsh Assembly Government not only to preventing and tackling homelessness but also to wider agendas of combating inequality and social exclusion. It reflects both the recommendations of the Homelessness Commission in Wales (NAW 2001b) and the *National Housing Strategy* (NAW 2001a), as well as the broader Assembly strategies such as *Better Wales*. The *Homeless Persons (Priority Need) (Wales) Order* 2001 was one of the first pieces of secondary legislation introduced by the Assembly in relation to housing. This policy change reflects not only the priority given to homelessness by the Welsh Assembly, particularly during its first term (1999-2003), but also the effective lobbying of organisations such as Shelter Cymru. The impact of these changes, of course, has been to see a dramatic increase in the levels of official homelessness – as a result of redefining priority need in such a way as to draw more people into the safety net. While these policy changes in Wales were accompanied by some additional Assembly funding for homelessness, there remains a lack of overall funding, both for sufficient additional social rented housing and for the provision of extra temporary accommodation. It, perhaps, highlights the fact that well-intentioned policy change needs to be accompanied by more forward planning of anticipated consequences.

In Scotland, legislative change (primarily through the *Homelessness (Scotland) Act* 2003) in relation to homelessness has been much more radical and far reaching than in England and Wales. Eligibility for permanent housing has been widened significantly, while 'local connection' and 'intentionality' rules have also been modified in favour of homeless people (Fitzpatrick 2004). As in Wales, the Scottish Executive's commitment reflects the advice of an independent commission (Scottish Executive 2002) and the devolved administration's own commitment to social justice (Kintrea forthcoming). However, potentially, the greatest impact may result from abolishing priority need, so that, by 2012, all homeless persons will have the right to a permanent home. It is also important to make the point that the Homelessness Task Force was seen as a flagship initiative of the Holyrood administration, not only identifying post-devolution Scotland with social justice, but making it difficult to oppose its recommendations in the local political or professional arenas, whatever the reservations. Meanwhile, however, there are warnings that inadequate investment in housing (particularly in the social sector) may undermine these policy changes.

Given the constraints on this chapter, it has not been possible to develop other outputs of the housing-policy agenda to examine issues of convergence and divergence between the three nations since political devolution. However, the final section begins to offer an assessment (albeit very preliminary) of progress so far.

Housing policy in post-devolution Britain: A preliminary assessment

So how successful have the Scottish Executive and Welsh Assembly been, so far, in developing and implementing their own housing policies? The creation of both bodies has been based on a dissatisfaction with what was achievable under the Westminster-led model of government; a sense of the two countries either being ignored or subject to 'hand-me-down' policies (or being used as a test-bed for controversial policies – such as the Poll Tax, which was tried in Scotland first). Although the administration of housing policy has long been decentralised, its formulation has generally been less so. In Wales, in particular, it has long been argued that housing-policy solutions developed in England have all too often been implemented without fully taking account of cultural, social and organisational differences between the two countries. In comparison, prior to political devolution, Scotland had a much more fully developed policy-formulation role, not only in terms of the role of the Scottish Office, but also through the work of Scottish Homes, which enjoyed considerable autonomy, even from the Scottish Office.

In Scotland, the availability of legislative powers has meant that there has been more extensive housing-related legislation in the Scottish Parliament than at Westminster. Reference has been made to the *Housing (Scotland) Act 2001* and the *Homelessness etc. (Scotland) Act 2003*, but legislation has also focused on related issues such as land rights, there have been private members' bills on housing issues, and secondary legislation has also been used to introduce housing reforms. The Welsh Assembly, in comparison, has not been able to underpin its national housing strategy through primary legislation. At the same time, tying the Assembly to the UK legislative programme and timetable has meant that housing issues identified as priorities within Wales (for example, the licensing of HMOs) have had to wait to be incorporated into legislation at Westminster. In addition, the Assembly's record of influencing UK legislation has been disappointing, while the retention of control over policies on housing benefit and taxation have constrained the development of policy in both Scotland and Wales. A lack of legislative powers has meant that Wales, in particular, has continued to follow an English-led agenda, echoing a pre-devolution view that housing policy in Wales has been little more than an adjunct to housing policy in England (Williams 1999b).

There are signs that both Scotland and Wales have made broader issues such as social justice, regeneration and equality matters of priority for the devolved administrations, and some of the reforms that have been introduced in the sphere of social housing policy (for example, in relation to access to housing and homelessness) have been primarily concerned with promoting greater social justice. At the same time, some of the debates about the quality of the physical housing product (for example, in relation to meeting the respective housing quality standards) and quality of services have been presented in terms of the wider economic and community benefits that might flow from increased investment in housing. It is doubtful that these arguments could have been made so forcefully in the absence of devolved responsibility. In both Scotland and Wales, there are encouraging signs that radical new policies can be developed and implemented – for example, the single social tenancy in Scotland, changes to the 'priority need' categories for acceptance as homeless (introduced in Wales ahead of England), and new rights in Scotland for those in temporary accommodation. Some of the specific programmes developed to assist those in the most disadvantaged communities (such as Communities First in Wales) have also been quite radical in their thinking, although it is too early to judge how successfully they might be implemented.

The focus on evidence-based policy-making post-1997 has also led to a substantially enlarged research programme around housing issues in Wales. While prior to devolution the former Scottish Office and Scottish Homes had significant research programmes, this was much less the case in Wales, where both the expansion and coherence of a research programme has become much more apparent since 1999. However, in Wales, in particular, there remains a need to build a local research capacity and for there to be clearer relationships between evidence and policy-making. In Scotland, progress in this respect is much less clear-cut, and it is arguable that housing research in Scotland since devolution has, in fact, been diminished both in output and coherence.

The early evidence suggests that devolution is a vehicle for making a difference. However, the variations in housing policy that have occurred to date may represent different processes of negotiation in the policy-making process within each of the different administrations. At the same time, policy may be starting from very different points – and involve reconciling different (and often competing) interests. However, policy differences may be only at the margins, suggesting that there is (unsurprisingly) a high degree of consistency in housing-policy-thinking across the different countries. There may be an unwillingness, politically, administratively or professionally, to break away from what are, at any one time, perceived as housing orthodoxies.

In conclusion, the period between 1999 and 2005 has shown some encouraging signs of what can be achieved through devolved housing policies, in terms of trying to develop more localised solutions to specific housing problems. However, limitations in the devolved powers and the capacity to deliver change, as well as the finance resource constraints imposed by the formula funding from the UK government, are undoubtedly limiting the prospects for reforming housing policy and achieving more substantial progress. At the end of the day, housing devolution may hold out the prospect of greater control over policy at the sub-national level, and opportunities for distinctive approaches to policy that may lead to detailed differences (and divergence), but, in other respects, strong similarities might be expected to continue.

Acknowledgements

The author would like to thank Hal Pawson (Heriot Watt University) and Steve Wilcox (University of York) for their comments on an earlier version of this paper. Thanks also to Keith Kintrea (University of Glasgow) for the sight of a yet-to-be-published paper (accepted by Housing Studies) on housing policy in Scotland post-devolution. The chapter has also benefited from the contributions of those who attended the ESRC/ippr north seminar in Edinburgh in June 2005 where it was first presented.

References

Bogdanor V (2001) *Devolution in the United Kingdom* Oxford University

Bramley G (1997) 'Housing policy: a case of terminal decline' in *Policy and Politics* 25:4, pp. 387-40

Burnett J (1986) *A Social History of Housing 1815-1985* 2nd edition, Methuen

Cole I (2003) 'The Development of Housing Policy in the English Regions: Trends and Prospects' in *Housing Studies* 18:2, pp. 219-234

Daunton MJ (1987) *Coal Metropolis, Cardiff 1870-1914* Leicester University Press

Department of Environment (DoE) (1977) *Housing Policy: A consultative document* HMSO

Department of Environment, Transport and the Regions / Department of Social Security (DETR/DSS) (2000) *Quality and Choice: A Decent Home for All: The housing green paper* DETR/DSS

Fisk MJ (2000) 'Historical perspectives on housing development' in Smith R, Stirling T and Williams P (eds.) *Housing in Wales: The Policy Agenda in an Era of Devolution* Chartered Institute of Housing, pp. 17-35

Fitzpatrick S (2004) 'Homessless Policy in Scotland' in Sim D (ed.) *Housing and Public Policy in Post Devolution Scotland* Chartered Institute of Housing pp. 183-198

Fraser M (1996) *John Bull's other homes* Liverpool University Press

Gauldie E (1974) *Cruel Habitations* George Allen and Unwin

Goodlad R (1993) *The Housing Authority as Enabler* Institute of Housing and Longman

Hills J (1998) 'Housing: a decent home within the reach of every family' in Glennester H and Hills J (eds.) *The State of Welfare* Oxford University Press

Jessop B (1998) 'The rise of governance and the risks of failure: the case of economic development' in *International Social Science Journal* 50:155, pp. 29-46

Karn V (1985) 'Housing' in Ranson S, Jones G and Walsh K (eds.) *Between Centre and Locality* George Allen and Unwin, pp. 163-184

Kemp P (1999) 'Housing Policy under New Labour' in Powell M (ed) *New Labour, New Welfare State?* The Policy Press, pp. 123-147

Kintrea K (forthcoming) 'Having it All? Housing Reform under Devolution' in *Housing Studies*

Kleinman M (1999) 'A commentary on "Housing policy: does it have a future?"' in *Policy and Politics* 27:2, pp. 229-230

Maclennan D (2000) *Changing Places, Engaging People* York Publishing Services.

Malpass P (1999) 'Housing policy: does it have a future?' in *Policy and Politics* 27:2, pp. 217-228

Malpass P and Murie A (1999) *Housing Policy and Practices* 5th edition Macmillan

Ministry of Housing and Local Government (MHLG) (1971) *Fair Deal for Housing* Cmnd 4728, HMSO

Murie A (1985) 'The Nationalisation of Housing Policy' in Loughlin M, Gelfand MD and Young K (eds.) *Half a Century of Municipal Decline 1935-1985* George Allen and Unwin pp. 187-201

Murie A (2004) 'Scottish Housing: the context' in Sim D (ed.) *Housing and public policy in post devolution Scotland* Chartered Institute of Housing, pp. 16-32.

National Assembly for Wales (NAW) (1999) *Framework for a National Housing Strategy for Wales* NAW

NAW (2000) *Proposals for a National Housing Strategy for Wales: Final reports by the Housing Strategy Task Groups* NAW

NAW (2001a) *Better Homes for People in Wales: A National Housing Strategy for Wales* NAW

NAW (2001b) *Homelessness Commission Report* NAW

NAW (2001c) *Report of the Working Group on Local Housing Strategies* NAW

O'Carroll A (1996) 'Historical perspectives on tenure development in two Scottish cities' in Currie H and Murie A (eds.) *Housing in Scotland* Chartered Institute of Housing

Office of the Deputy Prime Minister (ODPM) (2002) *How to Choose Choice: Lessons from the First Year of the ODPM's CBL Pilot Schemes* ODPM

ODPM (2005a) *Lessons from the past, challenges for the future for housing policy* ODPM

ODPM (2005b) *Sustainable Communities: Homes for all* TSO

Paris C (ed.) (2001) *Housing in Northern Ireland* Chartered Institute of Housing

Paris C, Gray P and Muir J (2003) 'Devolving Housing Policy and Practice in Northern Ireland 1998-2002' in *Housing Studies,* 18:2, pp. 159-176

Pierre J and Peters B (2000) *Governance, Politics and the State* Macmillan

Rhodes R (1994) 'The hollowing out of the state' *Political Quarterly* 65:2, pp. 138-151

Rhodes R (1997) *Understanding Governance* Open University Press

Richard Commission (2004) *Commission on the Powers and Electoral Arrangements of the National Assembly for Wales* NAW

Robinson D (2003) 'Housing Governance in the English Regions: Emerging Structures, Limits and Potentials' in *Housing Studies* 18:2, pp. 249-267

Rodger R (1992) 'Scotland' in Pooley CG (ed.) *Housing Strategies in Europe 1880-1930* Leicester University Press

Roof (2004) *The government's record on housing: evidence from the Roof inspection* November/December, pp. 21-29.

Satsangi M and Dunmore K (2003) 'The Planning System and the Provision of Affordable Housing in Rural Britain: A Comparison of the Scottish and English Experience' in *Housing Studies* 18:2, pp. 201-217

Scottish Executive (2000a) *Better Homes for Scotland's Communities: The Executive's Proposals for the Housing Bill* Scottish Executive

Scottish Executive (2000b) *Policy Memorandum to Accompany the Housing (Scotland) Bill* Scottish Executive

Scottish Executive (2002) *Helping Homeless People: An Action Plan for Prevention and Effective Response* Scottish Executive

Scottish Executive (2003) *Stewardship and Responsibility: A policy framework for private housing in Scotland* Scottish Executive

Scottish Office (1999) *Investing in Modernisation: An agenda for Scotland's housing* Stationery Office

Sim D (ed.) (2004) *Housing and public policy in post devolution Scotland* Chartered Institute of Housing

Slocombe L (2003) 'Integration in the Regions: Cross-sectoral housing policy co-ordination at regional level' in *Housing Studies* 18:2, pp. 235-248

Smith R, Stirling T and Williams P (eds.) (2000) *Housing in Wales: The Policy Agenda in an Era of Devolution* Chartered Institute of Housing

Smith R and Morgan K (2005) 'Regeneration: Housing at the Centre' in Clements A (ed.) *Game Plan* Chartered Institute of Housing Cymru

Stirling T and Smith R (2003) 'A Matter of Choice? Policy Divergence in Access to Social Housing Post Devolution' in *Housing Studies* 18:2, pp. 145-158

Wales Office (2005) *Better Governance for Wales* Cm 6582 TSO

Walker RM, Mullins D and Pawson H (2003) 'Devolution and Housing Associations in Great Britain: Enhancing Organisational Accountability' in *Housing Studies* 18:2, pp. 177-199

Welsh Assembly Government (WAG) (2004) *National Housing Strategy Task and Finish Advisory Group Review of the National Housing Strategy: Report to the Minister for Social Justice and Regeneration* WAG

Williams P (1999a) 'A commentary on "Housing policy: does it have a future?"' in *Policy and Politics* 27:2, pp. 231-232

Williams P (1999b) 'End of Empire: housing policy in a devolved Wales' in Wilcox S (ed.) *Housing Finance Review 1999/2000* Chartered Institute of Housing and Council of Mortgage Lenders

9 Regional economic development in a devolved United Kingdom

John Adams and Peter Robinson

It has traditionally been claimed, with much justification, that the United Kingdom is one of the most centralised of developed nations. London has been the seat of Parliament and government, the City of London is one of the world's leading financial centres, and the majority of UK media is based in London. The economic performance of the Greater South-East of England is superior to that of the other regions of the UK.

The creation of devolved institutions, following the election of a Labour Government in 1997, represented a fundamental step away from this portrait of an overcentralised polity. However, the link between political devolution and economic growth is not uncontroversial. While the UK's constitution, at least until 1997, was significantly more centralised than comparable nations in Europe, regional economic disparities within the UK are not worse than in other EU countries, despite the fact that many European nation states have had strong 'regional' governments for many years. Nevertheless, the creation of devolved institutions transformed the institutional landscape of economic development within the UK.

In this chapter, we shall first discuss divergence in economic development within the UK, and, as the authors have observed policy developments from their own vantage points, there is more information on events in Whitehall and Wales than other devolved administrations. We then discuss the geographical reach of Whitehall in a number of policy areas relevant to driving and facilitating economic growth, and, finally, we consider the developing quasi-federal role of the UK government.

Divergence within the UK

There are numerous similarities to the economic development strategies pursued in the different territories of the United Kingdom. In recent years, political pundits, media commentators and influential academics have developed a popular narrative on the causes and trends in economic growth in the UK.

This narrative starts with an emphasis on the impact of globalisation on the UK economy, and that the success of the regional economy in a devolved nation or English region depends on becoming a dynamic, 'knowledge-based economy'. This narrative is reflected in the economic development strategies of each of the UK's nations and regions, despite the fact that many of the assertions supporting this narrative are not supported by the evidence, and that some of the 'facts' are myths.

Although Gross Domestic Product (GDP) or Gross Value Added (GVA) per head is an imperfect measure of economic prosperity, it probably remains the best measure of the economic performance of a nation or region. At the most basic level, regional differences in GVA per capita will primarily be a function of regional variations in productivity and employment. Table 8.1 uses the most up-to-date figures that were available from official sources in the summer of 2005 to examine these three economic measures together. It should be noted that we have used, as a measurement of productivity, output per hour worked, rather than the UK Government's preferred index of output per person employed. The latter does not take into account any differences in working hours between different parts of the UK, and if one part of the nation decides to forego extra economic output to voluntarily work fewer hours this should not be a cause for concern.

The figures for GVA per head will come as little surprise to most people, detailing a broad North-South divide within the United Kingdom, with a 'winners' circle' in the Greater South-East. These regional disparities emerged during the depression of the 1930s, and there has been remarkably little change since then. Scotland is the most prosperous of the three devolved territories,

Table 8.1: Levels of regional prosperity, productivity and employment (UK=100)

	Productivity[1]	Employment[2]	Output[3]
Wales	91.9	97.7	79.0
Northern Ireland	84.3	93.3	81.2
Scotland	98.1	99.9	96.4
England	101.1	100.4	102.2
North East	95.1	91.3	79.7
Yorkshire & the Humber	93.7	99.2	89.0
North West	94.4	98.1	89.8
East Midlands	96.9	101.9	90.8
West Midlands	94.6	99.1	91.0
South West	95.4	105.2	94.1
East	97.1	105.1	109.2
South East	106.5	106.2	115.2
London	115.4	94.1	131.3
UK	100	100	100

Sources: ONS (2004) and (2005)

Notes
1 GVA per hour worked 2003)
2 Seasonally adjusted as a percentage of all people of working age – Spring 2003)
3 GVA per head 2003, residence-based)

with GVA per head slightly lower than the UK average. Wales and Northern Ireland lag significantly. England is the richest nation in the United Kingdom, but it is also by far the largest, and many of its regions are larger than the devolved territories. The North East of England is one of the poorest parts of the United Kingdom.

The relative importance of differences in employment and productivity in explaining these differences in GDP per head differs from region to region. The low GVA per head in the North East is explained, in large part, by low levels of employment; its productivity levels are similar to many regions with higher GDP per head. On the other hand, the South West has above average levels of employment, but relatively poor productivity (and a low working-age population share). Employment rates in Wales have risen significantly in recent years, and both employment rates and productivity levels are noticeably low in Northern Ireland. London's prosperity is due to its high levels of productivity, although it has a high working-age population share. London has had a very disappointing employment record in recent years.

It is worth stressing that much of the UK Government's initial focus on regional economic disparities seemed to stem from its concern to close the difference in productivity levels between the UK and comparable countries, in particular the USA, Germany and France. The Treasury has identified five key drivers of productivity growth: the level of business and public investment, the skills of the workforce, the role of innovation and enterprise, and the importance of competition (HMT 2000a). In itself this is a relatively uncontroversial list at the national level, but it does have limitations as a way of thinking of differences in prosperity between the nations and regions of the UK. Treasury documents, such as the *Productivity 3* report, initially seemed to struggle to make this framework fit easily with an analysis of regional disparities, as these five productivity drivers miss out some of the more important drivers at a local level, for example the efficiency with which labour and housing markets operate (HMT/DTI 2001).

This might be part of the explanation for a recent change in the thrust of UK Government policy. Whether one looks at the 'five-year plans' of the Department for Work and Pensions (DWP) or the Office of the Deputy Prime Minister (ODPM), the emphasis is on the Government's long-term aspiration of increasing the employment rate in the UK to eighty per cent of all adults of working age, although a timescale for achieving this aspiration is not specified (DWP 2005; ODPM 2005). This compares with about seventy-four per cent of working-age adults in employment in 2004, which indicates the scale of ambition. In terms of dealing with regional economic disparities, the ODPM now puts the focus squarely on tackling high levels of economic inactivity among key groups, especially those inactive due to sickness and disability. Because levels of economic inactivity are highest in the disadvantaged regions, including Northern Ireland and Wales, this agenda has an inbuilt 'bias' in favour of these regions; they simply have more to make up in terms of reducing economic inactivity. This is, perhaps, one of the most important ways in which gaps in regional economic prosperity can be closed.

It is within this context that the devolution settlement operates. Central government retains many of the regulatory functions at a UK level, notably competition policy. Most of the powers that could affect aggregate demand are reserved to Whitehall and Westminster – for example, taxation policies, the monetary-policy framework and policies in relation to the exchange rate. Furthermore, numerous active-labour-market policies are reserved, such as the Jobcentre Plus network, the various New Deal programmes and the various measures to improve work incentives, such as the Working Families Tax Credit. The devolved institutions do have a number of responsibilities that could help stimulate labour demand; for example, they are responsible for financial assistance to industry and for spending EU Structural Funds. The devolved institutions certainly have responsibility for a number of policy instruments that impact upon the supply side. To a greater or lesser degree, they are responsible for policies in the fields of education, training and skills, business-university links, transport, business advice and support for new firms.

Having discussed the approach of the UK Government, in the remainder of this section we will briefly discuss some of the policy developments within the devolved administrations.

Scotland

Prior to devolution, Scottish Enterprise had established itself as an effective institution, and, with the Scottish Office, had begun to pursue a number of quite distinct agendas several years before they were to appear on the English agenda (Gillespie and Benneworth 2002). Cluster policy, for example, was developed in Scotland in the early 1990s, several years before it was enthusiastically embraced by the Department for Trade and Industry (DTI) following the 1998 White Paper *Our Competitive Future* (DTI 1998). Clusters are geographic concentrations of interconnected companies that hold out the possibility of increasing knowledge spillovers, such as the IT cluster in Silicon Valley in the USA. While this was fashionable in the regional-development literature a few years ago, and is currently embraced by numerous policy-makers, it is worth noting that cluster policy also has its critics (Adams *et al.* 2003). In the 1990s, Scotland also promoted entrepreneurship, and, in particular, focused on new-firm formation, whereas the rest of the UK directed support towards established rather than new firms. At the start of the new century, policy across the UK seems to be returning to promoting new-firm start-ups (HMT/SBS 2002).

Policy divergence post-devolution has, in many ways, been less dramatic. The two strategies that govern economic development in Scotland are the *Framework for Economic Development in Scotland* (FEDS) and *Smart Successful Scotland*. The initial strategies were devised in 2000 and 2001, and then 'refreshed' in 2004 (Scottish Executive 2000, 2001, 2004a and 2004b). The *FEDS* documents set the broad parameters of economic governance, while the *Smart Successful Scotland* documents are more detailed implementation frameworks. Much of the Scottish Executive's approach to economic development seems to focus on improving levels of productivity in Scotland. Labour-market issues have a much lower profile in these four documents. However, other commentators would argue that social inclusion – also known as 'extending economic opportunities' – has, perhaps, a higher profile in Scottish economic development debates than it generally does in Whitehall (Keating 2005).

In Scotland, the institutions of economic development have been subject to less institutional restructuring than those of social policy. The only new implementation structures of economic governance in Scotland are the Local Economic Forums, created to facilitate joined-up governance (Goodwin *et al.* 2005). The Scottish Executive has also changed the constitution of Local Enterprise Companies (LECs), from private-sector companies limited by guarantee to public bodies. The LECs are now subsidiaries of Scottish Enterprise, and Highlands and Islands Enterprise, and their staffs are employees of these core organisations. Finally, the institutions concerned with Scotland's international linkages were merged in 2001, and Scottish Development International was created out of the Scottish Trade International and Locate in Scotland (Goodwin *et al.* 2005).

One of the more interesting initiatives of the Scottish Executive has been the *Fresh Talent Initiative*, which aims to attract newcomers to Scotland and encourage overseas students to stay in the country after graduation. It seems to be based less on an analysis of migration or demographic trends than on a desire to create a more entrepreneurial and innovative culture by attracting those whom it is hoped will be 'creative individuals' (Scottish Executive 2004c). While some themes of the *Fresh Talent Initiative* will resonate with institutions across the UK, this is clearly a significant divergence from policy pursued in other parts of the United Kingdom.

Wales

Whereas *FEDS* and *Smart Successful Scotland* focused very much on productivity issues, in the relevant strategies covering economic development – A Winning Wales – the Welsh Assembly Government (WAG) gave equal weight to both productivity and employment issues, particularly the need to reduce economic inactivity (WAG 2002). Raising economic activity rates is one of the four main priorities highlighted in the WAG's strategic plan *Wales: A Better Country* (WAG 2003). The issue of economic inactivity is of crucial importance to poorer regions, as a far larger number of people claim state benefits related to sickness or incapacity than claim Jobseeker's Allowance. However, it is not yet clear how actual policy instruments will be altered to reflect this divergent analysis and rhetorical commitment. As already emphasised, the situation is complicated by the fact that some of the most important policy instruments are reserved matters, particularly the Jobcentre Plus network, and the tax and benefit system.

The Welsh Assembly Government has tried to offer support for the DWP's *Pathways to Work* initiative, which is designed to offer employment-related support and financial incentives to people claiming benefits related to sickness and disability. However, the *Pathways to Work* initiative was developed in Whitehall, and the Welsh Assembly Government has been the junior partner. It is also important to stress that there will be a large number of local initiatives in this policy area, often run by the voluntary sector or local authorities and funded by EU Structural Funds. The Welsh Assembly Government has used £11 million of European Social Fund money to offer enhancements for the economically inactive under the 'Want2Work' scheme in certain wards in Merthyr Tydfil, Neath, Port Talbot and Cardiff. Like the *Pathways to Work* initiative, the scheme offers work-focused support from a personal advisor and condition management from healthcare professionals, but, unlike the *Pathways to Work* scheme, there are no back-to-work financial incentives. As discussed above, it does seem that there has been some convergence in policy, with Whitehall coming to the same conclusion as the Welsh Assembly Government in stressing the importance of strong labour-market policies.

In *A Winning Wales*, the Welsh Assembly Government committed to an 'aspiration' of raising Welsh GDP per head from about eighty per cent of the UK average to ninety per cent of the UK average by 2012. This target has been widely criticised as being wildly overoptimistic. However, the Welsh Assembly Government would argue that, at the time when the aspiration was developed, Welsh GDP per capita was consistently at or around eighty-five per cent of the UK average. Following the publication of *A Winning Wales*, Welsh GVA per head (which has become the Office of National Statistics's (ONS) preferred measure) both fell in relation to the UK average and was revised downwards by the ONS. The Welsh Assembly Government believed that this increase in prosperity would be achieved through an increase in employment rates, although this begs the question as to why their headline economic 'target' related to the GDP measure of economic prosperity, rather than employment rates.

While the Welsh Assembly Government has placed a greater emphasis on labour-market policy than some other parts of the United Kingdom, it does still bring forward a plethora of initiatives that aim to improve levels of productivity. Cluster policy, the Entrepreneurship Action Plan, science parks, and so on, form much of the bedrock of economic development strategy in Wales. Perhaps the most high-profile initiative has been the 'Technium' concept, which aims to improve levels of enterprise and innovation in Wales. A Technium is a building that offers 'state of the art facilities', including office space, business support, ICT infrastructure and access to venture capitalists. It aims to bring together fledgling start-ups, entrepreneurs from universities, researchers and firms at each site. In some respects, it is, at heart, a property-development initiative. The policy will have echoes in other parts of the United Kingdom, as will the trend in Wales to move away from a policy with inward investment as the centrepiece of economic development strategy. However, the success of initiatives such as these is far from proven.

One area where Wales will diverge substantially from the rest of the United Kingdom is in the changing institutional structure of economic governance. The Welsh Assembly Government has separate divisions for Economic Development and Transport; and for Education and Lifelong Learning. Furthermore, a number of institutional reforms were set in motion by the Welsh Office in the period between the Labour victory at the 1997 UK general election and the creation of the National Assembly for Wales in 1999. Specifically, a number of economic development agencies – the Development Board for Rural Wales, the Land Authority for Wales and the existing Welsh Development Agency – were merged into a new-style Welsh Development Agency (WDA), and a new agency – Education and Learning Wales (ELWa) – was made responsible for all post-sixteen education and skills, with both organisations to operate through four coterminous sub-regions (as does the Assembly).

Perhaps the most controversial economic development policy brought forward by the Welsh Assembly Government has been the announcement that the WDA, ELWa and the Wales Tourist Board would cease to remain as 'quasi-autonomous non-governmental organisations' and would come under the direct control of the Welsh Assembly Government. This decision is a significant divergence from the policy trend in the rest of the United Kingdom. The creation of Regional Development Agencies in England in 1999 and 2000 and the creation of Invest Northern Ireland in 2002 were in direct response to the perceived success of the Welsh Development Agency and Scottish Enterprise.

There seem to have been a number of factors that led to the announcement by First Minister Rhodri Morgan in July 2004. First, the decision reflected a desire by the First Minister and his Minister for Economic Development, Andrew Davies, to increase the political control of economic development. Second, the *Gershon Review* conducted from HM Treasury calls for efficiency savings across Whitehall (Gershon 2004). While the Review was confined to Whitehall, it does have implications for the block grant allocated to the devolved institutions, and both the Scottish Executive and the Welsh Assembly responded to the *Gershon Review* and are seeking to make their own efficiency gains. The abolition of three quangos could mean that certain back-office functions could be rationalised, or savings could be made from a joint procurement policy, with any savings allocated to 'frontline services'.

Finally, and perhaps most importantly, the abolition of the three agencies can be seen as a political response to a series of crises and scandals that characterised quangos in Wales in the 1990s under the then Conservative government. When an MP at Westminster, Rhodri Morgan was at the forefront of campaigns against the 'quango-state'; at the National Eisteddfod in 1995, the then Shadow Welsh Secretary Ron Davies announced that a Labour government would introduce a 'bonfire of the quangos' and the issue was one of the most important for Labour Party members in Wales. The three agencies will cease to be in 2006, and it is far too early to say what impact this initiative will have on prosperity in Wales. In particular, the Welsh Assembly Government faces a tough challenge to first digest the staff, functions and budget of the three agencies, before then improving on their delivery performance (Morgan and Upton 2005).

It is also worth noting that the standard of the analysis contained in *A Winning Wales* and associated documents is noticeably weaker than that in comparable documents in Scotland or Whitehall. This situation is perhaps unsurprising in light of Wales's traditionally weaker policy communities (Keating 2002).

Northern Ireland

In Northern Ireland, the two departments with lead responsibility in the field of economic development are the Department for Enterprise, Trade and Investment, and the Department for Employment and Learning. These structures were fixed in the Good Friday Agreement. There have been two significant post-devolution institutional changes to economic governance in Northern Ireland. First, a new economic development agency – Invest Northern Ireland – was created in April 2002, with the merger of three economic development agencies: the Local Enterprise Development Unit, the Industrial Development Board and the Industrial Research and Technology Unit. Second, post-sixteen education and training has moved from a 'Next Steps Agency' into the Northern Ireland civil service.

One of the key economic problems facing the Northern Ireland Executive during its all-too-brief existence was the widely-acknowledged deficiency in infrastructure investment. In a significant change to the devolution settlement, the UK Chancellor of the Exchequer and the Prime Minister visited Belfast in May 2002 to announce that a 'prudential' system for capital spending would be introduced to allow the Northern Ireland Executive to undertake borrowing to spend on infrastructure. The fact that Northern Ireland does not have the same system of local government as the rest of the UK would, undoubtedly, have influenced this decision.

Conclusion

As this brief overview indicates, much of the divergence in economic development has been institutional, reforming the structures of the devolved administrations and the public bodies within their remit. However, such reforms are time-consuming and expensive and often divert staff attention from fulfilling their responsibility to deliver frontline services. Structural reform also takes time to bed down, so it is too early to judge the impact of this institutional reform on the performance of the public sector, and certainly too early to judge its impact on actual policy outcomes. Nevertheless, as time goes by we might expect such structural differences to begin to impact on the provision of frontline services.

While there have been significant differences in the way economic development policies have evolved since the creation of the devolved institutions, the roots of this policy divergence can often be traced back to initiatives that emerged over the last twenty years or so. That is, during a period of administrative devolution. This has led some to argue that the initial step of administrative devolution has been more significant than the political follow-up (Gillespie and Benneworth 2002). Interestingly, the policy divergence that developed in Scotland and Wales during administrative devolution has proved to be influential for regional and industrial policy in the English regions.

Whitehall, its geographical reach and economic development

Being clear about the exact geographical reach of Whitehall is not a dry issue of importance only to constitutional anoraks, as a lack of clarity could lead to tensions between the UK government and the devolved administrations. Even despite regional economic disparities, England is the most prosperous part of the United Kingdom, and the Greater South-East of England is one of the most prosperous parts of Europe. Therefore, an England-only policy is more likely to be skewed towards affluence and affluent areas, and designed to deal with the pressure of success (Gordon 2002) while a UK-wide policy might take a very different approach. In addition, an England-only policy might well have adverse consequences for the poorer nations of the United Kingdom, such as Wales and Northern Ireland.

There are a number of Whitehall departments that have important responsibilities in the field of economic development. The two main departments are the Treasury, which is responsible for the Government's overall economic policy, and the DTI, responsible for science, innovation and enterprise. Other Whitehall departments with responsibilities that affect economic development include the DWP, the Department for Education and Skills (DfES), the Department for Transport (DfT) and the ODPM.

Within the DTI, a number of regional economic programmes are England-only initiatives, each of which will have some form of equivalent in the devolved territories. These include such programmes as the Regional Development Agencies, the Regional Innovation Fund, Regional Selective Assistance (now entitled 'Selective Finance for Investment in England'), the Higher Education Innovation Fund, and the Small Business Service. The DTI also delivers some quite straightforward economic development programmes on behalf of the UK as a whole, including inward-investment programmes, trade-development programmes and the Enterprise Fund/Small Firms Loan Guarantee Scheme.

The large amount of money spent by the DTI on science policy is regarded as a UK-wide policy – this includes spending on the Research Councils, the Office of Science and Technology, the Cambridge MIT Institute and numerous other science programmes. Clearly, some of the Research Council expenditure will be spent in the devolved territories, but only as part of a UK-wide research strategy that will need to be ratified by Whitehall ministers. By contrast, the spending on the Higher Education Funding Council for England by the DfES is, as its name implies, for England only.

The DTI also has a number of important functions that do not entail significant amounts of public expenditure. While financial assistance to industry is a devolved matter, the designation of Assisted Areas is a reserved function. Where the boundaries for the Assisted Areas are drawn will have a significant influence on the relative ability of the different nations and regions of the UK to attract mobile-investment projects, and is, therefore, a possible source of tension between the UK Government and the devolved administrations. The issue of regulating mobile investment is discussed further below, in the section on the role of the centre.

The DWP is a UK department, which carries out mostly reserved functions. The DWP's remit does not extend to Northern Ireland, and the Northern Ireland social security system is separate for historical reasons. However, the 1998 Northern Ireland Act provides for 'parity' in social security and it is extremely difficult, if not practically impossible, for Northern Ireland to depart from UK standards and the UK framework. Therefore, the DWP is best thought of as a 'Mostly UK' department (see Schmuecker and Adams in chapter 3). The few programmes that the DWP runs that are comparable to programmes within Scotland and Wales mostly relate to programmes funded by the European Union through the European Social Fund (ESF) and the European Regional Development Fund (ERDF).

There is no direct equivalent to the DWP in Northern Ireland – the main responsibilities are shared between the Department for Social Development and the Department for Education and Learning. As part of its 'Welfare Reform and Modernisation Programme' Northern Ireland policy converged with that in Great Britain, when Jobs and Benefits Offices were created as a mirror image to the British Jobcentre Plus network.

Interestingly a highly significant change to the devolution settlement occurred following the introduction of the Child Tax Credit in Britain, which resulted in Northern Ireland government departments losing responsibility for child benefit. When the Child Tax Credit was introduced on the mainland, the UK Government decided that only one agency should be responsible for support for children and that this agency should be the Inland Revenue. However, the Inland Revenue is a UK-wide agency and is responsible to UK Government ministers. Prior to this reform, central government had no responsibility for child benefit in Northern Ireland, but in November 2001 the Northern Ireland Assembly agreed to cede responsibility for child benefit to the Inland Revenue (DWP 2003). A reform introduced by Whitehall on the basis of administrative convenience, with little or no public debate on the merits of situating this policy responsibility in Whitehall or Stormont, significantly altered the devolution settlement, transferring a public-policy responsibility that involved a large amount of public expenditure. It is an excellent example of the ad hoc manner in which the boundaries of devolution are drawn in the UK.

The DfES is an England-only department. However, higher education occupies a somewhat ambiguous position in relation to the devolved administrations. While the research councils responsible to the DTI are UK-wide bodies, there are four devolved Higher Education Funding Councils. However, each of the devolved Higher Education Funding Councils subscribes to a common UK-wide system for quality assessment and the ranking of disciplines and departments – the Research Assessment Exercise (RAE) (Rees 2002). While the devolved funding councils can choose to allocate a different degree of funding to each RAE ranking – for example, unlike the rest of the UK, Scotland does not allocate higher levels of funding to a department ranked 5* than one ranked 5 – the RAE exercise does imply that the devolved administrations are expected to 'match' resources provided to departments elsewhere in the UK with similar RAE rankings. In practice, they accommodate funding levels for higher education on assessments that are largely outside their control.

However, the link between basic research and economic growth is not straightforward, and perhaps of more importance for economic development is the learning and skills sector. Again, policy in this field is almost completely devolved. One exception is the Sector Skills Development Agency (SSDA). The SSDA and the Sector Skills Councils (SSCs) are UK-wide agencies charged with improving levels of qualifications in numerous industry or business sectors, for example for the automotive industry or the hospitality sector. SSCs are licensed by the DfES Secretary of State, but in consultation with the Lifelong Learning Ministers of the devolved administrations.

The SSDA and the SSCs have the tricky task of pursuing this UK-wide agenda while simultaneously responding to the institutional and policy contexts of Scotland, Wales and Northern Ireland. Interestingly, the DfES agreed to fund the Sector Skills Development Agency in its entirety, and the devolved administrations do not contribute to the SSDA's core costs. However, many 'on the ground' programmes of the SSDA and the SSCs will be funded by local agencies: the Local Learning and Skills Councils in England, ELWa in Wales, the Local Enterprise Companies in Scotland and the Department for Education and Learning in Northern Ireland. It should be noted that, even prior to the creation of the SSDA, Northern Ireland already had a network of thirteen Sector Training Councils.

The role of the centre: regulating the new landscape

A nation state with devolved polities is still a nation state (albeit in the case of the UK, one consisting of four stateless nations). Westminster and Whitehall do retain a responsibility for all parts of the United Kingdom, and such 'quasi-federal' responsibilities must be exercised in a way that is compatible with the devolution settlement. Far from 'hollowing out' Whitehall, devolution means that it must develop important new roles, not least to manage territorial rivalries and try to ensure some degree of territorial justice.

Regional economic policy is undergoing something of a renaissance at the moment, with a specific commitment made in the Spending Review of 2002, and reiterated in 2004, to 'make sustainable improvements in the economic performance of all English regions and over the long term reduce the persistent gap in growth rates between the regions' (HMT 2002 and 2004). HM Treasury, the DTI and the ODPM jointly own this target. This PSA target can be criticised for a lack of ambition, as it simply aims to reduce the rate at which the South gets richer and the North gets poorer, rather than aiming to reverse regional disparities. Nevertheless, we do have an explicit UK Government commitment that focuses on regional economic disparities – at least in England.

Interestingly, the equivalent target in the 2000 Spending Review appeared to apply to the whole of the UK. This target was less ambitious in its scope, aiming only to 'improve the economic performance of all regions measured by the trend in growth of each region's GDP per capita' (HMT 2000b). However, in this case, the term 'regions' appears to have been taken to apply to all twelve of the UK's nations and regions (Scotland, Wales, Northern Ireland, and the nine English regions). Of the three departments that own the PSA 2004 target, both HM Treasury and the DTI exercise significant reserved powers on behalf of the UK. As a commitment to equity seems to be at the heart of the Government's approach, it is not clear what the basis is for the exclusion of the national territories.

The 2000 regional economic PSA target was jointly owned by the DTI and the Department for the Environment, Transport and the Regions (DETR) (which subsequently became the ODPM). In a sign of the rising interest of HM Treasury in regional economic policy, it became a joint signatory to the PSA target during the 2002 Spending Review process, when the commitment to reduce 'the persistent gap in growth rates between the regions' was added.

There are two other areas that it is traditionally thought have the potential to ignite territorial rivalries: regulating financial assistance to industry, and distributing public expenditure.

The DTI is responsible for regulating financial assistance to industry in order to prevent zero-sum competition. Inward investors could seek to play off different devolved or regional agencies against each other with the objective of maximising financial subsidies. There is, clearly, an argument that policies designed to capture mobile investment are ineffective and wasteful, and that regional and local agencies should concentrate on nurturing the successful firms already present and promoting enterprise. Although this is a powerful argument, there will still be occasions when devolved, regional and local agencies pursue policies that may have a positive economic impact when viewed from the perspective of the territory, but which are zero-sum when viewed from a wider perspective. This situation is most likely to occur in the pursuit of mobile investment. There is, therefore, a powerful case for a strong framework at the UK (and European) level for regulating territorial competition.

It is worth noting that the devolution White Papers produced in the summer of 1997 specifically said that, while financial assistance to industry would be devolved to the Scottish Parliament and the National Assembly for Wales, it would 'remain subject to common UK guidelines and consultation arrangements, to be set out in a published concordat' (this quote from Welsh Office 1997, but see also Scottish Office 1997). Subsequently, one of the supplementary agreements incorporated with the Memorandum of Understanding first produced in July 2000 concerned financial assistance to industry (LCD 2000). The political importance given to this form of regulation at this time may well have reflected the concerns of the then Secretary of State for Trade and Industry, Margaret Beckett.

At the beginning of 2005, levels of Foreign Direct Investment were lower than in previous years, and were disproportionately concentrated in the Greater South-East of England. Therefore, there were few major inter-regional tensions concerning incentives to attract mobile investment. The importance of incentives, such as Regional Selective Assistance, in relation to inward investment is continually being reappraised, and some recent research indicates that expenditure on government subsidies has little correlation to levels of inward investment. Partly as a result, there seems less of a desire to pursue such investment by devolved, regional and local decision-makers. Nevertheless, such tensions will not disappear entirely – for example, a National Audit Office report in 2003 referred to a grant being paid to retain an American-owned plant in the West Midlands in the face of enticements from Northern France and the Welsh Assembly and the Welsh Development Agency (NAO 2003). The DTI has been criticised for failing to regulate this form of pointless zero-sum competition with sufficient urgency (Adams *et al.* 2003).

The potential for conflicts of interest is written into the structure of the DTI. It is supposed to protect the interests of consumers and safeguard the rights of the workforce, yet it also sees itself as the voice of business in Whitehall and provides various forms of support for industry. At the same time, it has difficulty in separating its 'English' responsibilities (for example, relating to innovation, business support or the English RDAs) from its 'UK' responsibilities (for example, relating to competition and trade policy, consumer protection and employment relations) (Adams and Robinson 2002). There is a strong case for a fundamental rethink of the DTI's role and structure in the light of devolution and in the light of the potential conflicts of interest in its roles (Robinson 2001).

The other issue that runs a particular risk of territorial rivalry concerns the distribution of public expenditure – the so-called 'Barnett debate'. All advanced industrial countries consciously redistribute resources across regions and localities to achieve more equitable outcomes in terms of public spending. In some countries with federal constitutions, the processes that achieve this are very formalised. As befits a country without a codified constitution, the UK's system of fiscal equalisation has evolved over time in response to particular political pressures and requirements. This does not, however, necessarily mean that an uncodified system is any less effective at achieving a desirable distribution of resources when compared with other countries (see also Heald and McLeod 2002).

When the Treasury publishes its figures in April of each year, in the *Public Expenditure Statistical Analysis* (PESA) publication, they are invariably the subject of much comment in the Scottish, Welsh and English regional newspapers. The Treasury figures indicate that the difference in public spending between the different nations of the United Kingdom have changed little since the devolution took place (HMT 2005). In theory, the Barnett formula ought to produce a convergence in per-capita spending; the so-called 'Barnett squeeze'. As the Barnett mechanisms distribute equal per-capita increments to each country, smaller percentage-spending increases are automatically delivered to those territories with the highest spending levels. As far as Scotland and Wales are concerned, the 'Barnett squeeze' is not yet in operation and concerns on this score would seem to be unfounded. Levels of spending in Northern Ireland, however, may be converging towards the UK average. This might be partly explained by lower security costs due to the peace process, expenditure on which falls to the Northern Ireland Office.

It is hard to see how reform of the Barnett formula could be achieved in the near future, given the reluctance of the UK Government to open up a politically divisive issue when the achievable public expenditure savings are likely to be limited. In particular, one would assume that, as a Scottish MP, the current Chancellor of the Exchequer would be understandably concerned that levels of spending in Scotland are not disadvantaged. Nevertheless, this it is still the issue most likely to ignite divisive territorial rivalries in the UK.

However, the Treasury's post-devolution role has not been limited to public expenditure issues. One of the unexpected consequences of devolution has been the strengthening of the role of HM Treasury. Because of its responsibility for allocating public expenditure to the various territories of the United Kingdom, the Treasury was always going to be an important institution after devolution. This is, after all, perhaps the issue whose handling is the most important in ensuring that the UK does not fall into divisive territorial rivalry (Morgan 2002). However, the Treasury has developed an interesting post-devolution role in an unanticipated way.

It is the Treasury, not the DTI, that has been the driving force behind the current renaissance of debates over the 'North-South divide' and Labour's 'new regional policy' (Balls and Healey 2000). The explicit commitment to narrow regional economic disparities – to 'reduce the persistent gap between regions' – is perhaps the closest the UK Government has come to admitting a responsibility for promoting territorial justice (HMT/DTI 2001).

The Treasury has also been active in developing UK-wide policies in areas that are almost completely devolved to Scotland, Wales and Northern Ireland. For example, in 2003, the Treasury and ODPM commissioned Kate Barker to 'conduct a review of issues underlying the lack of supply and responsiveness of housing in the UK' (Barker 2004). The review was established with a clear UK remit, and numerous consultation meetings were held with the Scottish and Welsh devolved administrations, and with local authorities, quangos and NGO bodies based in Scotland and Wales. Similarly HM Treasury, DTI and DfES commissioned the Lambert Review in 2002 to explore the links between business and industry. Again, this review had a UK wide remit (Lambert 2002). Even the Wanless Review into health spending had a UK remit (Wanless 2002). In this case, the Treasury commissioned Wanless and only subsequently invited the participation of the devolved administrations – the idea of the four constituent parts of the UK jointly commissioning the work was apparently not considered.

While a number of these reviews were commissioned jointly with other Whitehall departments, it seems clear that the Treasury was the driving force behind these public-policy reviews. There are a number of reasons that might explain the rise of the Treasury in these 'quasi-federal' policy matters. Clearly the intellectual appetite and political authority of the current Chancellor of the Exchequer, Gordon Brown, will partly explain the current dominance of the Treasury. The failure of other Whitehall departments to develop their post-devolution role compounds the matter. Certainly, the DTI could have become the locus for UK-wide regional economic policy, but handed that role, by default, to HM Treasury. Similarly, the DWP could well have been the logical place to co-ordinate important elements of social policy post-devolution.

Nevertheless, the Treasury has been the most effective department in thinking through the implications of devolution and the concept of territorial justice in relation to the policy areas on which devolution has impacted. Interestingly, it now seems as if the Treasury was one of the more important Whitehall Departments in dealing with the elected government of Northern Ireland at Stormont, prior to the imposition of direct rule in the early 1970s (Mitchell 2005). However, more recently, the ODPM and DWP have been more proactive than in the past, and have somewhat taken the initiative with their appreciation of the importance of the issue of employment in driving economic prosperity.

Conclusion

Within the UK there has been a traditional unease on the left of British politics with the notion of devolution. The process does highlight the historic tensions between subsidiarity and solidarity, and many have argued that what matters is class or group identity, not territory. Bevan famously said 'there is no Welsh problem', and thirty years later the future Labour leader Neil Kinnock led the charge against the Welsh devolution proposals in similar terms (Bevan 1944; Kinnock 1975). This is compounded by the fact that devolution and decentralisation are more popular when political parties are in opposition, and enthusiasm tends to wane when parties get closer to a return to power at the centre.

The rise of territorial politics from 1960 onwards seems to have been accompanied (possibly fuelled) by a growing lack of confidence in the ability of Whitehall to deal with territorial inequalities within the United Kingdom. Pressure for decentralisation and devolution has been greatest in the stateless nations and historical communities of Scotland, Wales and Northern Ireland. In the regions of England, on the other hand, regional identity is much weaker – yet some of the English regions are, and have persistently been, among the poorest areas in the United Kingdom.

There is a broad consensus that strong economic development institutions are necessary at the regional level in order to promote balanced economic growth. However, this does not mean that either regional elites or the general public believe that regional devolution will provide an economic dividend. The 'North-South' regional economic divide did not have a significant impact on the North East Assembly referendum in November 2004. In contrast to Scotland, where support for devolution was closely linked to policy expectations, support in the North East (such as there was) seemed to be based on quite straightforward political grounds and antipathy to 'far-away London'. In conclusion, it seems that the demand for self-government is less likely to be caused by the level of regional economic disparities, and more likely to emerge if regional needs are perceived to be ignored, or if regional policy demands are resisted. Such a situation could very easily arise in regional economic policy, but it could also arise in numerous other policy areas.

References

Adams J and Robinson P (2002) 'Divergence and the Centre' in Adams J and Robinson P (eds.) *Devolution in Practice* ippr, pp. 198-227

Adams J, Robinson P and Vigor A (2003) *A New Regional Policy for the UK* ippr

Balls E and Healey J (2000) *Towards a New Regional Policy: Delivering growth and full employment* The Smith Institute

Barker K (2004) *Review of Housing Supply – Delivering Stability: Securing our Future Housing Needs – Final Report* TSO

Bevan A (1944) *Hansard* 10 October 1944, col 231

Department for Trade and Industry (DTI) (1998) *Our Competitive Future: Building the Knowledge Driven Economy* TSO

Department for Work and Pensions (DWP) (2003) *Departmental Report 2003* Cm 5921, TSO

Department for Work and Pensions (DWP) (2005) *Five Year Strategy: opportunity and security throughout life* Cm 6447, TSO

Gershon P (2004) *Releasing Resources to the Front Line: independent review of public sector efficiency* HMT

Gillespie A and Benneworth P (2001) 'Industrial and Regional Policy in a devolved United Kingdom' in Adams J and Robinson P (eds.) *Devolution in Practice* ippr, pp. 69-85

Goodwin M, Jones M and Jones R (2005) 'Devolution, Constitutional Change and Economic Development: Explaining and Understanding the New Institutional Geographies of the British State' in *Regional Studies* 39:4, pp. 397-403

Gordon I (2002) 'Industrial and Regional Policy: a London perspective' in Adams J and Robinson P (eds.) *Devolution in Practice* ippr, pp. 86-89

Heald D and McLeod A (2002) 'Beyond Barnett? Financing Devolution' in Adams J and Robinson P (eds.) *Devolution in Practice* ippr, pp. 147-175

HM Treasury (HMT) (2000a) *Productivity in the UK: the evidence and the Government's approach* HMT

HMT (2000b) *2000 Spending Review: Public Service Agreements July 2000* Cm 4808, TSO

HMT (2002) *2002 Spending Review: Public Service Agreements 2003-2006* Cm 5571, TSO

HMT (2004) *2004 Spending Review: Public Service Agreements 2005-2008* Cm 6238, TSO

HMT (2005) *Public Expenditure Statistical Analyses 2005* TSO

HM Treasury and the Department for Trade and Industry (HMT/DTI) (2001) *Productivity in the UK: 3 – The Regional Dimension* HMT

HM Treasury and the Small Business Service (HMT/SBS) (2002) *Enterprise Britain: A Modern Approach to Meeting the Enterprise Challenge* London: HM Treasury

Keating M (1998) *The New Regionalism in Western Europe – Territorial Restructuring and Political Change* Edward Elgar

Keating M (2002) 'Devolution and Public Policy in the United Kingdom: divergence or convergence?' in Adams J and Robinson P (eds.) *Devolution in Practice* ippr, pp. 3-21

Keating M (2005) *The Government of Scotland: Public Policy Making after Devolution* Edinburgh University Press

Kinnock N (1975) *Hansard* 3 February 1975, col 1031

Lambert R (2003) *Lambert Review of Business-University Collaboration: Final Report* TSO

Lord Chancellor's Department (LCD) (2000) *Memorandum of Understanding and supplementary agreements between the United Kingdom Government, Scottish Ministers, the Cabinet of the National Assembly for Wales and the Northern Ireland Executive Committee* Cm 4806, TSO

Mitchell J (2005) *Understanding Stormont-London Relations* available online at http://www.strath.ac.uk/Departments/Government/staff_pages/jm/pdf/understanding_stormont-london_relations.pdf

Morgan K (2002) 'The English Question: Regional Perspectives on a Fractured Nation' in *Regional Studies* 36:7, pp. 797-810

Morgan K and Upton S (2005) 'The New Centralism' in *agenda* IWA

National Audit Office (NAO) (2003) 'The Department for Trade and Industry: regional grants in England' Report *by the Comptroller and Auditor General* TSO

Office of National Statistics (ONS) (2004) *Regional Trends 38* TSO

ONS (2005) *First Release: Productivity* 23 March ONS

Office of the Deputy Prime Minister (ODPM) (2005) *Sustainable Communities: People, Places and Prosperity - a five year plan from the Office of the Deputy Prime Minister* Cm 6425, TSO

Rees G (2002) 'Devolution and the restructuring of post-16 education and training' in Adams J and Robinson P (eds.) *Devolution in Practice* ippr, pp. 104-114

Robinson P (2001) 'Comment' *New Economy* 8:3, pp. 148-150

Scottish Executive (2000) *Framework for Economic Development in Scotland* Scottish Executive

Scottish Executive (2001) *A Smart Successful Scotland: Ambitions for the Enterprise Networks* Scottish Executive

Scottish Executive (2004a) *Framework for Economic Development in Scotland* Scottish Executive

Scottish Executive (2004b) *A Smart Successful Scotland* Scottish Executive

Scottish Executive (2004c) *New Scots – attracting fresh talent to meet the challenge of growth* Scottish Executive

Scottish Office (1997) *Scotland's Parliament* Cm 3658 TSO

Wanless D (2002) *Securing Our Future Health: Taking a long-term view* HMT

Welsh Assembly Governemtn (WAG) (2002) *A Winning Wales* National Assembly for Wales

Welsh Assembly Government (WAG) (2003) *Wales: A Better Country* National Assembly for Wales

Welsh Office (1997) *A Voice for Wales: The Government's Proposals* Cm 3718, TSO

10 Devolution and the economy: a Scottish perspective

Brian Ashcroft, Peter McGregor and Kim Swales

In their interesting and challenging chapter, John Adams and Peter Robinson (chapter 9) assess the consequences for economic development policy of the devolution measures enacted by the UK Labour Government post-1997. Their chapter ranges widely over current UK regional disparities, the balance of responsibilities in policy between Whitehall and the devolved administrations, and, finally, they raise questions about the developing 'quasi-federal' role of Whitehall in regulating or co-ordinating the new devolved-policy landscape.

In response, we propose to focus on four issues that we believe are key to understanding the economic consequences of devolution both at the Scottish and UK levels. First, we argue that Scotland's devolutionary experience in economic policy is both significant and innovative. Secondly, we examine the role of devolution in regional economic performance. Our third section highlights a crucial area for Scotland and the other devolved UK territories: the funding of the devolution settlement. Here we consider some of the implications of funding arrangements for economic performance and the options for a new funding settlement. Finally, we deal with the difficult issue of co-ordination between the centre and the devolved regions. We contend that co-ordination is largely conspicuous by its absence. Moreover, where co-ordination is deployed it reflects an inadequate understanding of the extent to which the economies of the regions and devolved territories of the UK are linked.

Scottish experience

Adams and Robinson argue that the Scottish devolutionary experience in economic policy is that policy divergence has been 'less dramatic' post-devolution than it was before. In this, they echo Gillespie and Benneworth (2002), who stress that administrative devolution from the mid-1970s onwards, and the response to pressures from nationalist movements, led to policy innovations such as the creation of the Scottish Development Agency (SDA) in 1975, and the formation of Scottish Enterprise and Highlands and Islands Enterprise in 1991.[1] Thus, economic policy in Scotland began to diverge considerably, long before political devolution commenced in 1999. Moreover, the innovations adopted by Scottish Enterprise, such as an emphasis on clusters, and a well-

---

1 The Highlands and Islands Development Board (HIDB) preceded the creation of the SDA by at least a decade and both were merged with the Training Agency to form, respectively, Scottish Enterprise, and Highlands and Island Enterprise in 1991.

researched and specified business-birth-rate policy, led the English regions, through the Department for Trade and Industry (DTI) and the Regional Development Agencies (RDAs) to seek to adopt some of these earlier Celtic innovations.[2] Gillespie and Benneworth (2002) argue that these developments offer examples of some policy *convergence* post-1999, but we would point to a number of innovative examples in economic policy after the creation of the Scottish Parliament.

As Adams and Robinson note, the *Framework for Economic Development in Scotland* (FEDS) is the Scottish Executive's first economic development policy strategy document, which was introduced in 2000. This was followed in 2001 by *Smart Successful Scotland* (SSS) a strategy document for the enterprise networks. Both strategies were 'refreshed' in 2004. FEDS emphasised the importance of supply-side drivers of productivity such as innovation and skills, stressed the key role of market forces, and offered the primary justification for policy intervention as market failure. SSS established policy along three dimensions:

- *Growing Businesses*: which pioneered a Business Growth Fund, allowing small companies to access Regional Selective Assistance (RSA) through less bureaucratic procedures; Proof of Concept Fund; Scottish Co-Investment Fund; the Edinburgh University-Stanford link; the Intermediary Technology Institutes (ITIs); and enterprise education in primary and secondary schools sponsored by Scottish entrepreneurs.

- *Skills and Learning*: the creation *inter alia* of Careers Scotland, offering all-age careers advice and development of industry-skills plans to address skills gaps.

* *Global Connections*: merged Locate in Scotland and Scottish Trade International to create Scottish Development International, one organisation focused on attracting high-value Research and Development (R&D), creating partnerships and seeking to assist the commercialisation of Scottish-generated knowledge; created Global Scot – a network of Scottish business expatriates to draw on their knowledge and expertise; and Event Scotland to bring major international events to Scotland. The subsequent creation of the *Fresh Talent Initiative* represents a broadening out of the Global Connections approach to the attraction of mobile skilled labour as well as knowledge capital.

Cooke (2005) characterises economic development policy in the devolved administrations as *visionary* in Scotland, *precautionary* in Wales and *constrained* in Northern Ireland. Cooke acknowledges the innovation in Scottish eco-

---

2   It can be argued that these policy exemplars have moved on in Scotland with, for example, the business-birth-rate strategy now, following a review, focusing on high-growth starts and, following a 'refreshed' SSS, a greater emphasis on life-cycle support for businesses and developing businesses of scale (Scottish Enterprise 2005).

nomic development policy prior to 1999, but highlights the visionary nature of post-devolution policy through the attempt to promote a science-based economy as charted in SSS. This regional development strategy can be viewed as the first attempt in the UK, and perhaps in Europe, to recognise the importance of linking scientific commercialisation and entrepreneurship within a specifically open economy context.

Gillespie and Benneworth, in contrast, take the view that the Scottish Executive has not been particularly innovative in using its powers of industrial intervention, citing Regional Selective Assistance (RSA) as a specific example. According to these authors, RSA has simply been 're-badged and streamlined rather than more comprehensively re-aligned with the interventionist approach alluded to in FEDS' (Gillespie and Benneworth 2002, p. 76). Clearly, judgements as to whether a policy change is innovative or not are likely to be subjective. However, we take the view that the Scottish Executive's Review of RSA in 2001 was substantial and led to significant changes in both the nature and operation of policy. The application of the scheme was aligned with the objectives of SSS, and a greater emphasis was placed on supporting investments in indigenous high-growth companies, with support for R&D and investment in intangible assets such as know-how, patents and other intellectual property. The Executive also acknowledged the need to accept a greater degree of risk to public funds in its assessment of RSA applications involving university spinouts, hi-tech start-ups and other knowledge-intensive activities. In addition, the rationale for awarding support was changed in several ways. First, the procedures for small companies was streamlined. Second, the generation of value-added rather than job creation was given a greater weight in assessment. Finally, a sizeable part of the budget that had previously been assigned for RSA purposes – £20 million – was diverted to support equity investments in innovation through the creation of the Scottish Co-investment Fund. Further developments to this funding package have since been announced. All of these preceded any comparable change in RSA in the rest of the UK.

Adams and Robinson end their discussion of policy developments in the devolved territories by concluding that most divergence has been institutional and that, where significant differences in economic development policies have occurred, their roots lie in the earlier administrative, rather than the later political, devolution. While this may be true of England, Wales and Northern Ireland, it is worth noting that, in Scotland, the principal delivery agencies of economic policy – Scottish Enterprise, Highlands and Islands Enterprise, the Local Enterprise Companies – have not changed.[3] Moreover, under political devolution, the changes in policy did mark a major break with the past. First,

---

3   Change has occurred within these agencies as they have sought to streamline their back-office functions.

FEDS and SSS placed economic development policy, for the first time, in a strategic framework and a framework that differed in several important respects from elsewhere (Ashcroft 2002). Secondly, devolved policy built on the successful economic policy innovations introduced in the 1990s, but adapted them to meet the requirements of the new strategic vision within a specific open economy context, which, as Cooke argues, sought 'to position Scotland to exploit to the full the Knowledge Economy (Cooke 2005, p. 44). Finally, as Cooke further points out, the implementation of this strategic vision led to the adoption of some major policy innovations, the *Intermediary Technology Institutes* (ITIs) being a prime example. The ITIs are one of the key components of Scottish Enterprise's approach to strengthening innovation and R&D in Scotland. Three Intermediary Technology Institutes – Life Sciences, Energy and Techmedia – have been created. Scottish Enterprise is investing heavily in them with £450 million earmarked to be spent over the next ten years. Each ITI operates as a 'hub' for identifying, commissioning and diffusing pre-competitive research, embracing emerging markets, maximising the value of intellectual-property rights and seeking to integrate new technologies into the market place. And, they are open for membership to companies and research institutions that will actively participate in their activities.

Devolution and economic performance

From a conventional fiscal-federalist perspective, the economic arguments for devolution concern the provision and financing of local public goods, such as health and education expenditures.[4] There would appear to be three broad routes through which devolution might affect 'economic efficiency': in the allocation of public goods and services to meet Scottish preferences and needs; in the allocation of inputs or resources to productive public use; and in the allocation of resources between present and future consumption, in other words, through growth.[5] But *a priori*, devolution may incur costs as well as benefits to economic efficiency, as table 9.1 indicates.

Table 9.1 suggests that political devolution in Scotland may have had favourable or unfavourable effects on information, resources, incentives, and co-ordination in the formulation and implementation of policy. In Ashcroft,

---

4   The literature suggests that national public goods, such as defence or foreign affairs, should be provided nationally and that the external, or spillover, effects of local macroeconomic and distributional policies warrants that they be reserved to the national level. Conversely, compatibility of expenditure choices on local public goods with local preferences is best ensured by appropriate devolution. Devolution to Scotland and Wales has broadly followed this approach in the specification of the powers reserved to the centre. Tiebout (1956), Musgrave (1959), and Oates (1972) are the classic accounts and Oates (1999) provides a survey.

5   The effect of devolution on policy therefore embraces both static economic efficiencies (that is, one-off effects on the allocation of goods and resources) and dynamic efficiencies (that is, growth)

Table 9.1. The economic benefits and costs of Scottish devolution

Potential benefits	Potential costs
Provision better reflecting local preferences.	The direct administration costs of an additional layer of government (in this case the Scottish Parliament).
Local democratic accountability improving: efficiency of policy formulation, implementation, innovation.	Inadequate monitoring, implementation and evaluation. (Is HM Treasury tougher than the Scottish Parliament?)
Better information on the local economic environment.[6]	The loss of economies of scale in the conduct of policy.
Headquarters effect stimulating local services	Increased rent-seeking.
Barnett imposes strict limit on Executive's discretionary expenditures and the tax-varying power allows marginal changes in taxation and spending.	Smaller budget due to strict adherence to Barnett.
	No mechanism linking public spending with tax revenues raised in Scotland.[7]
Lower co-ordination/ compliance costs.	Reduced co-ordination with the rest of the UK.

Source: Ashcroft, McGregor and Swales (2005a).

McGregor and Swales (2005a and 2005b) we discuss the issues surrounding the impact of devolution on the Scottish economy outlined in table 9.1 above. We also look at some evidence and conclude that the impact of devolution on the Scottish economy requires further research and that the effect is likely to be complex, subtle and difficult to measure.

Anecdotally there is only limited evidence of policy changing to better reflect Scottish preferences. Policy has diverged in areas of indirect consequence for the economy, such as university tuition fees, care for the elderly and in the economic development policies underpinning SSS noted above. And some of these policies, such as care for the elderly, are likely

---

6   'Local' informational advantages are often regarded as one of the benefits of decentralisation. Given that Scotland enjoyed administrative decentralisation prior to devolution, this is a less obvious source of gain in this case. However, if, as seems likely, democratic accountability results in pressures that improve local information, then devolution may bring genuine gains through this mechanism.

7   Aspects of this are not costs of devolution per se, but relevant to whether a greater degree of fiscal independence would generate larger gains.

to have a bigger impact on the pattern of expenditure in the future than at present.

However, there is concern in Scotland that the adoption and implementation of policy does not 'fit' fully with the declared preferences of the Scottish Executive and, we must assume, the preferences of the Scottish electorate. The Scottish Executive has made economic growth its paramount policy priority and placed much emphasis on securing improvements in the efficiency of delivery. But Wood (2005) finds that the share of primary expenditure on economic development policy has fallen from 7.4 per cent to 5.5 per cent between 1999 and 2005. Other expenditures classified as supporting development grew more slowly than overall public expenditure in Scotland (thirty per cent compared to forty-one per cent) implying a declining share, although less severe than that of primary development spend. Moreover, Wood also found that the share of such expenditures going to rural areas was significantly in excess of their population share. The latter might be an example of the possible increased opportunities for rent-seeking following devolution, which created a number of new agents with influence over policy, most obviously MSPs, that in turn has stimulated a host of lobbying organisations and other interest groups. Added to this is the finding of the Parliament's Finance Committee that the revealed commitment to efficiency savings within the Executive was less than that promised by the UK Government and less than originally claimed by the Executive itself (Finance Committee 2004, paragraphs 77-92).

Funding

The financial resources available to the Scottish Executive and the other devolved administrations principally depend on the budget assigned by Westminster.[8] The Barnett formula, which determines the assigned budget, allocates a population share to Scotland of increments to public spending on comparable programmes in England and Wales. Since devolution, the formula has been applied more rigorously with population weights updated annually (Heald and McLeod 2005). At the start of devolution, public expenditure in Scotland on comparable programmes was in excess of its population share and so the effect of a rigid adherence to Barnett will be to reduce relative public spending in Scotland, ultimately – although over a much-extended period – moving to the English figure in real per-capita terms. This has adverse consequences for GDP and employment in Scotland, as well as in the other devolved territories (Ferguson *et al.* 2003).

---

8   In Scotland, other sources of revenue include Council Tax, Non-Domestic Rate Income, charges, and realised efficiency savings. The variable income-tax provision of a 3p change in the basic rate - the Tartan tax - has not been used in the first two Parliaments.

Barnett is simply a convergence formula and is independent of a desired territorial distribution of resources, although a desired distribution may influence the rigour with which the formula is applied. Adams and Robinson recognise that the so-called 'Barnett squeeze' – both actual in Northern Ireland and potential in Scotland and Wales – is 'the issue most likely to ignite divisive territorial rivalries in the UK' (chapter 9). But perhaps it has reached the limits of appropriateness as the principal territorial funding mechanism in the UK, and may, in any event, become unsustainable as long-term convergence in per-capita spending levels raises the demands for an alternative.

Hallwood and Macdonald (2005) survey the range of fiscal-federal systems around the world – all reflecting different trade-offs between equity and efficiency. They argue that a form of fiscal federalism should be adopted in the funding of the devolved territories in the UK, with a greater alignment of revenue and spending powers to overcome the present vertical imbalance implicit in Barnett. They take the view that the current funding mechanism unduly trades efficiency off in favour of equity, and that moving to a more fiscal-federalist system would require some sacrifice of equity in favour of potentially greater efficiency. While their approach, perhaps, does not fully acknowledge the hard budget constraint implicit in Barnett, and hence the presence of an incentive to efficient spending, it is also correct that the present funding mechanism provides no link between public spending and tax revenues raised in Scotland. The incentive to promote growth is weakened by the resultant absence of any direct and automatic link between economic growth and tax revenues accruing to the Scottish Parliament. But it should also be noted that the evidence on fiscal decentralisation and the promotion of growth is ambiguous (Hallwood and MacDonald 2005). Nevertheless, this is a debate that will increasingly come to dominate devolution in the UK and, in our judgement, merits considerably greater emphasis.

Co-ordination

One important consequence of devolution is the actual and potential tension between the (economic) interests of the devolved territories and the UK as a whole. While such tensions between region and nation are not new, devolution has given them institutional significance. Scotland and Wales are free to pursue their own economic development policies that may conflict with the economic policy objectives of the UK government.

Clearly devolution increases the need for greater co-ordination from the centre, while preserving the spirit of the devolution settlement. However, if the UK is to deal with the issue of co-ordination effectively, there needs to be a clearer understanding of the nature of regional interdependence in the UK and the institutional arrangements to deal with it. This issue is fundamental: in principle, at least, inter-regional interdependence is important for all economic policies with a spatially differentiated impact, whether administered by devolved or delegated authorities or by the Westminster government. While inward investment, for example, brings inter-regional competition into very sharp relief, economic interdependence renders virtually every policy at least a potential source of both inter-regional spillovers and gains from co-ordination.

Spillovers

Co-ordination is an issue principally because regions are interdependent. Regions and small countries are interdependent because they more open to trade and resource flows than larger jurisdictions. Hence, changes in economic activity in one region spill over to other regions through movements in trade, migration and capital flows. The problem for policy is that our understanding of the nature and extent of economic spillovers between regions generally, and UK regions in particular, is limited (for more on this see McGregor and Swales 2005). The theoretical possibilities are understood but, as McGregor and Swales (2005) point out, the issue is essentially an empirical one. Inter-regional interdependence depends on the specific conditions affecting demand and supply in each region. And in the UK, the empirical research is lacking, with matters not helped by a lack of data on inter-regional flows of trade and finance.

This lack of understanding has not, however, stopped governments from taking and promoting a view of the UK inter-regional macroeconomy. Until the election of the Labour Government in 1997, the UK Treasury took the very restrictive view that a policy disturbance in a UK region would be met by 100 per cent crowding out in other regions, and so would have no net impact on national economic activity (McGregor and Swales 2005). In contrast, the 'new regional policy' of the Labour Government appears to be underpinned by a view that each region is independent, with no significant spillovers from one to the other. McVittie and Swales (2003) characterise this about-face by the Treasury as 'very odd'.

Two implications appear to follow from this *volte-face*. First, the focus of UK regional policy is on each region fulfilling its potential, with each English region treated as a mini-UK in the adoption of the Treasury supply-side agenda and the pursuit of policies to improve performance on the Treasury's five productivity drivers. Adams and Robinson rightly note that these drivers exclude some of the more important drivers at the local level. The openness of regional economies suggests the importance of trade, migration and capital flows to regional development. In Scotland, this is recognised to some degree through the promotion of global connections within SSS[9] and the adoption

---

9 Although, in the 2004 'refresh' of *Smart Successful Scotland*, the emphasis on promoting global connections appears to have diminished somewhat.

of a migration policy: the *Fresh Talent Initiative* to help stem Scotland's declining population. But at the UK Government level, probable inter-regional links are not considered. So, for example, the link between the problems of congestion and overdevelopment in the South East of England and the lower rates of job creation in the north, and the attendant policy solutions, are both ignored. Second, the perceived lack of regional interdependence has led to a failure by the UK Government to develop the appropriate institutional arrangements to co-ordinate policy across the devolved – and English – regions, to move closer to the joint maximisation of economic welfare (McGregor and Swales 2005).

Institutions

Devolution led to the adoption of new institutional arrangements in the UK to encourage co-operation among the devolved territories and the different levels of government: Concordats; Joint Ministerial Committees; and Committee of the Isles. But the view of political analysts is that such arrangements promote minimal co-operation and offer no formal policy co-ordination (Jeffery 2004; Mitchell and Lodge 2004). Adams and Robinson, in contrast, see the Treasury as playing a binding role, both in thinking through the implications of devolution for territorial justice and in promoting UK-wide policies. We acknowledge that the Treasury is ideally placed to perform a co-ordinating role. But that role is currently only exercised – with the DTI and ODPM – through the PSA target on regional growth, which, as Adams and Robinson note, no longer applies to the whole of the United Kingdom. We can think of no examples of the Treasury playing a binding or co-ordinating role with respect to Scottish economic development policy or any other Scottish Executive policy. The potential UK-wide implications and tensions of unique Scottish policies on care for the elderly, teachers' pay, university tuition fees, and economic migration through the *Fresh Talent Initiative*, appear simply to have been ignored. Overall, the UK Government has adopted a disjointed incremental approach to spatial institutional change, which is very fluid in England, but which does not appear to be guided by an overall spatial institutional strategy.[10]

Conclusions

We consider Adams and Robinson's analysis to be a useful and stimulating contribution. Our response from a Scottish perspective highlights the significance of four key issues. First, we believe Scotland's post-devolution experience has seen a significant degree of innovation in Scottish policy. Second, devolu-

---

10   At the level of the English regions, targets, evaluation procedures, democratic accountability (the role of regional chambers and regional government offices), and long-term regional planning all appear to be in a state of flux.

tion in Scotland (and elsewhere, and decentralisation more generally) has potentially important economic effects. None the less, while the traditional fiscal-federalism literature tends to emphasise the potential gains of devolution, there are also, undoubtedly, potential costs. The economic impacts of devolution are likely to be subtle and difficult to measure, but are no less important for this.

Third, we consider the funding of the devolved (and delegated) authorities to be of central importance to the long-term future of the devolution process in the UK. The sustainability of Barnett is a major issue, not least because its rigorous implementation is likely to impact adversely on the economies of the devolved territories. Consideration of alternatives is, therefore, an issue of some concern, and the debate on the appropriate degree of autonomy is likely to increase in importance through time, and not just for Scotland. And, fourth, we feel the issue of the role of the centre and co-ordination is of key importance, but we would place much emphasis on the importance of regional spillovers and the appropriateness of the institutional structure to deal with them. In principle, any devolved, delegated or central economic policy may, in a system of interdependent regional economies, have important inter-regional spillover effects. This, in turn, may imply the potential for overall gains from the appropriate co-ordination of policies across the same and different levels of the governance structure.

Finally, while identification of the key issues is comparatively straightforward, our current understanding of, for example, the likely macroeconomic consequences of alternatives to the Barnett formula and the scale and direction of various spillover effects is in its infancy. We are some way away from providing the evidence-base that should ideally be informing the conduct of spatially differentiated policies in the UK.

References

Ashcroft B (2002) 'The Scottish Economy' in Hood N, Peat J, Peters E and Young S (eds.) *Scotland in a Global Economy: the 2020 Vision* Palgrave Macmillan

Ashcroft B, McGregor PG and Swales JK (2005a) 'Is Devolution Good for the Scottish Economy?' *Presentation to conference on Governing Scotland: Open Questions on the Future of Scottish Politics* organised by the ESRC's Research programme Devolution and Constitutional Change Edinburgh, 18 March 2005

Ashcroft B, McGregor PG and Swales JK (2005b) 'Is Devolution Good for the Scottish Economy? A Framework for Analysis', in the ESRC's Research programme Devolution and Constitutional Change *Devolution Briefing No. 26*, March

Bell D and Christie A (2001) 'Finance – The Barnett Formula: Nobody's Child?' in Trench A (ed.) *The State of the Nations 2001: The Second Year of Devolution in the United Kingdom* Imprint Academic, pp. 135-151

Cooke P (2005) 'Devolution and Innovation: the Financing of Economic Development in the UK's Devolved Administrations' in *Scottish Affairs* 50, pp. 39-50

Ferguson L, Learmonth D, McGregor PG, Swales JK and Turner K (2003) 'The Impact of the Barnett Formula on the Scottish Economy: A General Equilibrium Analysis' in *Strathclyde Papers in Economics* No. 03-04, March 2003, available at http://www.economics.strath.ac.uk/Dpapers/strath.econ.03-04.pdf

Finance Committee (2004) 'Report on Stage 2 of the 2005-06 Budget Process', 8th Report, 2004 (Session 2), Scottish Parliament, available at http://www.scottish.parliament.uk/business/committees/finance/reports-04/fir04-08-01.htm

Gillespie A and Benneworth P (2002) 'Industrial and regional policy in a devolved United Kingdom' in Adams J and Robinson P (eds.) *Devolution in Practice* ippr, pp. 69-85

Hallwood P and MacDonald R (2005) 'The Economic Case for Fiscal Federalism' in Coyle D, Alexander W and Ashcroft B (eds.) *New Wealth for Old Nations: Scotland's Economic Prospects* Princeton University Press, pp. 96-116

Heald DA and McLeod A (2005) 'What is in Scotland's Interest? Reviving the Barnett Formula or Fiscal Autonomy?' Paper presented to the conference Governing Scotland: Open Questions on the Future of Scottish Politics organised by the ESRC's Research programme Devolution and Constitutional Change Edinburgh, 18 March 2005.

Jeffery C (2004) *Devolution: What Difference Has It Made? Interim findings of the ESRC Devolution and Consitutional Change Programme* available at http://www.devolution.ac.uk/pdfdata/Interim_Findings_04.pdf

McGregor PG and Swales JK (2005) 'Economics of Devolution/ Decentralization in the UK: Some Questions and Answers' in *Regional Studies* 39:4, pp. 477-494

McVittie EP and Swales JK (2003) *Constrained Discretion in UK Monetary and Regional Policy* available at http://www.weru.org.uk/Esrc/London/Swales_Lon.pdf

Mitchell J and Lodge G (2004) 'The Treasury and Devolution' paper presented at the Devolution and the Centre conference, University of Strathclyde, May

Musgrave R (1959) *The Theory of Public Finance* McGraw-Hill

Oates WE (1972) *Fiscal Federalism* Harcourt Brace Jovanovich

Oates WE (1999) 'An Essay on Fiscal Federalism' in *Journal of Economic Literature* 37, pp. 1120-1149

Oates WE (2004) 'Toward a second-generation theory of fiscal federalism' (unpublished paper)

Scottish Enterprise (2005) *Operating Plan 2005-2008: Ambitious for Scotland* Scottish Enterprise

Tiebout C (1956) 'A Pure Theory of Local Expenditures' in *Journal of Political Economy* 64, pp. 416-424

Wood P (2005) 'Is the growth of the Scottish economy the 'first priority' for public spending in Scotland?' in *Quarterly Economic Commentary* 30:1, University of Strathclyde: Fraser Allander Institute

11 Child poverty and devolution

Liane Asta Lohde

Child poverty has been on the national political agenda since 1999, following the Prime Minister's pledge to eradicate it within a generation. The current Government has acknowledged that poverty is not just about low income but also about the manifestations of disadvantage in other areas of life, including education, health and housing. In short, the understanding of child poverty seemingly extends beyond income poverty to social exclusion and the lack of equal opportunities.

The Prime Minister's commitment to eradicate child poverty has been underlined by the setting of targets and the creation of indicators that measure progress. The UK child poverty strategy has primarily consisted of income-focused policies, but they have been supplemented by an array of initiatives aimed at attenuating other manifestations of poverty and at tackling drivers of social exclusion. While the Government, thus far, has had a lucid vision of how to reduce the number of children living in poverty through tax credits and benefit, it seems to have proved more difficult to articulate a broader set of policies that clearly add up to a strategy directed at tackling the multi-dimensional nature of child poverty.

The *Child Poverty Review*, led by HM Treasury in the latter half of 2003, was set up to identify how the income-focused strategy can be best complemented through the improvement of public services related to education, health, housing, and so on. Most likely, public services will have to become more important in the Government's plan to address child poverty and increase future life-chances of disadvantaged children. There are challenges ahead. While income-related poverty indicators are moving in the right direction, the picture looks less clear-cut with respect to educational attainment or child health (DWP 2004a). Apart from the challenge to further mainstream the child poverty strategy across departments, the devolution of social policy areas is likely to complicate the formulation of a coherent and comprehensive strategy to eradicate child poverty by 2020 across the UK.

The Prime Minister's child poverty pledge holds across the nations. However, the responsibility over key social policy areas that impact on the extent and experience of poverty are devolved. In particular, the nations have authority over education, health, housing and economic development, limiting Westminster's influence in these areas. There are differences among the nations in the way that they have articulated an explicit child poverty strategy, and there are nuances between the adopted policy initiatives across the devolved areas. Policy measures are developing within the co-ordinates of established priorities and the political structures of each nation. As a result, whether the child poverty pledge will be met will depend, in part, on what happens in the nations. Therefore, eradicating child poverty will require, among other things, more and better exchange of information, and policy co-ordination and co-operation across Westminster and the devolved administrations.

This chapter aims to contribute to the sharing of information. It will explore the differences and similarities in the national child poverty strategies and will attempt to chart their underlying drivers. A short overview is given of the policy strategies to tackle child poverty as adopted by Westminster and the national governments in Scotland, Wales and Northern Ireland. The nations' approaches are compared across three broad dimensions and common themes and emerging issues are highlighted. The dimensions across which the nations' strategies are contrasted reflect, first, attempts to develop a comparative framework, and they include policy and delivery, and cultural and political context, as well as rhetoric and language.

The UK-wide approach

The UK Government's concern with poverty and social exclusion has crystallised around the Prime Minister's child poverty pledge. Westminster has used a broad array of policies to tackle child poverty, but welfare support, through tax credits and child benefit, has driven the improvement, and has helped to redistribute income towards families with children in general, and towards those on lower incomes in particular. Crucial to the Government's overall anti-poverty strategy has been paid work as the key route out of poverty, and its thrust has been to encourage and compel people into work. Lisa Harker provides a useful summary of the key policies that have been used to advance the child poverty strategy, and they evolve around the following themes: tackling worklessness and increasing opportunities, tackling low income, preventing disadvantage, and improving communities (Harker 2003).

Tackling worklessness and increasing opportunities

Worklessness is associated with a high risk of low income and poverty, and employment reduces this risk. The UK Government has utilised active labour market policies across Britain to raise the number of individuals in the labour market. Welfare-to-work programmes, like the New Deals, have been introduced to facilitate the entry and return into paid work. Jobcentre Plus has been launched to better assist unemployed people and the economically inactive with their job search.

Government initiatives have also focused on improving job prospects and enhancing employability through the promotion of skill development, training and higher educational attainment. Examples that apply to England include the National Skills Strategy, Education Action Zones and the Education Maintenance Allowance.

Other measures have been aimed at reducing barriers to work in deprived areas. The UK Government has established Employment Zones and created Action Teams to help reduce unemployment and economic inactivity. Insufficient childcare facilities frequently hamper labour-market participation, and resources have been allotted under the *National Childcare Strategy* to improve the childcare infrastructure in deprived areas.

More recently, the Government has set out its aspiration to achieve the equivalent of eighty per cent of the working-age population in work (DWP 2005). The 2005 Labour manifesto took this further by aspiring to 'full employment in every region and nation' by 2010 (Labour 2005, p. 14). The recent shift of focus to tackling economic inactivity through reforming incapacity benefit and supporting people back into work will be vital if these aspirations are to be met.

Tackling low income

The introduction of the minimum wage and reforms of the tax-benefit system have positively influenced incomes at the lower levels. The minimum wage has increased steadily since its introduction, and is set to rise to the level recommended by the Low Wage Commission following the 2005 Budget (HMT 2005). Also, with respect to families with children in particular, child benefits have risen, and the child-related element of the Child Tax Credit will be raised as announced in the Pre-Budget Report 2004 (HMT 2004b). Overall, families with children have benefited, and, among these families, resources have been redistributed towards those at the lower end of the income spectrum. The Child Trust Fund is also now in operation for children born since 1 September 2002 (HM Government 2004). This is a universal programme offering asset-building support for families and children.

Preventing disadvantage

Sure Start is the most prominent programme in the early-years strategy at present, and national versions of Sure Start have been established across the devolved nations. The Treasury's ten-year strategy for childcare includes a number of measures aimed at preventing disadvantage, including the rollout of Sure Start to create 3,500 family centres in England by 2010. While a number of items in this strategy are reserved (for example, tax credits and maternity leave), there are also overlaps with a number of devolved areas (for example, the quality of childcare places). The strategy notes this and states that responsibility for delivering the strategy is shared between the UK Government and devolved administrations and commits to involving all four countries of the UK in discussing its implementation (HMT 2004a).

An area-based approach has been a key component of the strategy to tackle poverty across the UK. Programmes such as the Neighbourhood Renewal Strategy in England, Communities First in Wales, and Closing the Opportunity Gap and the Community Regeneration Fund in Scotland are all aimed at improving quality of life in the most deprived areas.

Measuring poverty

There is no single, comprehensive dataset yet available that records poverty and deprivation statistics for the UK and the nations, which makes country and regional comparisons difficult. Currently, one of the most commonly used ways of reporting on income poverty is the benchmark of sixty per cent of contemporary median income (CMI). This benchmark is quoted both on a before-housing-costs (BHC) and after-housing-costs (AHC) basis. The Household Below Average Income publication supplies figures on low income in England and the English regions, Scotland and Wales, but does not contain any information on Northern Ireland. Across England, Scotland and Wales, in 2003/2004, children were most at risk of living below the sixty per cent mark (CMI AHC) in Wales, at thirty per cent, followed by England (twenty-nine per cent) and Scotland (twenty-seven per cent) (DWP 2004b). But the most at-risk area was within England, with fifty-four per cent of children in Inner London at risk. Judging from survey and administrative data, child poverty rates vary more significantly within rather than across regions. For example, child poverty rates by ward vary most dramatically within Scotland (Bradshaw 2002).

In order to monitor specifically the impact of policy on tackling poverty and social exclusion, the UK Government established a series of indicators, which are published annually in *Opportunities for All* (DWP 2003a). The indicators are arranged around life-cycle stages and cover low income and other dimensions such as educational attainment, health issues and so on. Currently, many indicators in *Opportunities For All* are only applicable to England, failing to report on regional differences. In the future, however, *Opportunities For All* reports will draw on boosted datasets that will include more detailed regional information.

There have been separate efforts across the nations to collect data on low income and deprivation. For example, in Northern Ireland, the Office of First Minister and Deputy First Minister (OFMDFM) has collected data. It shows that thirty-eight per cent of children in Northern Ireland live in households that are in the bottom thirty per cent of equivalised household income after housing costs (McLaughlin and Dignam 2002). Wales and Scotland also collect their own data. For example, the Welsh Office commissioned a Welsh Index of Deprivation in 1999, while the Scottish Household Survey provides information by local authority area, and, recently, the Scottish Index of Multiple Deprivation has enabled data to be analysed on a smaller geographic scale known as 'data zones' (areas of between 500-1000 household residents).

At the end of 2003, the UK Government introduced the official measure that will track childhood poverty in the UK. It is tiered, with three indicators tracing absolute and relative poverty and material deprivation. The new measure will include data from all nations. The introduction of this measure has been largely welcomed. However, several issues regarding its precise nature are outstanding, including a lack of clarity regarding which one of the three indicators (absolute, relative or material deprivation) will be the headline figure. Depending on which one the Government chooses, it will make a difference to how easily it can claim to having succeeded on its child poverty pledge. Besides, it remains unclear what exactly will be included in the material deprivation indicator. Moreover, while statistics will be reported on both a before- and after-housing-costs basis, they are reported on a Great Britain-wide basis, which will hide the regional dimension of housing costs. Housing costs take up a larger proportion of disposable income of poor families, particularly disadvantaging those who live in areas with high housing costs.

It is widely accepted that the UK Government has made progress in reducing the number of children living in poverty. Between 1996/97 and 2001/02, the number of children living in households below sixty per cent of contemporary median income after housing costs fell from 4.3 million to 3.8 million (Brewer *et al.* 2003). However, the reduction was smaller than expected. In order to increase the likelihood of meeting its first child poverty target of reducing the number of children in income poverty by a quarter to 3.1 million (AHC) in 2004/05, an extra £885 million would have to be committed to the child element of the child tax credit. The latest figures, released in 2004, show that 3.6 million children in Britain (excluding Northern Ireland), or twenty-eight per cent of all children, live in low-income households, down from thirty-four per cent in 1996/97 (DWP 2004a).

The first five years of the UK Government's child poverty strategy have been characterised by policies to raise the income of poor families. Child-related benefits have become more generous and tax credits have been introduced to make moving off benefits and into employment a more viable option. In the future, there will have to be a sustained financial effort to tackle income poverty at a time when there is extreme pressure to limit public spending. None the less, serious consideration will have to be given to distributing more resources still to poorer families with children. However, in a climate of competing spending priorities and public wariness of tax increases, financial redistribution is unlikely to be high up on the policy agenda.

Public-service improvements are also key to tackling poverty and deprivation. Increasing their quality and effectiveness is essential to making progress with respect to the UK Government's Public Service Agreements, which cover, among other things, children's health and educational attainment. To ensure further progress, the UK Government will need to increase its efforts to mainstream its child poverty strategy across the key Whitehall departments beyond HM Treasury and the Department for Work and Pensions (DWP). However, given the devolution of key social policy areas and public services, improvements in these areas often fall within the remit of the devolved administrations, and, by extension, outside the control of the UK Government. It is to the nature of devolution that we now turn.

The nature of devolution

Devolution was one of the keynote initiatives of the Labour Government elected in 1997, and different devolution settlements were agreed with Scotland, Northern Ireland and Wales. These settlements define the general, executive and legislative competences of each nation and set out the devolved and reserved matters

There is a complex mix of reserved, devolved and concurrent powers that varies between Scotland, Wales and Northern Ireland. The key devolved areas pertinent to tackling child poverty, however, can be summarised as follows: education, health, housing and economic development, which are devolved to all the administrations; of the devolved administrations, only Northern Ireland is able to exert control over policy areas such as the tax-benefit system or employment legislation.

Policy in England continues to be determined by the Government in Westminster and is taken forward by Whitehall, with some decentralisation to the regions through government offices for the regions, regional development agencies and unelected regional assemblies. It is unlikely, however, that these institutions will help stake out a significant English child poverty strategy, as, while they have some influence over economic growth, planning, culture and housing, they have no powers in health or education, where grave inequalities exist between children.

The changes in formal structures due to devolution have introduced policy differentiation, but the scale of future divergences remains unclear. Not only is it too early to tell, but there are a number of factors that are likely to constrain policy divergence. Among others, Keating highlights that functional (and financial) dependence between devolved and reserved questions may curb the extent to which the nations will take different policy directions. Furthermore, the fact that the UK is a common security area, a market and an integrated welfare state that has fostered a common sense of social citizenship will further rein in the extent to which policies are expected to be able to diverge (Keating 2002).

Significant administrative devolution preceded constitutional reform, however, and it would be wrong to ignore the differentiation in administrative infrastructures and powers that existed before devolution. In particular, it has been argued that the distinctive administrative structures across the nations have considerable influence in directing policy and setting priorities (Rees 2002).

In terms of policies, there have been some high-profile divergences between the nations, such as free personal care for the elderly or the abolition of upfront tuition fees in Scotland. However, the picture is more subtly differentiated in relation to child poverty, not least because of its multi-dimensional nature and the array of policy instruments that need to be enlisted to reduce it. Initiatives to tackle child poverty will have a bearing on multiple policy areas, and they are likely to be fitted around already existing emphases with regard to health, education, housing, and so on, in as much as they are characteristic of each nation.

There is potential for a dynamic relationship between divergence and convergence of policy: the diversification of policy initiatives multiplies the chance of finding a successful strategy that can be shared and adopted in other places, leading in turn to policy convergence. Policy-learning, particularly with respect to child poverty, however, is complicated by the multifaceted nature of poverty, increasing the difficulty of comparing policies and evaluating their impact. This paper will limit itself to outlining the broad similarities and differences in the nations' child poverty strategies.

England

England does not have a dedicated child poverty strategy at this point but follows Westminster's approach by default. Following the No vote in the North East referendum on regional government, English priorities will continued to be determined by the centre.

The only exception is London, with its directly elected Mayor and Assembly. Section 30 of the *Greater London Authority Act* (1999) gives the London Mayor the authority to promote social development. However, the Mayor acts on behalf of the Authority as a whole and is restricted in his/her power and resources. S/he cannot pass primary legislation or provide services that are offered by other public bodies, such as housing, education, health or other social services (GLA 2003). *London Divided* is the GLA's keynote report on poverty and was published in November 2002 (GLA 2002). Following this, the Mayor consulted with London boroughs, community organisations and central government to identify the options available to local and regional government to address poverty in London. Some of the specific recommendations have included increased affordable childcare, promotion of flexible employment and recruitment of ethnic-minority young people (GLA 2003).

Interestingly, HM Treasury has also introduced specific initiatives in London to improve incentives to work, particularly for those in lower-paid jobs. The 2003 Pre-Budget Report introduced a £40 per week in-work credit to parents, including lone parents, to boost earnings over the first year of employment (HMT 2003). This initiative took many in the GLA by surprise, both by its timing and by the resources committed to London. This was followed by the announcement in *Choice for Parents*, the *Best Start for Children* of a £5 million pilot, in partnership with the GLA, to tackle the availability of affordable childcare in London (HMT 2004a). It seems to emphasise the importance that central government places on poverty in London.

Scotland

In 1999, the Scottish Executive followed the Prime Minister's lead when it explicitly stated its own pledge to eradicate child poverty within a generation. The commitment to eradicate child poverty is part of the Scottish Executive's overall objective to promote social justice and to mainstream those principles across departments. The promotion of social justice has been a priority for the Scottish Executive since it was created in 1999. However, there has been no clear-cut definition of what is meant by social justice, as such. Achieving social justice seems require a commitment to tackle poverty and social exclusion, to rebuild and strengthen communities and to increase opportunities. The social justice strategy is complemented by an equality strategy, which focuses more directly on issues of discrimination and prejudice.

In its first session (1999-2003), the Scottish Executive consolidated its social justice agenda by choosing ten long-term objectives and twenty-nine milestones that would monitor the progress in increasing opportunities across life stages and communities. The statistics that relate to the twenty-nine milestones have been published annually in the *Social Justice Annual Report – Indicators of Progress* (Scottish Executive 2003). The format and conceptualisation of the different dimensions of poverty and social exclusion are similar to those of the DWP's *Opportunities for All*, which applies primarily to England (DWP 2004a).

Child poverty has been recognised as a complex problem. The proportion of children living in poverty is similar to that of England and Wales (DWP 2003b). As in the other nations, poverty is concentrated in particular areas. In Social Inclusion Partnership areas (deprived areas targeted by the Executive for regeneration) twice as many children were living in poverty than in other areas (Kemp, Dean and Mackay 2002). Solutions are unlikely to have a single policy location. Rather, as poverty is correlated with a roster of risk factors that embody disadvantage (low income, poor housing, health inequalities, lack of educational opportunities), the Executive has a broad definition of child poverty, which is reflected in the targets that have been set to monitor progress towards the ambitious long-term goal of eradicating it.

Six of the twenty-nine social justice milestones, measuring progress on poverty and social exclusion indicators, relate directly to children. They monitor the change related to educational attainment, health status, housing, and the proportion of children in workless or low-income households.

The anti-poverty strategy is pursued across departments, and the Minister for Communities (formerly called the Social Justice Minister) co-ordinates the joined-up efforts. S/he is also responsible for equality issues, community regeneration, housing, the voluntary sector and digital inclusion. All ministers are required to prioritise helping the most disadvantaged groups and areas in their mainstream programmes. Budget proposals are to reflect the ministers' contributions to the anti-poverty agenda.

A high-profile policy to tackle poverty is the new Community Regeneration Fund, which combines and replaces the Social Inclusion Partnership fund, Better Neighbourhood Services fund and the Tackling Drugs Misuse fund. It takes a similar local area-regeneration approach, with two thirds of the fund targeted at the most deprived fifteen per cent of data zones based on the Scottish Index of Multiple Deprivation. The remaining third has been allocated to Community Planning Partnerships in areas with higher than average (above fifteen per cent) concentration of deprivation in their area. The Community Regeneration Fund seeks to move from a project-based approach to regeneration to a more strategic approach, through the agreement of a small number of outcome agreements, focused on the Executive's core objectives of improving access to services, the local environment and the education, health, and job prospects of those living in Scotland's most deprived communities (Scottish Executive, 2004). This reflects the Executive's multifaceted anti-poverty strategy, which concentrates on various policy areas, based on the belief that low income is only one dimension of poverty and that an effective policy approach must have a wider scope. 'This is why the Scottish budget concentrates our resources in tackling poor quality housing, homelessness, ill health, educational attainment, access to training and employment and deprived communities' (Curran 2002).

Paid work is seen as the key route out of poverty, and resources are channelled towards supporting the transition into employment, enhancing educational opportunities and providing skills training to raise employability. There has been a concerted effort to provide childcare to enable the employment of low-income parents, and economic development has focused on promoting the supply of job opportunities. Besides policies that are directly related to employment, the Scottish Executive has also launched initiatives that aim to reduce inequalities in other areas, such as educational attainment and health, particularly because Scotland has a relatively poor health record. Other measures that have been taken to alleviate the experience of poverty and attendant disadvantages include initiatives to promote financial inclusion.

The following provides an overview of some policy initiatives over the last few years. Some programmes have the explicit objective of alleviating child poverty, while others mainstream the anti-poverty agenda. The needs of chil-

dren in poverty are to be met through universal services for children, programmes targeted at disadvantaged children directly and policies that support
poor families and poor neighbourhoods.

Policies that ...

... relate to children and their health status
- Breakfast Services Fund, which provides money for breakfast services for
  children in deprived areas.

- Free fruit for first two years of primary school, which is provided in the
  context of the Health Improvement Campaign.

- National Sexual Health Strategy, which aims to reduce unintended pregnancies.

- Scottish Health Promoting Unit, which supports all schools to become
  health-promoting schools.

... focus on early years, education and children's services
- Early Years Strategy, including Sure Start Scotland, which targets very young
  children, and gives all three- to four-year-olds access to quality care and
  learning before entering primary school.

- Integrated Community Schools, which aim to raise social inclusion and
  educational attainment by following a more integrated approach to supporting children. The approach is to be rolled out across all schools in
  Scotland by 2007.

- Changing Children's Services Fund, which is a cross-Executive fund and a
  joint strategy to provide better integrated services for children.

... enable participation in the labour market and increase parents' opportunities
- Working Family Fund, organized by the Minister for Communities, which
  makes available £10 million for provision of flexible childcare and support
  for disadvantaged parents to access training and employment.

- Lone Parent Mentoring Service, which provides advice for parents about
  how to access education, training and employment. The service is accessible by phone, and lone parents in Glasgow can have face-to-face appoint-
  ments.

- Support for lone parent students, which entails childcare grants to lone
  parents in full-time higher education. Money is also given to Further
  Education colleges to meet locally identified childcare needs.

Northern Ireland

Northern Ireland's main policy framework for addressing poverty and social exclusion is called New Targeting Social Need (New TSN). New TSN was a relaunch of a previous initiative, Targeting Social Need (TSN), which was announced in 1991 to redress the significant socioeconomic inequalities between the two communities in Northern Ireland and the attendant political problems that have pronounced the experience of disadvantage. However, Targeting Social Need had implementation problems, not least due to ambiguous definitions of poverty and inequality. This made it difficult to develop initiatives and monitor progress, and to mainstream the policy across departments.

During the Northern Ireland Peace Agreement negotiations, TSN became integral to the equality agenda and served as the template for New TSN, which was announced by the devolved government in 1999 to be its main vehicle for tackling inequality, social exclusion and social need. Northern Ireland's anti-poverty strategy operates within a clear equality framework whose dimensions are articulated in Section 75 of the *Northern Ireland Act* 1998. It sets out that a public authority has the responsibility to promote equality of opportunity, irrespective of religious belief, political opinion, age, racial group, marital status, sexual orientation, gender, disability or dependants.

The New TSN programme is mainstreamed across departments. The New TSN Unit, which is part of the OFMDFM, has the responsibility for promoting the programme and other elements of the equality agenda. In particular, the New TSN Unit drives forward policy by setting overall objectives and challenging departments to prioritise meeting the needs of the most disadvantaged people, groups and areas. Every department produces a New TSN Action Plan, in which it identifies the needs it will address and how it will do so. Departments are expected to skew their resources appropriately in their existing and new programmes. Annual reports chart the departments' successes in delivering on the New TSN agenda and the targets that had been set.

A recent formal evaluation of New TSN found examples of good practice and effective co-ordination, and success in mainstreaming the New TSN into departments' budgeting, planning and implementation processes. However, the problem of departments using different definitions of 'social need' was highlighted. Furthermore, the problem of departments' New TSN Action Plans setting too many targets and not being strategic in their target-setting was raised. One third of targets were not output-focused and could not, therefore, be measured, a further third of targets had not been met.

How the New TSN will develop following the evaluation is currently out for consultation. Key proposals include moving towards an explicit anti-poverty strategy (including changing the name to the Northern Ireland Anti-Poverty Strategy), widening the scope of the strategy to include reducing financial exclusion as a core aim and putting a greater emphasis on assistance for lone parents (OFMDFM 2005)

Three core objectives are proposed, which focus on building capacity: to participate in the labour market and the social and cultural life of the community; to increase employment opportunities and reduce barriers to employment; and to reduce financial inclusion. As with the New TSN, the anti-poverty strategy will be targeted at helping the most disadvantaged groups and areas. It is also proposed to continue Promoting Social Inclusion (PSI), the existing initiative through which departments co-ordinate cross-departmental initiatives on specific issues of social exclusion that do not sit comfortably with any one department. Examples of PSI actions include a review on the social exclusion problems faced by travellers, and the problem of teenage pregnancy. It is proposed that a new group be formed to develop a strategy to tackle social exclusion and poverty experienced by lone parents, of whom there seems to be a growing number in Northern Ireland (OFMDFM 2005).

Northern Ireland has not yet articulated a dedicated child poverty strategy, but has identified poor children as a priority group for action in accordance with the Prime Minister's pledge to eradicate child poverty by 2020. Child poverty is currently addressed within the New TSN/anti-poverty-strategy framework, and consultations with third-sector organisations are to help identify what actions need to be undertaken to meet the pledge. Furthermore, the Children's and Young People's Unit (CYPU) of the OFMDFM is developing a ten-year Children's Strategy for Northern Ireland, due to be published in autumn 2005. The objective of the strategy is to guide policy-making across government departments, as well as to influence service development and delivery across all sectors. Child poverty and patterns of social exclusion that affect children's lives were recognised as an area deserving special attention. While the CYPU Strategy aims to improve the wellbeing of all children, poor children are seen to require targeted interventions to meet their particular needs. Overall, for political and other reasons, Northern Ireland has not yet committed significant efforts to tackle child poverty. None the less, there have been some initiatives that are likely to have had some attenuating effects.

Some initiatives that address child poverty have included ...

- ... the Breakfast Club Programme, which provided breakfast to school children in deprived areas.

- ... a joint initiative between the PSI unit and the Department of Health to address teenage pregnancy.

- ... the Children's Fund, which is an Executive fund that has been set up to provide direct support to children and young people in need by assisting in areas such as child abuse, homelessness, health and wellbeing, disability and educational outcomes.

Wales

The Welsh Assembly Government (WAG) outlined, in *A Plan for Wales* 2001, its long-term vision for Wales, and the values and principles that should influence its work (WAG 2001). The *Government of Wales Act* 1999 placed the Assembly under a statutory duty to promote sustainable development and the equalities agenda. However, the Welsh Assembly Government took the political decision to give the same priority to social inclusion. Therefore, *A Plan for Wales* set out a tripartite commitment to social inclusion, equality and sustainable development to guide the Welsh Assembly Government's strategy to address the problems of deprived communities and tackle disadvantage and poverty. The objectives have included the regeneration of Wales's most deprived communities, provision of employment, training, and learning opportunities – both in the early years and throughout life – improvement of the health status of the Welsh population, and delivery of better and more accessible public services.

Ministerial responsibility for promoting the social inclusion agenda and community regeneration initially rested with the Minister for Finance, Local Government and Communities. However, following the elections in 2003, the Assembly's commitment to social inclusion was seemingly reinforced by establishing a dedicated Minister for Social Justice. The Minister is responsible for leading and co-ordinating policies and initiatives to tackle social exclusion across departments, and publishing an annual report setting out progress on achieving social justice (WAG 2004). Rhetorically, at least, 'social justice' seems to frame the social inclusion agenda more explicitly. The agenda has been central to the Assembly's policies and programmes in assisting those most at risk of poverty and social disadvantage. The focus appears to be on communities as the natural unit and context of policy delivery, rather than on targeting particular groups of people.

The Welsh Assembly Government reports annually on the state of affairs across various policy areas and outlines the activities aimed at improvement. Indicators to track progress are not uniformly provided, and advancement is also reported by summarising the actions taken across the following policy and programme areas: social inclusion, economic opportunity, health, children and young people, community and housing.

In 2003, the Assembly Government set up a Task Group on Child Poverty, which consulted with children and young people and the general public in order to inform the Government's child poverty strategy *A Fair Future for our Children* (WAG 2005). This document covers all aspects of policy relating to child poverty, which is analysed in a framework of income poverty, participation poverty and services poverty. Furthermore, a commitment has been made to a rights-based approach, based on the UN Convention on the Rights of the Child. However, much of the strategy seems to reiterate policies and targets that the Assembly is already committed to. A number of these have been focused on paid work and reducing barriers to employment, through the provision of childcare and schemes that increase employability through training. There are also some explicit initiatives targeted at disadvantaged children to provide support and soften the experience of poverty. Furthermore, anti-poverty and social inclusion initiatives across the devolved policy areas, which address the underlying drivers of disadvantage, also benefit poor children.

Interestingly, the strategy also includes a number of areas that are reserved matters, such as a call to further raise the level of Child Benefit and to look again at the Single Room Rent Rule. These are areas where the Assembly Government is making representations to ministers in Westminster regarding reform (WAG 2005). Progress on the measures set out in the strategy will be monitored by the full cabinet, and progress reported through an annual report. Monitoring will also include mechanisms for gathering the views of children on progress being made, most likely through ministers' annual meeting with Funky Dragon, the Children and Young People's Assembly for Wales.

The following gives an overview of some of the key anti-poverty and social inclusion initiatives and programmes, of which some have an explicit focus on child poverty and child wellbeing.

Policies that ...

... affect children and families
- Cymorth, the Children and Youth Support Fund, which is a grant fund that supports children and young people. The Assembly considers this fund one of its main instruments for tackling child poverty. While funding will not only be targeted at children from disadvantaged backgrounds, priority will be given to Community First areas. These are Wales's most deprived areas. The fund, which is also incorporated in the Assembly's *Childcare Action Plan* to improve and expand childcare options and provision, will, in addition, be used to expand childcare facilities. Other activities include family support (training, mentoring, information, benefit support), health promotion, empowerment, participation and active citizenship. Cymorth aims to respond to needs from early to teenage years in an integrated fashion, but weight is given to early years to break the cycle of deprivation.

- Early-years integrated centres, to provide daycare and other support services from prenatal parenting advice to adult learning. Their remit is it to tackle wider social problems. These centres are being rolled out so there is at least one in each local authority area.

... focus on education and training
- The Basic Skills strategy, which is part of the Assembly's *Skills and Employment Action Plan* 2002 (WAG 2002a). The objective specifically rele-

vant to children is to support language development in the early years. This
initiative also aims to promote basic-skills provision and support for adults
to enhance participation in society.

- Reaching Higher, through which financial support is being provided to
help disadvantaged young people enter higher education (WAG 2002b).

... focus on community regeneration and development

- The Communities First programme is one of the most prominent initiatives to address disadvantage and poverty in Wales. With a budget of £83
million over the first three years (2002-2005), 142 of Wales's most deprived
areas are targeted. The programme aims to improve the circumstances of
people in the most deprived communities in Wales through a multi-dimensional approach that includes building confidence, increasing income,
improving health and wellbeing, encouraging and improving education
and skills training, creating jobs, and making changes to how public services are delivered.

... address health issues

- Initiatives under the *Strategic Framework for Promoting Sexual Health* in Wales
(WAG 2000) provide sexual-health advice and service provision targeted at
vulnerable groups to reduce the rate of teenage pregnancies.

Similarities and differences

While it is early in the process of devolution and in developing strategies to
tackle child poverty across the nations, it is, none the less, a useful exercise to
compare the different approaches when considering that successful policies
may inspire policy development elsewhere. Although child poverty has
declined in the last five years, there is evidence that poverty reduction in the
future is likely to prove more difficult and will require increased government
effort. Public service improvements will have a greater role; and the role of the
nations in making a difference to child poverty is likely to increase. Given the
nations' powers in key policy areas, the UK Government will have to clearly
articulate a coherent strategy that builds on, complements and accommodates
the different national policy frameworks.

Comparisons of the national strategies and their outcomes are challenging
and limited beyond a certain degree of simplicity due to a lack of data, comparable statistics and indicators. Equally, sharing best practice is frequently
hampered because evaluations of new programmes are not completed yet, or
are simply not undertaken because of a lack of resources. As a result, this is a
first attempt at contrasting the national approaches across three dimensions:

- To what extent do the nations differ in formulating dedicated *policy* and how does *delivery* vary?

- What is the *cultural* and *political* context and how may it drive differences?

- How different is *rhetoric* and *language* and does it influence or reflect policy direction?

Policy and delivery

On the most basic level, all nations have formulated a strategy or policy framework that articulates the commitment to address poverty and social disadvantage. Scotland has a social justice strategy, Northern Ireland is a working towards an anti-poverty strategy to replace the New TSN approach, and Wales pursues a social inclusion strategy and has recently published a dedicated child poverty strategy. Integral to all approaches is the notion that poverty is multi-dimensional and extends beyond low income to poverty of opportunity and disadvantage in education, health and housing. The anti-poverty agendas are complemented by equality strategies across the nations, with Northern Ireland, in particular, taking a human-rights-based approach.

While the Prime Minister's pledge applies across the UK, only Scotland restated it, making an overt commitment to end child poverty within a generation and taking joined-up action across all portfolios to meet it. Northern Ireland is committed to 'making a contribution' to achieving the UK target (OFMDFM 2005) and the WAG 'wishes to play its full part in meeting that target' (WAG 2005). This reflects the nations' disparate political realities, articulating strategies at different speeds, and recognising that non-devolved policy is not the only way to tackle poverty. The Welsh Assembly Government was slower to produce an explicit child poverty strategy, although it seems to appreciate that child poverty must be addressed through a combination of devolved and reserved activities, and is currently lobbying the UK Government on key reserved policies that it argues will help to alleviate poverty in Wales. Northern Ireland is yet to articulate an explicit child poverty strategy, although the new anti-poverty strategy will include many measures likely to alleviate child poverty, and the CYPU's ten-year Children's Strategy will give special attention to child poverty as a crosscutting issue for Northern Ireland government departments.

The organisational responsibilities for implementing the anti-poverty strategies vary: Scotland and Wales have ministers who both steer their own initiatives and co-ordinate actions, across departments, aimed at tackling poverty and social disadvantage. They ensure that the commitments to social justice are mainstreamed across all ministerial portfolios. However, it is difficult to assess how far the appointment of a Minister of Social Justice simply reflects, or potentially propels, a particularly progressive strategy to tackle poverty and disadvantage. Northern Ireland has no dedicated minister, but the

New TSN unit within the OFMDFM, which is set to be replaced by an anti-poverty forum (performing a similar role), ensures that the principles of the New TSN/anti-poverty strategy are integrated into each department's initiatives. A joined-up and cross-departmental co-operation seems to be equally emphasised across the nations.

The position of a Children's Commissioner is an example of a policy innovation in one nation that has been taken up across the UK. Wales appointed its first Commissioner in 2001. The remit of Children's Commissioners is to ensure that the rights of children and young people are upheld, to monitor the standards of children's services and to provide both advice and information. Children's Commissioners across the nations have been involved in promoting child poverty policies to varying degrees. The Welsh Commissioner, for example, has taken a relatively active role in calling attention to child poverty in Wales.

The commitment to tackle poverty and social exclusion is mainstreamed across ministerial portfolios and is to be reflected in budgetary commitments. However, it is difficult to monitor whether expenditure on universal services or targeted programmes always meets the needs of poor and disadvantaged children, because of the multiple levels of government and involvement of third sector organisations that deliver services. Local authorities and other spending agencies have control over how they allocate resources, albeit within the bounds of statutory obligations. In other words, it is difficult to analyse to what extent commitments to tackle child poverty translate into poverty alleviation on the ground.

There is a mixture of mainstream and targeted programmes dedicated to tackling poverty and childhood disadvantage across the nations, but it is not clear what the future directions of policy are likely to be. *A Fair Future for Our Children* argues for mainstream services to underpin the targeted Welsh child poverty strategy. A recent report on crosscutting expenditure on child poverty in Scotland showed that significant resources were allocated both to mainstream and targeted programmes, but the growth of the latter was greatest, up to 2002.

The different nations place somewhat different emphases on the different policy areas. This may reflect the relatively greater or lesser extent to which a problem exists (or is perceived to exist). In Scotland, for example, where health problems in the population are greater in certain respects than the UK average (Palmer *et al.* 2003), various initiatives across ministerial responsibilities have addressed health inequalities and their lifelong effects (examples are the *Health Improvement Strategy* and health promotion in schools). Housing seems less of a priority. Wales seems to tackle poverty across the devolved policy areas by focusing on the most deprived areas and pockets of deprivation. Communities First is the main framework through which social exclusion is being addressed. This is not to say that Scotland or Northern Ireland lack an area-based approach. The new Community Regeneration Fund in Scotland is, clearly, evidence to the contrary, and Northern Ireland's New TSN and developing anti-poverty strategy explicitly state its remit to influence policy to deliver improvement for the most disadvantaged individuals and areas.

While there are nuances of emphasis across the devolved policy areas, employment is seen as the key route out of poverty across all nations. Resources are also targeted to reduce barriers to employment and training that may enhance employability. Scotland has committed significant resources for the provision of childcare to disadvantaged parents and lone parents in higher or further education, to allow employment to become possible. Wales has also committed funds for the provision of childcare to enable parents to enter paid work.

National governments are likely to be challenged to provide significant support for people who are in transition into or out of employment. Frequent transitions between economic states are linked to labour-market conditions, type of employment and labour-market policies. Given the relative weakness of many local economies and pockets of intense deprivation, transitions into low-paid and unstable employment are likely to be a frequent occurrence. These transitions are accompanied by extreme vulnerability for the participants involved, and children require particular protection and care during these periods. Moreover, people with complex needs frequently fall into the category of the hard-to-reach, even though any single need may not be of great intensity. Rather, as recent research shows, the breadth of needs that people experience makes them extremely vulnerable, due to insufficiently integrated public services (Rankin and Regan 2004). Another way devolved nations can alleviate the experience of poverty and social exclusion is by promoting financial inclusion (McCormick, Spencer and Gamble 2004; Regan and Paxton 2003), a theme recently picked up in Northern Ireland.

Culture and political context

The cultural and political context influences the approach that is taken to particular policy problems. The nations have developed their anti-poverty programmes at varying levels of speed and with differences in emphasis. As mentioned earlier, administrative devolution had set certain pathways for policy development and set accents on particular policy areas. It remains to be seen to what extent this divergence will persist and what other divergences will occur. It is too early to try to identify any clear-cut push or pull factors with regard to child poverty policies, especially since the development of dedicated strategies is relatively recent.

In the case of Northern Ireland, the suspension of the Assembly has inevitably slowed the process of developing responses to the problem of child poverty and has shifted priorities somewhat. Sectarianism and concern with violence have shaped the policy agenda. The TSN strategy was adopted to alleviate socio-economic inequalities between the two communities, which fuelled tension and violence. The New TSN has been firmly established within an equality and human-rights framework, and anti-poverty strategies are to take account of Section 75, which outlines nine dimensions along which equality of opportunity must be upheld.

The fact that Labour is now in power and has a long-standing tradition in Scotland and Wales suggests that progressive ideas regarding social justice may be more prominent. Adams and Robinson, however, argue that the Welsh and Scottish, in general, and their Labour parties, in particular, are not necessarily more progressive and left-wing (Adams and Robinson 2002). If not necessarily based in practice or fact, Welsh and Scottish Labour rhetoric suggests a greater affinity with equality of outcome as well as universal and citizenship-based services. For example, First Minister Rhodi Morgan emphasised the interpretation of the individual in society as citizen, and highlighted that concerns with equality of choice privilege an individualistic model of society, with little or no regard for the wider community. It has been argued that the Welsh anti-poverty approach takes the community as its starting point, instead of targeting the individual or a particular vulnerable group at a certain life stage (Osmond and Mugaseth 2004).

Rhetoric and language

A comparison of language reveals that the rhetoric of poverty and social exclusion is strikingly similar across the nations, and the similarity extends to the frequently ambiguous usage of terms such as social inclusion, social justice, opportunity, and so on. Broadly speaking, there seems to be a greater emphasis on social and economic equalities in Wales and Scotland, while the UK approach has focused on extending opportunities and promoting inclusion of the disadvantaged, with little concern of overall inequality. Northern Ireland has taken a human-rights stance to address the needs of the most disadvantaged. Similarly, in chapter 6, Wincott argues that, rather than a fundamental difference in levels or quality of service, differences are better characterised as a difference of emphasis, as broadly similar policy approaches are adapted to differing local circumstances.

Scotland has pursued a social justice approach, of which the anti-poverty strategy is a part. Social justice in the Scottish context is about extending opportunities to give everyone the chance of an equal outcome. The social justice framework guides policy to provide equality of opportunity, particularly to the disadvantaged, and to promote a socially inclusive society, with the twenty-nine social justice milestones used to monitor progress towards social justice. However, it is not quite clear how, exactly, these indicators relate to social justice, or, indeed, that they are the best ones to track the Executive's progress towards social justice. Moreover, the social inclusion agenda is juxtaposed with an Equalities Strategy, which was adopted in 2000 and mainstreamed across the Executive's policy areas. As Fitzgerald highlights, it is not clear how these two strategies intersect, compete or complement each other (Fitzgerald 2002). Recently, more rhetorical emphasis seems to have been placed on 'closing the opportunities gap'. It may be an attempt to align anti-poverty and equality thinking or be a new proxy for 'social justice'.

Wales also pursues a socially inclusive society and rhetoric. It has, more explicitly, adopted a social justice stance through the recent creation of the position of a Minister of Social Justice. The language surrounding social justice focuses on 'providing equal opportunities' to the most deprived individuals and communities. In addition, there is a separate commitment to equality by the Welsh Assembly, and, as in Scotland, it is unclear how these two agendas interact. With respect to children, and child poverty, in particular, Welsh rhetoric is influenced by references to the UN Convention on the Rights of the Child. Moreover, it also seems to put emphasis on citizenship participation and engagement. Northern Ireland's New TSN sits firmly within the equality unit, and the rhetoric around New TSN, and poverty and social inclusion policy is articulated with a strong human-rights angle. Both Wales and Scotland are explicitly pursuing their poverty strategies from a social justice perspective, more so than either Westminster or Northern Ireland.

Variations in rhetoric reflect, to a greater or lesser extent, differences in values, and, crucially, communicate a government's priorities to the public, raising potential expectations. The question is whether differences in language will effect disparate settlements in the long term. Will a social justice framework, which is concerned with inequality as well as tackling poverty, lead to a different settlement in the future? Will a rights-based approach, which is more prominent in Wales and Northern Ireland, and a focus on communities lead to different policies being introduced?

Conclusion

Central government has made steady progress in reducing the number of children living in child poverty since 1999. While Westminster has adopted a broader definition of poverty to include dimensions of social exclusion, child poverty policies have, thus far, had a focus on increasing household income. This emphasis does not detract from the initiatives that have been undertaken in areas such as regional regeneration, education, health or housing. However, Whitehall departments do not seem to have heeded the child poverty pledge with similar vigour to the Treasury and DWP.

The need for a coherent child poverty strategy has increased over the years for a number of reasons. First, unless taxation becomes more redistributive, public services are likely to become more important in attenuating the experience of poverty. Public services span various departments and it is more difficult to track progress and impact. Second, devolved governments have control over policy areas such as education, health, housing and other social services, effectively limiting what the UK Government can do in these devolved policy areas in the nations. Devolved institutions have constrained resources and depend on the centre but none the less have considerable liberty to define priorities and create policy. The pivotal role for devolved governments in helping to deliver the pledge is clear, at least by the sheer number of children living in poverty in Scotland, Wales and Northern Ireland. What remains unclear, however, is how the devolved nations and the UK can best complement each other, particularly in the context of distinctly evolving welfare structures. There is a complex relationship between reserved and devolved powers, which each nation is grappling with, and the centre and the nations should do more to resolve these tensions.

In order to resolve these tensions, there is a need to bring together the different experiences, share the particular national needs and experiences, and set out the co-operation and co-ordination of anti-poverty policy pursued by the centre and the nations. However, it is early in the process of devolution, and even earlier in the development of dedicated strategies to tackle child poverty. As this paper demonstrates, the nations have pursued approaches at different speeds and with differing emphases. In order to compare and contrast what policies and programmes are successful, it is imperative to better evaluate progress. As outlined in this paper, every nation has some kind of monitoring framework, but indicators are not necessarily comparable. The Joint Ministerial Committee (Poverty) has committed an officials' working group to take this forward, but it is currently unclear what progress has been made in this forum. Furthermore, there is a multitude of ideas and initiatives across social policy areas that could be shared across the nations, and networks and forums should be fostered. How do we ensure good practice is shared within and between nations? A website setting out the strategies, component parts and range of different initiatives would be a good starting point. Other forums may be needed, as well as existing networks and relationships, to make sharing good practice happen effectively.

In short, the campaign against child poverty has been developing in the right direction, but, in order to achieve further progress on the pledge, the UK Government will have to outline more clearly how it will pursue a coherent strategy, and how it will work alongside and in co-operation with the devolved administrations.

Acknowledgements

This chapter is based on research originally conducted for the End Child Poverty Coalition.

References

Adams J and Robinson P (2002) 'Divergence and the Centre' in Adams J and Robinson P (eds) *Devolution in Practice* ippr, pp.198-227

Bradshaw J (ed.) (2002) *The Well-being of Children in the UK* Save the Children

Brewer M, Goodman A and Shephard A (2003) *How has child poverty changed under the Labour Government? An Update* IFS Briefing Note 32, available at www.ifs.org.uk

Children's and Young People's Unit (2003) *The Next Step – Developing a Strategy for Children and Young People in Ireland* OFMDFM

Curran M (2002) *Third Social Justice Annual Report* Scottish Executive Press Release SESJ082, 18 November 2002, Scottish Executive, available at www.scotland.gov.uk/pages/news/2002/11/p_SESJ082.aspx

Department for Work and Pensions (DWP) (2003a) *Opportunities For All: Fifth Annual Report 2003* TSO

DWP (2003b) *Households Below Average Income 1994/95-2001/02* TSO

DWP (2004a) *Opportunity for All: Sixth annual report 2004* DWP

DWP (2004b) *Households Below Average Income 1994/95-2002/03* TSO

DWP (2005) *Five Year Strategy: opportunity and security throughout life* TSO

Fitzgerald R (2002) 'Equalities and Poverty' in Brown U, Scott G, Mooney G and Duncan B (eds.) *Poverty in Scotland 2002* Child Poverty Action Group

Greater London Authority (GLA) (2002) *London Divided: Income Inequality and Poverty in the capital* GLA

GLA (2003) *Tackling Poverty in London: Consultation Paper* GLA

Harker L (2003) *Dimensions of poverty and social exclusion – Persistence of Childhood Poverty* (unpublished Report for Save the Children Fund UK)

HM Government (2004) *The Child Trust Funds Act 2004* TSO

HM Treasury (HMT) (2003) *Pre-Budget Report 2003 – The Strengrh to Take the Long-Term Decisions for Britain: Seizing the opportunities of the global recovery* TSO

HMT (2004a) *Choice for Parents, the Best Start for Children: A ten year strategy for childcare* TSO

HMT (2004b) *Pre-Budget Report 2004 - Opportunity for All: The strength to take the long-term decisions for Britain* TSO

HMT (2005) *Budget 2005 - Investing for our Future: Fairness and opportunity for Britain's hard-working families* HC 372, TSO

Keating M (2002) 'Devolution and Public Policy in the UK: Divergence or convergence?' in Adams J and Robinson P (eds.) *Devolution in Practice* ippr, pp. 3-21

Kemp PA, Dean J and Mackay D (2002) *Child Poverty in Social Inclusion Partnerships* Edinburgh

Labour Party (2005) *Britain Forward not Back: The Labour Party Manifesto 2005* Labour Party

McCormick J, Spencer F and Gamble C (2004) 'Beyond the bounds: Resources for tackling disadvantage in JRF' in *Overcoming disadvantage – an agenda for the next 20 years* JRF

McLaughlin E and Dignam T (2002) *New TSN Research: Poverty in Northern Ireland* report to the OFMDFM Research Branch, available at www.research.ofmdfmni.gov.uk/powerfull/fullpoverty.pdf

Office of the First Minister and Deputy First Minister (OFMDFM) (1999) *New Targeting Social Need* OFMDFM

Office of the First Minister and Deputy First Minister (OFMDFM) (2005) *New TSN – The Way Forward: Towards an anti-poverty strategy. A consultation document, phase 2* OFMDFM

Osmond J and Mugaseth J (2004) 'Community Approaches to poverty in Wales' in *Overcoming disadvantage – an agenda for the next 20 years* JRF

Palmer G, North J, Carr J and Kenway P (2003) *Monitoring Poverty and Social Exclusion 2003* JRF and NPI

Rankin J and Regan S (2004) *Meeting Complex Needs: the future of social care* ippr

Rees G (2002) 'Devolution and the restructuring of post-16 education and training in the UK' in Adams J and Robinson P (eds.) *Devolution in Practice* ippr, pp. 104-114

Regan S and Paxton W (2003) *Beyond bank accounts – full financial inclusion* ippr

Scottish Executive (2002) *Social Justice – where everyone matters* available at *http://www.scotland.gov.uk/library5/social/emsjm-00.asp*

Scottish Executive (2003) *A Social Justice where everyone matters: Indicators of Progress* Scottish Executive

Scottish Executive (2004) *New Focus and Targets for Anti-Poverty Work* available at http://www.scotland.gov.uk/News/Releases/2004/12/09151556

Scottish Parliament (2003) *Report on Cross-cutting expenditure in relation to child poverty*, Finance Committee 2nd Report 2003, available at www.scottish.parliament.uk/finance/reports

Welsh Assembly Government (WAG) (2000) *Strategic Framework for Promoting Sexual Health in Wales* available at http://www.hpw.wales.gov.uk/English/topics/sexualhealth/strategy.htm

WAG (2001) *A Plan for Wales* available at www.planforwales.wales.gov.uk

WAG (2002a) *Skills and Employment Action Plan for Wales* WAG, available at
http://www.wales.gov.uk/subieducationtraining/content/employment/skillsem
ployment-actionplan-e.pdf

WAG (2002b) *Reaching Higher: Higher Education and the Learning Country – A
Strategy for the Higher Education Sector in Wales* WAG, available at
http://www.wales.gov.uk/subieducationtraining/content/higher/reachinghighe
r-e.pdf

WAG (2004) *Social Justice Report 2004* WAG

WAG (2005) *A Fair Future for our Children: The Strategy of the Welsh Assembly for
Tackling Child Poverty* available at
http://www.wales.gov.uk/subichildren/content/child-poverty-e.htm